Cosmetology Vocabulary Workbook

By Cosmetology Exam Success Group Copyright ©

Network4Learning, Inc. 2019.

www.insiderswords.com/cosmetology

ISBN-13: 978-1694121370

Copyright © 2019, Network4Learning, inc.
All rights reserved. No part of this publication may be
reproduced, distributed, or transmitted in any form or by any
means, including photocopying, recording, or other electronic
or mechanical methods, without the prior written permission
of the publisher

We hope you find this vocabulary workbook helpful with your
studies. If you do, please consider leaving a brief review at this link:
http://www.amazon.com/review/create-review?&asin=1694121372

Table of Contents

Introduction	5
Crossword Puzzles	24
Multiple Choice	84
Matching	132
Word Search	188

What is "Insider Language"?

Recent research has confirmed what we have known for decades: The strongest students and leaders in industry have a mastered an Insider Language in their subject and field. This Insider language is made up of the technical terms and vocabulary necessary to communicate effectively in classes or the workplace. For those who master it, learning is easier, faster, and much more enjoyable.

Most students who are surveyed report that the greatest challenge to any course of study is learning the vocabulary. When we examine typical college courses, we discover that there is, on average, 250 Insider Terms a student must learn over the course of a semester. Further, most exams rely heavily on this set of words for assessment purposes. The structure of multiple choice exams lends itself perfectly to the testing of this Insider Language. Students who can differentiate between Insider Language terms can handle challenging exam questions with ease and confidence.

From recent research on learning and vocabulary we have learned:

- Your knowledge of any subject is contained in the content-specific words you know. The more of these terms that you know, the easier it is to understand and recall important information; the easier it will be to communicate your ideas to peers, professors, supervisors, and co-workers. The stronger your content-area vocabulary is, the higher your scores will be on your exams and written assignments.

- Students who develop a strong Insider Language perform better on tests, learn faster, retain more information, and express greater satisfaction in learning.

- Familiarizing yourself with subject-area vocabulary before formal study (pre-learning) is the most effective way to learn this language and reap the most benefit.

- The vocabulary on standardized exams come directly from the stated objectives of the test-makers. This means that the vocabulary found on standardized exams is predictable. Our books focus on this vocabulary.

- Most multiple-choice exams are glorified vocabulary quizzes. Think about the format of a multiple-choice question. The question stem is a definition of a term and the choices (known as distractors) are 4 or 5 similar words. Your task is to differentiate between the meanings of those terms and choose the correct word.

- It takes a person several exposures to a new word to be able to use it with confidence in conversation or in writing. You need to process these words several different ways to make them part of your long-term memory.

The goals of this book are:
- To give you an "Insider Language" for your subject.
- Pre-teach the most important words before you set out on a traditional course of review or study.
- Teach you the most important words in your subject area.
- Teach you strategies for learning subject-area words on your own.
- Boost your confidence in your ability to master this language and support you in your study.
- Reduce the stress of studying and provide you with fun activities that work.

How it works:

The secret to mastering Insider Language is through repetition and exposure. We have eleven steps for you to follow:

1. Read the word and definition in the glossary out loud. "See it, Say it"
2. Identify the part of speech the word belongs to such as noun, verb, adverb, or adjective. This will help you group the word and identify similar words.
3. Place the word in context by using it in a sentence. Write this sentence down and read it aloud.
4. Use "Chunking" to group the words. Make a diagram or word cloud using these groups.
5. Make connections to the words by creating analogies.
6. Create mnemonics that help you recognize patterns and orders of words by substituting the words for more memorable items or actions.
7. Examine the morphology of the word, that is, identify the root, prefix, and suffix that make up the word. Identify similar and related words.
8. Complete word games and puzzles such as crosswords and word searches.
9. Complete matching questions that require you to differentiate between related words.
10. Complete Multiple-choice questions containing the words.
11. Create a visual metaphor or "memory cartoon" to make a mental picture of the word and related processes.

By completing this word study process, you will be exposed to the terminology in various ways that will activate your memory and create a lasting understanding of this language.

The strategies in this book are designed to make you an independent expert at learning insider language. These strategies include:

- Verbalizing the word by reading it and its definition aloud ("See It, Say It"). This allows you to make visual, auditory, and speech connections with its meaning.

- Identifying the type of word (Noun, verb, adverb, and adjective). Making this distinction helps you understand how to visualize the word. It helps you "chunk" the words into groups, and gives you clues on how to use the word.

- Place the word in context by using it in a sentence. Write this sentence down and read it aloud. This will give you an example of how the word is used.

- "Chunking". By breaking down the word list into groups of closely related words, you will learn them better and be able to remember them faster. Once you have group the terms, you can then make word clouds using a free online service. These word clouds provide visual cues to remembering the words and their meanings.

- Analogies. By creating analogies for essential words, you will be making connections that you can see on paper. These connections can trigger your memory and activate your ability to use the word in your writing as you begin to use them. Many of these analogies also use visual cues. In a sense, you can make a mental picture from the analogy.

- Mnemonics. A device such as a pattern of letters, ideas, or associations that assists in remembering something. A mnemonic is especially useful for remembering the order of a set of words or the order of a process.

- Morphology. The study of word roots, prefixes, and suffixes. By examining the structure of the words, you will gain insight into other words that are closely related, and learn how to best use the word.

- Visual metaphors. This is the most sophisticated and entertaining strategy for learning vocabulary. Create a "memory cartoon" using one or more of the vocabulary terms. This activity triggers the visual part of your memory and makes fast, permanent, imprints of the word on your memory. By combining the terms in your visual metaphor, you can "chunk" the entire set of vocabulary terms into several visual metaphors and benefit from the brain's tendency to group these terms.

The activities in this book are designed to imprint the words and their meanings in your memory in different ways. By completing each activity, you will gain the necessary exposures to the word to make it a permanent part of your vocabulary. Each activity uses a different part of your memory. The result is that you will be comfortable using these words and be able to tell the difference between closely related words. The activities include:

A. Crossword Puzzles and Word Searches- These are proven to increase test scores and improve comprehension. Students frequently report that they are fun and engaging, while requiring them to analyze the structure and meaning of the words.

B. Matching- This activity is effective because it forces you to differentiate between many closely related terms.

C. Multiple Choice- This classic question format lends itself to vocabulary study perfectly. Most exams are in this format because they are simple to make, easy to score, and are a reliable type of assessment. (Perfect for the Vocabulary Master!) One strategy to use with multiple choice questions that enhance their effectiveness is to cover the answer choices while you read the question. After reading the question, see if you can answer it before looking at the choices. Then look at the choices to see if you match one of them.

Conducting a thorough "word study" of your insider language will take time and effort, but the rewards will be well worth it. By following this guide and completing the exercises thoughtfully, you will become a stronger, more effective, and satisfied student. Best of luck on your mastery of this Insider Language!

Insider Language Strategies

"See It, Say It!" Reading your Insider Language set aloud

"It is better to fail in originality than to succeed in imitation."
–Herman Melville

Reading aloud is the foundation for the development of an Insider Language. It is the single most important thing you can do for vocabulary acquisition. Done correctly, it engages the visual, auditory, and speech centers of the brain and hastens its storage in your long-term memory.

Reading aloud demonstrates the relationship between the printed word and its meaning.

You can read aloud on a higher level than you can initially understand, so reading aloud makes complex ideas more accessible and exposes you to vocabulary and patterns that are not part of your typical speech. Reading aloud helps you understand the complicated text better and makes more challenging text easier to grasp and understand. Reading aloud helps you to develop the "habits of mind" the strongest students use.

Reading aloud will make connections to concepts in the reading that requires you to relate the new vocabulary to things you already know. Go to the glossary at the end of this book and for each word complete the five steps outlined below:

1. Read the word and its definition aloud. Focus on the sound of the word and how it looks on the paper.
2. Read the word aloud again try to say three or four similar words; this will help you build connections to closely related words.
3. Read the word aloud a third time. Try to make a connection to something you have read or heard.
4. Visualize the concept described in the term. Paint a mental picture of the word in use.
5. Try to think of the opposite of the word. Discovering a close antonym will help you place this word in context.

Create a sentence using the word in its proper context

"OPPORTUNITIES DON'T HAPPEN. YOU CREATE THEM." –CHRIS GROSSER

Context means the circumstances that form the setting for an event, statement, or idea, and which it can be fully understood and assessed. Synonyms for context include conditions, factors, situation, background, and setting.
Place the word in context by using it in a sentence. Write this sentence down and read it aloud. By creating sentences, you are practicing using the word correctly. If you strive to make these sentences interesting and creative, they will become more memorable and effective in activating your long-term memory.

Identify the Parts of Speech
"SUCCESS IS NOT FINAL; FAILURE IS NOT FATAL: IT IS THE COURAGE TO CONTINUE THAT COUNTS." –WINSTON S. CHURCHILL

Read through each term in the glossary and make a note of what part of speech each term is. Studying and identifying parts of speech shows us how the words relate to each other. It also helps you create a visualization of each term. Below are brief descriptions of the parts of speech for you to use as a guide.

VERB: A word denoting action, occurrence, or existence. Examples: walk, hop, whisper, sweat, dribbles, feels, sleeps, drink, smile, are, is, was, has.

NOUN: A word that names a person, place, thing, idea, animal, quality, or action. Nouns are the subject of the sentence. Examples: dog, Tom, Florida, CD, pasta, hate, tiger.

ADJECTIVE: A word that modifies, qualifies, or describes nouns and pronouns. Generally, adjectives appear immediately before the words they modify. Examples: smart girl, gifted teacher, old car, red door.

ADVERB: A word that modifies verbs, adjectives and other adverbs. An "ly" ending almost always changes an adjective to an adverb. Examples: ran swiftly, worked slowly, and drifted aimlessly. Many adverbs do not end in "ly." However, all adverbs identify when, where, how, how far, how much, etc. Examples: run hot, lived hard, moved right, study smart.

Chunking

"YOUR POSITIVE ACTION COMBINED WITH POSITIVE THINKING RESULTS IN SUCCESS." SHIV KHERA

Chunking is when you take a set of words and break it down into groups based on a common relationship. Research has shown that our brains learn by chunking information. By grouping your terms, you will be able to recall large sets of these words easily. To help make your chunking go easily use an online word cloud generator to make a set of word clouds representing your chunks.

1. Study the glossary and decide how you want to chunk the set of words. You can group by part of speech, topic, letter of the alphabet, word length, etc. Try to find an easy way to group each term.
2. Once you have your different groups, visit www.wordclouds.com to create a custom word cloud for each group. Print each one of these clouds and post it in a prominent place to serve as constant visual aids for your learning.

Analogies

"CHOOSE THE POSITIVE. YOU HAVE CHOICE, YOU ARE MASTER OF YOUR ATTITUDE, CHOOSE THE POSITIVE, THE CONSTRUCTIVE. OPTIMISM IS A FAITH THAT LEADS TO SUCCESS."– BRUCE LEE

An analogy is a comparison in which an idea or a thing is compared to another thing that is quite different from it. Analogies aim at explaining an idea by comparing it to something that is familiar. Metaphors and similes are tools used to create analogies.

Analogies are useful for learning vocabulary because they require you to analyze a word (or words), and then transfer that analysis to another word. This transfer reinforces the understanding of all the words.

As you analyze the relationships between the analogies you are creating, you will begin to understand the complex relationships between the seemingly unrelated words.

 A is to B as C is to D

This can be written using colons in place of the terms "is to" and "as."

A:B::C:D

The two items on the left (items A & B) describe a relationship and are separated by a single colon. The two items on the right (items C & D) are shown on the right and are also separated by a colon. Together, both sides are then separated by two colons in the middle, as shown here: Tall: Short :: Skinny: Fat. The relationship used in this analogy is the antonym.

How to create an analogy

Start with the basic formula for an analogy:

____ : ____ :: ____ : ____

Next, we will examine a simple synonym analogy:

<u>automobile</u> : <u>car</u> :: <u>box</u> : <u>crate</u>

The key to figuring out a set of word analogies is determining the relationship between the paired set of words.

Here is a list of the most common types of Analogies and examples

Synonym	Scream : Yell :: Push : Shove
Antonym	Rich : Poor :: Empty : Full
Cause is to Effect	Prosperity : Happiness :: Success : Joy
A Part is to its Whole	Toe : Foot :: Piece : Set
An Object to its Function	Car : Travel :: Read : Learn
A Item is to its Category	Tabby : House Cat :: Doberman : Dog
Word is a symptom of the other	Pain : Fracture :: Wheezing : Allergy
An object and it's description	Glass : Brittle :: Lead : Dense
The word is lacking the second word	Amputee : Limb :: Deaf : Hearing
The first word Hinders the second word	Shackles : Movement :: Stagger : Walk
The first word helps the action of the second	Knife : Bread :: Screwdriver : Screw
This word is made up of the second word	Sweater : Wool :: Jeans : Denim
A word and it's definition	Cede: Break Away :: Abolish : To get rid of

Using words from the glossary, make a set of analogies using each one. As a bonus, use more than one glossary term in a single analogy.

_____ : _____ :: _____ : _____

Name the relationship between the words in your analogy:_____

_____ : _____ :: _____ : _____

Name the relationship between the words in your analogy:_____

_____ : _____ :: _____ : _____

Name the relationship between the words in your analogy:_____

Mnemonics

> "IT ISN'T THE MOUNTAINS AHEAD TO CLIMB THAT WEAR YOU OUT; IT'S THE PEBBLE IN YOUR SHOE." —MUHAMMAD ALI

A mnemonic is a learning technique that helps you retain and remember information. Mnemonics are one of the best learning methods for remembering lists or processes in order. Mnemonics make the material more meaningful by adding associations and creating patterns. Interestingly, mnemonics may work better when they utilize absurd, startling, or shocking examples and references. Mnemonics help organize the information so that you can easily retrieve it later. By giving you associations and cues, mnemonics allow you to form a mental structure ordering a list or process to help you remember it better. This mental structure allows you to create a structure of association between items that may not appear to have any relationship. Mnemonics typically use references that are easy to visualize and thus easier to remember. Through visualization of vivid images and references, the information is much easier to imprint into long-term memory. The power of making mnemonics lies in converting dull, inert and uninspiring information into something vibrant and memorable.

How to make simple and effective mnemonics
Some of the best mnemonics help us remember simple rules or lists in order.

Step 1. Take a list of terms you are trying to remember in order. For example, we will use the scientific method:

observation, question, hypothesis, methods, results, and conclusion.

Next, we will replace each word on the list with a new word that starts with the same letter. These new words will together form a vivid sentence that is easy to remember:

Objectionable Queens Haunted Macho Rednecks Creatively.

As silly as the above sentence seems, it is easy to remember, and now we can call on this sentence to remind us of the order of the scientific method.

Visit http://www.mnemonicgenerator.com/ and try typing in a list of words. It is fun to see the mnemonics that it makes and shows how easy it is to make great mnemonics to help your studying.

Using vivid words in your mnemonics allows you to see the sentence you are making. Words that are gross, scary, or name interesting animals are helpful. Profanity is also useful because the shock value can trigger memory. The following are lists of vivid words to use in your mnemonics:

Gross words
Moist, Gurgle, Phlegm, Fetus, Curd, Smear, Squirt, Chunky, Orifice, Maggots, Viscous, Queasy, Bulbous, Pustule, Putrid, Fester, Secrete, Munch, Vomit, Ooze, Dripping, Roaches, Mucus, Stink, Stank, Stunk, Slurp, Pus, Lick, Salty, Tongue, Fart, Flatulence, Hemorrhoid.

Interesting Animals
Aardvark, Baboon, Chicken, Chinchilla, Duck, Dragonfly, Emu, Electric Eel, Frog, Flamingo, Gecko, Hedgehog, Hyena, Iguana, Jackal, Jaguar, Leopard, Lynx, Minnow, Manatee, Mongoose, Neanderthal, Newt, Octopus, Oyster, Pelican, Penguin, Platypus, Quail, Racoon, Rattlesnake, Rhinoceros, Scorpion, Seahorse, Toucan, Turkey, Vulture, Weasel, Woodpecker, Yak, Zebra.

Superhero Words
Diabolical, Activate, Boom, Clutch, Dastardly, Dynamic, Dynamite, Shazam, Kaboom, Zip, Zap, Zoom, Zany, Crushing, Smashing, Exploding, Ripping, Tearing.

Scary Words
Apparition, Bat, Chill, Demon, Eerie, Fangs, Genie, Hell, Lantern, Macabre, Nightmare, Owl, Ogre, Phantasm, Repulsive, Scarecrow, Tarantula, Undead, Vampire, Wraith, Zombie.

There are several types of mnemonics that can help your memory.

1. Images
Visual mnemonics are a type of **mnemonic** that works by associating an image with characters or objects whose name sounds like the item that must be memorized. This is one of the easiest ways to create effective mnemonics. An example would be to use the shape of numbers to help memorize a long list of them. Numbers can be memorized by their shapes, so that: 0 -looks like an egg; 1 -a pencil, or a candle; 2 -a snake; 3 -an ear; 4 -a sailboat; 5 -a key; 6 -a comet; 7 -a knee; 8 -a snowman; 9 -a comma.

Another type of visual mnemonic is the word-length mnemonic in which the number of letters in each word corresponds to a digit. This simple mnemonic gives pi to seven decimal places:

3.141582 becomes "How I wish I could calculate pi."

Of course, you could use this type of mnemonic to create a longer sentence showing the digits of an important number. Some people have used this type of mnemonic to memorize thousands of digits.

Using the hands is also an important tool for creating visual objects. Making the hands into specific shapes can help us remember the pattern of things or the order of a list of things.

2. Rhyming
Rhyming mnemonics are quick ways to make things memorable. A classic example is a mnemonic for the number of days in each month:
"30 days hath September, April, June, and November.
All the rest have 31
Except February, my dear son.
It has 28, and that is fine
But in Leap Year it has 29."

Another example of a rhyming mnemonic is a common spelling rule:
"I before e except after c
or when sounding like a
in neighbor and weigh."

Use **rhymer.com** to get large lists of rhyming words.

3. Homonym
A homonym is one of a group of words that share the same pronunciation but have different meanings, whether spelled the same or not.

Try saying what you're attempting to remember out loud or very quickly, and see if anything leaps out. If you know other languages, using similar-sounding words from those can be effective.

You could also browse this list of homonyms
at http://www.cooper.com/alan/homonym_list.html.

4. Onomatopoeia
An Onomatopeia is a word that phonetically imitates, resembles or suggests the source of the sound that it describes. Are there any noises made by the thing you're trying to memorize? Is it often associated with some other sound? Failing that, just make up a noise that seems to fit.

Achoo, ahem, baa, bam, bark, beep, beep beep, belch, bleat, boo, boo hoo, boom, burp, buzz, chirp, click clack, crash, croak, crunch, cuckoo, dash, drip, ding dong, eek, fizz, flit, flutter, gasp, grrr, ha ha, hee hee, hiccup, hiss, hissing, honk, icky, itchy, jiggly, jangle, knock knock, lush, la la la, mash, meow, moan, murmur, neigh, oink, ouch, plop, pow, quack, quick, rapping, rattle, ribbit, roar, rumble, rustle, scratch, sizzle, skittering, snap crackle pop, splash, splish splash, spurt, swish, swoosh, tap, tapping, tick tock, tinkle, tweet, ugh, vroom, wham, whinny, whip, whooping, woof.

5. Acronyms

An acronym is a word or name formed as an abbreviation from the initial components of a word, such as NATO, which stands for North Atlantic Treaty Organization. If you're trying to memorize something involving letters, this is often a good bet. A lot of famous mnemonics are acronyms, such as ROYGBIV which stands for the order of colors in the light spectrum (Red, Orange, Yellow, Green, Blue, Indigo, and Violet).

A great acronym generator to try is: www.all-acronyms.com.

A different spin on an acronym is a backronym. A **backronym** is a specially constructed phrase that is supposed to be the source of a word that is an acronym. A backronym is constructed by creating a new phrase to fit an already existing word, name, or acronym.

The word is a combination of *backward* and *acronym*, and has been defined as a "reverse acronym." For example, the United States Department of Justice assigns to their Amber Alert program the meaning "**A**merica's **M**issing: **B**roadcast **E**mergency **R**esponse." The process can go either way to make good mnemonics.

Visit: https://arthurdick.com/projects/backronym/ to try out a simple backronym generator.

6. Anagrams

An anagram is a direct word switch or word play, the result of rearranging the letters of a word or phrase to produce a new word or phrase, using all the original letters exactly once; for example, the word anagram can be rearranged into nag-a-ram.

Try re-arranging letters or components and see if anything memorable emerges. Visit http://www.nameacronym.net/ to use a simple anagram generator.

One particularly memorable form of anagram is the spoonerism, where you swap the initial syllables or letters of words to make new phrases. These are usually humorous, and this makes them easier to remember. Here are some examples:

"Is it kisstomary to cuss the bride?" (as opposed to "customary to kiss")
"The Lord is a shoving leopard." (instead of "a loving shepherd")
"A blushing crow." ("crushing blow")
"A well-boiled icicle" ("well-oiled bicycle")
"You were fighting a liar in the quadrangle." ("lighting a fire")
"Is the bean dizzy?" (as opposed to "is the dean busy?")

7. Stories

Make up quick stories or incidents involving the material you want to memorize. For larger chunks of information, the stories can get more elaborate. Structured stories are particularly good for remembering lists or other sequenced information. Have a look at https://en.wikipedia.org/wiki/Method_of_loci for a more advanced memory sequencing technique.

Visual Metaphors

"Limits, like fear, is often an illusion." –Michael Jordan

What is a Metaphor?

A metaphor is a figure of speech that refers to one thing by mentioning another thing. Metaphors provide clarity and identify hidden similarities between two seemingly unrelated ideas. A visual metaphor is an image that creates a link between different ideas.

Visual metaphors help us use our understanding of the world to learn new concepts, skills, and ideas. Visual metaphors help us relate new material to what we already know. Visual metaphors must be clear and simple enough to spark a connection and understanding. Visual metaphors should use familiar things to help you be less fearful of new, complex, or challenging topics. Metaphors trigger a sense of familiarity so that you are more accepting of the new idea. Metaphors work best when you associate a familiar, easy to understand idea with a challenging, obscure, or abstract concept.

How to make a visual metaphor

1. Brainstorm using the words of the concept. Use different fonts, colors, or shapes to represent parts of the concept.

2. Merge these images together

3. Show the process using arrows, accents, etc.

4. Think about the story line your metaphor projects.

Examples of visual metaphors:

A skeleton used to show a framework of something.

A cloud showing an outline.

A bodybuilder whose muscles represent supporting ideas and details.

A sandwich where the meat, tomato, and lettuce represent supporting ideas.

A recipe card to show a process.

Your metaphor should be accurate. It should be complex enough to convey meaning, but simple and clear enough to be easily understood.

Morphology
"SCIENCE IS THE CAPTAIN, AND PRACTICE THE SOLDIERS." LEONARDO DA VINCI

Morphology is the study of the origin, roots, suffixes, and prefixes of the words. Understanding the meaning of prefixes, suffixes, and roots make it easier to decode the meaning of new vocabulary. Having the ability to decode using morphology increases text comprehension when initially reading as well.

The capability of identifying meaningful parts of words (morphemes), including prefixes, suffixes, and roots can be helpful. Identifying morphemes improves decoding accuracy and fluency. Reading speed improves when you can decode larger chunks of text quickly. When you can recognize morphemes in words, you will be better able to make sense of new words in context. Below are charts containing the most common prefixes, suffixes, and root words. Use them to help you decode your vocabulary terms.

Prefixes

Prefix	Meaning	Example words and meanings	
a, ab, abs	away from	absent abdicate	not to be present, to give up an office or throne.
ad, a, ac, af, ag, an, ar, at, as	to, toward	Advance advantage	To move forward To have the upper hand
anti	against	Antidote antisocial antibiotic	To repair poisoning refers to someone who's not social
bi, bis	two	bicycle binary biweekly	two-wheeled cycle two number system every two weeks
circum, cir	around	circumnavigate circle	Travel around the world a figure that goes all around
com, con, co, col	with, together	Complete Complement	To finish To go along with
de	away from, down, the opposite of	depart detour	to go away from to go out of your way
dis, dif, di	apart	dislike dishonest distant	not to like not honest away
En-, em-	Cause to	Entrance	the way in.
epi	upon, on top of	epitaph epilogue epidemic	writing upon a tombstone speech at the end, on top of the rest
equ, equi	equal	equalize equitable	to make equal fair, equal
ex, e, ef	out, from	exit eject exhale	to go out to throw out to breathe out
Fore-	Before	Forewarned	To have prior warning

Prefix	Meaning	Example Words and Meanings	
in, il, ir, im, en	in, into	Infield Imbibe	The inner playing field to take part in
in, il, ig, ir, im	not	inactive ignorant irreversible irritate	not active not knowing not reversible to put into discomfort
inter	between, among	international interact	among nations to mix with
mal, male	bad, ill, wrong	malpractice malfunction	bad practice fail to function, bad function
Mid	Middle	Amidships	In the middle of a ship
mis	wrong, badly	misnomer	The wrong name
mono	one, alone, single	monocle	one lensed glasses
non	not, the reverse of	nonprofit	not making a profit
ob	in front, against, in front of, in the way of	Obsolete	No longer needed
omni	everywhere, all	omnipresent omnipotent	always present, everywhere all powerful
Over	On top	Overdose	Take too much medication
Pre	Before	Preview	Happens before a show.
per	through	Permeable pervasive	to pass through, all encompassing
poly	many	Polygamy polygon	many spouses figure with many sides
post	after	postpone postmortem	to do after after death
pre	before, earlier than	Predict Preview	To know before To view before release
pro	forward, going ahead of, supporting	proceed pro-war promote	to go forward supporting the war to raise or move forward
re	again, back	retell recall reverse	to tell again to call back to go back
se	apart	secede seclude	to withdraw, become apart to stay apart from others
Semi	Half	Semipermeable	Half-permeable

Prefix	Meaning	Example Words and Meanings	
Sub	under, less than	Submarine	under water
super	over, above, greater	superstar superimpose	a start greater than her stars to put over something else
trans	across	transcontinental transverse	across the continent to lie or go across
un, uni	one	unidirectional unanimous unilateral	having one direction sharing one view having one side
un	not	uninterested unhelpful unethical	not interested not helpful not ethical

Roots

Root	Meaning	Example words & meanings	
act, ag	to do, to act	Agent Activity	One who acts as a representative Action
Aqua	Water	Aquamarine	The color of water
Aud	To hear	Auditorium	A place to hear music
apert	open	Aperture	An opening
bas	low	Basement Basement	Something that is low, at the bottom A room that is low
Bio	Living thing	Biological	Living matter
cap, capt, cip, cept, ceive	to take, to hold, to seize	Captive Receive Capable Recipient	One who is held To take Able to take hold of things One who takes hold or receives
ced, cede, ceed, cess	to go, to give in	Precede Access Proceed	To go before Means of going to To go forward
Cogn	Know	Cognitive	Ability to think
cred, credit	to believe	Credible Incredible Credit	Believable Not believable Belief, trust
curr, curs, cours	to run	Current Precursory Recourse	Now in progress, running Running (going) before To run for aid
Cycle	Circle	Lifecycle	The circle of life
dic, dict	to say	Dictionary Indict	A book explaining words (sayings)

Root	Meaning	Examples and meanings	
duc, duct	to lead	Induce Conduct Aqueduct	To lead to action To lead or guide Pipe that leads water somewhere
equ	equal, even	Equality Equanimity	Equal in social, political rights Evenness of mind, tranquility
fac, fact, fic, fect, fy	to make, to do	Facile Fiction Factory Affect	Easy to do Something that is made up Place that makes things To make a change in
fer, ferr	to carry, bring	Defer Referral	To carry away Bring a source for help/information
Gen	Birth	Generate	To create something
graph	write	Monograph Graphite	A writing on a particular subject A form of carbon used for writing
Loc	Place	Location	A place
Mater	Mother	Maternity	Expecting birth
Mem	Recall	Memory	The recall experiences
mit, mis	to send	Admit Missile	To send in Something sent through the air
Nat	Born	Native	Born in a place
par	equal	Parity Disparate	Equality No equal, not alike
Ped	Foot	Podiatrist	Foot doctor
Photo	Light	Photograph	A picture
plic	to fold, to bend, to turn	Complicate Implicate	To fold (mix) together To fold in, to involve
pon, pos, posit, pose	to place	Component Transpose Compose Deposit	A part placed together with others A place across To put many parts into place To place for safekeeping
scrib, script	to write	Describe Transcript Subscription	To write about or tell about A written copy A written signature or document
sequ, secu	to follow	Sequence	In following order

Root	Meaning	Examples and Meanings	
Sign	Mark	Signal	to alert somebody
spec, spect, spic	to appear, to look, to see	Specimen Aspect	An example to look at One way to see something
sta, stat, sist, stit, sisto	to stand, or make stand Stable, steady	Constant Status Stable Desist	Standing with Social standing Steady (standing) To stand away from
Struct	To build	Construction	To build a thing
tact	to touch	Contact Tactile	To touch together To be able to be touched
ten, tent, tain	to hold	Tenable Retentive Maintain	Able to be held, holding Holding To keep or hold up
tend, tens, tent	to stretch	Extend Tension	To stretch or draw out Stretched
Therm	Temperature	Thermometer	Detects temperature
tract	to draw	Attract Contract	To draw together An agreement drawn up
ven, vent	to come	Convene Advent	To come together A coming
Vis	See	Invisible	Cannot be seen
ver, vert, vers	to turn	Avert Revert Reverse	To turn away To turn back To turn around

Crossword Puzzles

1. Using the Across and Down clues, write the correct words in the numbered grid below.

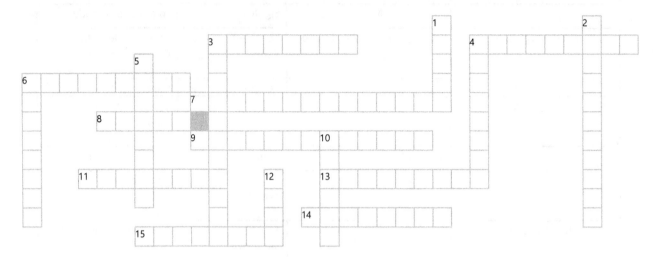

ACROSS

3. Allergen is a substance that causes an allergic reaction.
4. A deep cleansing process which strips the hair lightly before a chemical service. Also known as clarifying.
6. A collection of fat cells resulting from poor lymphatic drainage, fluid retention, poor circulation, not drinking enough water, a sedentary lifestyle and hormones.
7. An antiandrogen and is used in the treatment of androgen related disorders such as female pattern baldness and hirsutism.
8. The oily secretion of the sebaceous glands of the scalp, composed of keratin, fat or cellular debris.
9. Term used to measure the output energy for Lasers and Pulsed Light Sources.
11. Surgical procedure that lifts and stretches the patient's skin to provide a firmer more youthful look.
13. A medical term for blackheads.
14. Flaking scalp due to excessive cell production.
15. The space between the eyebrows.

ACROSS

3. Allergen is a substance that causes an allergic reaction.
4. A deep cleansing process which strips the hair lightly before a chemical service. Also known as clarifying.
6. A collection of fat cells resulting from poor lymphatic drainage, fluid retention, poor circulation, not drinking enough water, a sedentary lifestyle and hormones.
7. An antiandrogen and is used in the treatment of androgen related disorders such as female pattern baldness and hirsutism.
8. The oily secretion of the sebaceous glands of the scalp, composed of keratin, fat or cellular debris.
9. Term used to measure the output energy for Lasers and Pulsed Light Sources.
11. Surgical procedure that lifts and stretches the patient's skin to provide a firmer more youthful look.
13. A medical term for blackheads.
14. Flaking scalp due to excessive cell production.
15. The space between the eyebrows.

A. FINASTERIDE   B. ESCHAR   C. ENERGY DENSITY   D. GLABELLA
E. ALLERGEN   F. FACE LIFT   G. CELLULITE   H. SPRIONOLACTONE
I. SEBUM   J. ACUPUNCTURE   K. CUTICLES   L. CHILLTIP
M. COMEDONES   N. CHELATING   O. DANDRUFF   P. T ZONE
Q. DIABETES   R. PABA

2. Using the Across and Down clues, write the correct words in the numbered grid below.

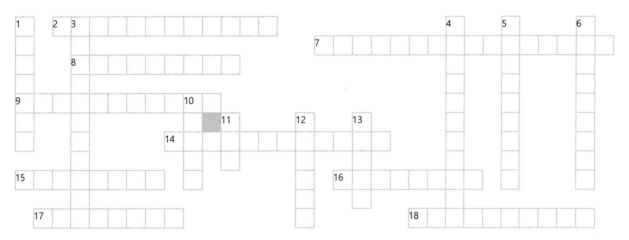

ACROSS

2. A lining around a hair.
7. This refers to hair loss which occurs due to traction being placed on hair. Traction alopecia is commonly seen with braids, pony tails and other hairstyles which cause tension on the scalp.
8. The hair follicle is the tiny blub under your scalp from which the hair grows.
9. Commonly used in the treatment of acne and other skin conditions.
14. Blocks the effects of androgens, normally by blocking the receptor sites.
15. A recessive hereditary trait which presents as white hair due to defective melanin production thought to be caused by a mutation within genes.
16. Products that reflect all the sun's rays, such as zinc oxide and titanium dioxide. They permit minimal tanning, and are a good choice for those who are sensitive to chemicals.
17. Flaking scalp due to excessive cell production.
18. A mixture of wax, thickeners, and a group of chemicals used to coat the hair shaft and detangle after shampooing.

ACROSS

2. A lining around a hair.
7. This refers to hair loss which occurs due to traction being placed on hair. Traction alopecia is commonly seen with braids, pony tails and other hairstyles which cause tension on the scalp.
8. The hair follicle is the tiny blub under your scalp from which the hair grows.
9. Commonly used in the treatment of acne and other skin conditions.
14. Blocks the effects of androgens, normally by blocking the receptor sites.
15. A recessive hereditary trait which presents as white hair due to defective melanin production thought to be caused by a mutation within genes.
16. Products that reflect all the sun's rays, such as zinc oxide and titanium dioxide. They permit minimal tanning, and are a good choice for those who are sensitive to chemicals.
17. Flaking scalp due to excessive cell production.
18. A mixture of wax, thickeners, and a group of chemicals used to coat the hair shaft and detangle after shampooing.

A. DERMAL SHEATH
B. DANDRUFF
C. IONIC
D. SUNBLOCK
E. BRASSY
F. CREAM RINSE
G. FOLLICLES
H. ALBINISM
I. ANAGEN CYCLE
J. ANTIANDROGEN
K. SERUM
L. TRACTION ALOPECIA
M. AZELAIC ACID
N. WIG
O. DONOR SITE
P. MICRO FINE
Q. EXFOLIATION
R. HYDRATE

3. Using the Across and Down clues, write the correct words in the numbered grid below.

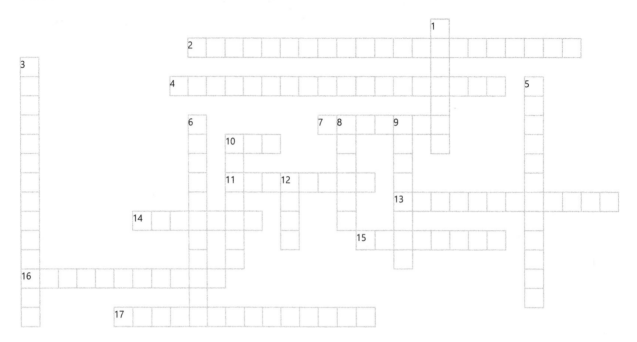

ACROSS

2. The process of attaching hair wefts without braids. The links are sewn on to the wefted hair. The user's natural hair is pulled through and locked secure.
4. Also known as a CO2 laser, these are commonly used to perform skin resurfacing.
7. The resting stage of the hair cycle.
10. The classic look of the 50s and 60s; the style was short and straight but blow-dried and curled under.
11. A female hormone sometimes linked to increased hair growth.
13. The essence of a plant, removed by compressing, steaming, dissolving or distilling.
14. An alkaline ingredient used in some permanent hair color. An ingredient that results in a chemical action that decolorizes the hair.
15. The hair follicle houses the root of the hair. A pore in the skin from which a hair grows.
16. A substance used to relieve all feeling.
17. A hairspray with medium hold used on a finished style to maintain its shape and hold.

ACROSS

2. The process of attaching hair wefts without braids. The links are sewn on to the wefted hair. The user's natural hair is pulled through and locked secure.
4. Also known as a CO2 laser, these are commonly used to perform skin resurfacing.
7. The resting stage of the hair cycle.
10. The classic look of the 50s and 60s; the style was short and straight but blow-dried and curled under.
11. A female hormone sometimes linked to increased hair growth.
13. The essence of a plant, removed by compressing, steaming, dissolving or distilling.
14. An alkaline ingredient used in some permanent hair color. An ingredient that results in a chemical action that decolorizes the hair.
15. The hair follicle houses the root of the hair. A pore in the skin from which a hair grows.
16. A substance used to relieve all feeling.
17. A hairspray with medium hold used on a finished style to maintain its shape and hold.

A. BETAINE
D. ESSENTIAL OIL
G. CARBON DIOXIDE LASER
J. MICRO LINKING TECHNIQUE
M. SUBCUTANEOUS
P. FOLLICLE

B. BLEMISH
E. GLABELLA
H. ANAESTHETIC
K. LANUGO HAIRS
N. CATOGEN
Q. AMPERE

C. BOB
F. FINISHING SPRAY
I. AMMONIA
L. REMI
O. FOLLICLE SHEATH
R. ESTROGEN

4. Using the Across and Down clues, write the correct words in the numbered grid below.

ACROSS

2. A device that removes hair by grasping hairs above the skin's surface with an electrified tweezers.
6. Makes smooth or slippery by using oil to overcome friction.
7. A non-living hair in the last stages of the hair growth cycle, it is detached from the follicle but has not yet shed.
8. A bodily reaction to an irritant. Skin allergies can be exacerbated by solutions put on the skin.
12. The amount of moisture available in the air.
13. A discoloration of skin from blood, sometimes caused by electrolysis, plucking, or waxing. Also known as Purpura.
14. An inflammation of the skin, a result of over production of oil and bacteria.
15. A fibrous protein found in hair, nails, and skin.
16. An oil or oil rich crème or lotion designed to lubricate the skin and slow moisture loss.
17. Increases wet and dry combability.
18. has been called a more extensive and severe form of dandruff.

ACROSS

2. A device that removes hair by grasping hairs above the skin's surface with an electrified tweezers.
6. Makes smooth or slippery by using oil to overcome friction.
7. A non-living hair in the last stages of the hair growth cycle, it is detached from the follicle but has not yet shed.
8. A bodily reaction to an irritant. Skin allergies can be exacerbated by solutions put on the skin.
12. The amount of moisture available in the air.
13. A discoloration of skin from blood, sometimes caused by electrolysis, plucking, or waxing. Also known as Purpura.
14. An inflammation of the skin, a result of over production of oil and bacteria.
15. A fibrous protein found in hair, nails, and skin.
16. An oil or oil rich crème or lotion designed to lubricate the skin and slow moisture loss.
17. Increases wet and dry combability.
18. has been called a more extensive and severe form of dandruff.

- A. RELAX
- B. AUTOCLAVE
- C. SILICONE
- D. KERATIN
- E. BRUISE
- F. LUBRICATES
- G. ELECTRIC TWEEZER
- H. SEBORRHOEIC DERMATITIS
- I. FEATHERING
- J. SURFACTANTS
- K. ACNE
- L. LUBRICANT
- M. REMI
- N. HUMIDITY
- O. ALLERGY
- P. ALEXANDRITE
- Q. CLUB HAIR
- R. LIQUID HAIR

27

5. Using the Across and Down clues, write the correct words in the numbered grid below.

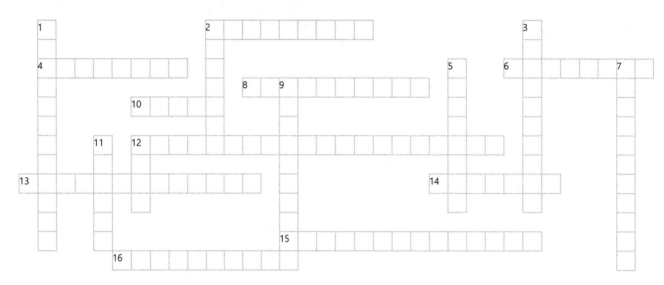

ACROSS

2. An ingredient in skin or hair products that draws moisture from the air to moisturize.
4. The process by which most synthetic fiber is curled at the factory.
6. Flaking scalp due to excessive cell production.
8. A very small hair graft usually consisting of one or two hairs.
10. Medical term for beard.
12. This is the common name for male or female pattern baldness which depends on the genetic predisposition of the hair follicles and the levels of DHT in the body.
13. Products so labeled may still contain small amounts of fragrances to mask the fatty odor of soap or other unpleasant odors.
14. Pertaining to a substance, product or drug that is not protected by trademark. It is identical in chemical composition but not necessarily equivalent in therapeutic effect.
15. An antiandrogen and is used in the treatment of androgen related disorders such as female pattern baldness and hirsutism.
16. Highly effective active anti-dandruff ingredient. Combats bacteria on the scalp.

ACROSS

2. An ingredient in skin or hair products that draws moisture from the air to moisturize.
4. The process by which most synthetic fiber is curled at the factory.
6. Flaking scalp due to excessive cell production.
8. A very small hair graft usually consisting of one or two hairs.
10. Medical term for beard.
12. This is the common name for male or female pattern baldness which depends on the genetic predisposition of the hair follicles and the levels of DHT in the body.
13. Products so labeled may still contain small amounts of fragrances to mask the fatty odor of soap or other unpleasant odors.
14. Pertaining to a substance, product or drug that is not protected by trademark. It is identical in chemical composition but not necessarily equivalent in therapeutic effect.
15. An antiandrogen and is used in the treatment of androgen related disorders such as female pattern baldness and hirsutism.
16. Highly effective active anti-dandruff ingredient. Combats bacteria on the scalp.

A. PARFUM
D. GENERIC
G. BARBA
J. MICRO GRAFT
M. HUMECTANT
P. CREAM RINSE

B. HYDRATE
E. CLIMBAZOLE
H. ACNE
K. TEA TREE OIL
N. FIBROBLASTS
Q. TESTOSTERONE

C. CANITIES
F. SPRIONOLACTONE
I. FRAGRANCE FREE
L. DANDRUFF
O. ALOPECIA ANDROGENETIC
R. STEAMING

6. Using the Across and Down clues, write the correct words in the numbered grid below.

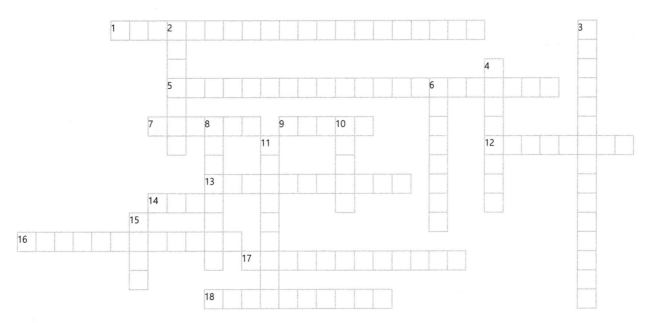

ACROSS

1. This is the common name for male or female pattern baldness which depends on the genetic predisposition of the hair follicles and the levels of DHT in the body.
5. The process of attaching hair wefts without braids. The links are sewn on to the wefted hair. The user's natural hair is pulled through and locked secure.
7. This is the growing phase of the hair cycle which lasts about seven years in a healthy person. The active stage in a hair growth cycle.
9. A unit of energy. Describes energy output for pulsed light based systems.
12. The greying of hair. A pigment deficiency frequently seen in middle-aged people of either sex.
13. Causes blackheads
14. A small opening of the sweat glands of the skin.
16. A common disorder characterized by inflammation of the hair follicle.
17. Refers to a congenital absence of pigment in a lock of hairs which will show as grey or white.
18. Discolored skin that should be examined and approved by a physician before hair removal.

ACROSS

1. This is the common name for male or female pattern baldness which depends on the genetic predisposition of the hair follicles and the levels of DHT in the body.
5. The process of attaching hair wefts without braids. The links are sewn on to the wefted hair. The user's natural hair is pulled through and locked secure.
7. This is the growing phase of the hair cycle which lasts about seven years in a healthy person. The active stage in a hair growth cycle.
9. A unit of energy. Describes energy output for pulsed light based systems.
12. The greying of hair. A pigment deficiency frequently seen in middle-aged people of either sex.
13. Causes blackheads
14. A small opening of the sweat glands of the skin.
16. A common disorder characterized by inflammation of the hair follicle.
17. Refers to a congenital absence of pigment in a lock of hairs which will show as grey or white.
18. Discolored skin that should be examined and approved by a physician before hair removal.

A. GLYCERIN
D. TREATMENT
G. COMEDOGENIC
J. MICRO LINKING TECHNIQUE
M. BIRTHMARKS
P. JOULE

B. ANAGEN
E. CANITIES
H. PIGMENT
K. PORE
N. FOLLICULITIS
Q. CARBOMER

C. LASER
F. ALOPECIA SENILIS
I. SILICONE
L. LEUCOTRICHIA
O. RUBY
R. ALOPECIA ANDROGENETIC

7. Using the Across and Down clues, write the correct words in the numbered grid below.

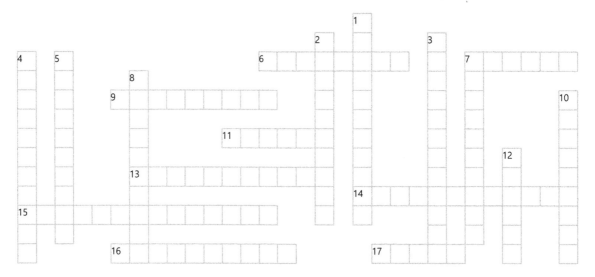

ACROSS

6. A term meaning how well or effectively a cosmetic device works.
7. To become shed or cast off.
9. A chemical ingredients that is specifically added to hair bleach to speed up the action of the bleach without unnecessarily damaging the hair.
11. The most concentrated and most fragrant scent and therefore the most expensive.
13. A product that works under the surface of the skin and provides the necessary ingredients for melanin production, which will accelerate the rate at which the skin tans.
14. The most commonly used scale for the classification of hair loss.
15. A method of cooling the epidermis immediately prior to laser irradiation in hopes of reducing or eliminating damage to the skin's surface.
16. The temporary removal of hair.
17. A group of genetically identical cells or organisms derived from a single common cell.

ACROSS

6. A term meaning how well or effectively a cosmetic device works.
7. To become shed or cast off.
9. A chemical ingredients that is specifically added to hair bleach to speed up the action of the bleach without unnecessarily damaging the hair.
11. The most concentrated and most fragrant scent and therefore the most expensive.
13. A product that works under the surface of the skin and provides the necessary ingredients for melanin production, which will accelerate the rate at which the skin tans.
14. The most commonly used scale for the classification of hair loss.
15. A method of cooling the epidermis immediately prior to laser irradiation in hopes of reducing or eliminating damage to the skin's surface.
16. The temporary removal of hair.
17. A group of genetically identical cells or organisms derived from a single common cell.

A. DEPILATION B. CONTACT COOLING C. ACCELERATOR D. SLOUGH
E. ACTIVATOR F. ANAGEN CYCLE G. EFFICACY H. PARFUM
I. CLONE J. ACID MANTLE K. NORWOOD SCALE L. ANTIANDROGEN
M. BIRTHMARKS N. SEBACEOUS O. SACRUM P. SCRUNCH DRY
Q. TRANSLUCENT R. TOURMALINE

8. Using the Across and Down clues, write the correct words in the numbered grid below.

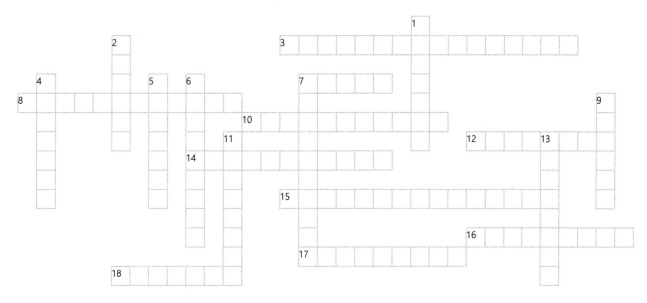

ACROSS

3. Also known as eczema.
7. To weave strands of hair together. On the scalp braiding is used to form a base or track to sew on a commercial weft.
8. A chemically based permanent waving product that has a pH from 7.5 to 9.5. Stronger than acid perms, alkaline perms are designed to produce tight, firm, springy curls.
10. A technique under development which could make an unlimited crop of donor hair available for transplanting.
12. A measurement across the width of the hair.
14. Are usually shed during the 7th month of fetal life following primary folliculo-genesis.
15. Positively charges the hair to provide manageability and reduces static.
16. A small hair graft usually consisting of between three to ten hair roots.
17. Trichoptilosis
18. The resting phase in the hair cycle.

ACROSS

3. Also known as eczema.
7. To weave strands of hair together. On the scalp braiding is used to form a base or track to sew on a commercial weft.
8. A chemically based permanent waving product that has a pH from 7.5 to 9.5. Stronger than acid perms, alkaline perms are designed to produce tight, firm, springy curls.
10. A technique under development which could make an unlimited crop of donor hair available for transplanting.
12. A measurement across the width of the hair.
14. Are usually shed during the 7th month of fetal life following primary folliculo-genesis.
15. Positively charges the hair to provide manageability and reduces static.
16. A small hair graft usually consisting of between three to ten hair roots.
17. Trichoptilosis
18. The resting phase in the hair cycle.

A. CORTEX
B. BLEMISH
C. SPLIT ENDS
D. ANDROGEN
E. ESTROGEN
F. CATIONIC POLYMER
G. ALKALINE PERM
H. DEVELOPER
I. TELOGEN
J. KERATIN
K. HAIR CLONING
L. LANUGO HAIRS
M. BIRTHMARKS
N. BETAINE
O. SPRITZ
P. DIAMETER
Q. ATOPIC DERMATITIS
R. MINI GRAFT
S. BRAID

31

9. Using the Across and Down clues, write the correct words in the numbered grid below.

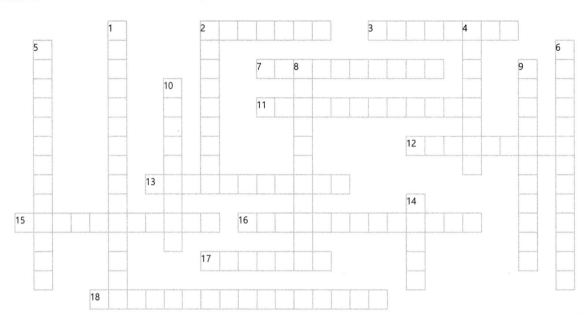

ACROSS

2. The flow of electricity.
3. Reducing skin discomforts from irritation, blemishes, burning skin, etc.
7. A natural or neutral color.
11. A common disorder characterized by inflammation of the hair follicle.
12. A machine used to sterilize medical utensils and some hair removal devices.
13. Detangling aid which conditions, protects against humidity, and adds shine.
15. Are usually shed during the 7th month of fetal life following primary folliculo-genesis.
16. Light that stays focused, a property of lasers.
17. A combination of water containing alcohol and fragrant oils. Not to be confused with a concentrated perfume.
18. This form of hair loss is caused by pulling out one's own hair, usually without realizing it.

ACROSS

2. The flow of electricity.
3. Reducing skin discomforts from irritation, blemishes, burning skin, etc.
7. A natural or neutral color.
11. A common disorder characterized by inflammation of the hair follicle.
12. A machine used to sterilize medical utensils and some hair removal devices.
13. Detangling aid which conditions, protects against humidity, and adds shine.
15. Are usually shed during the 7th month of fetal life following primary folliculo-genesis.
16. Light that stays focused, a property of lasers.
17. A combination of water containing alcohol and fragrant oils. Not to be confused with a concentrated perfume.
18. This form of hair loss is caused by pulling out one's own hair, usually without realizing it.

A. TERMINAL HAIRS
B. BASIC SHADE
C. DEXAMETHOSONE
D. INFUSION
E. FOLLICULITIS
F. COLOGNE
G. OXIDATION COLOUR
H. DIMETHICONE
I. MINOXIDIL
J. TRICHOTILLOMANIA
K. LANUGO HAIRS
L. SOOTHING
M. CURRENT
N. CILIA
O. AUTOCLAVE
P. COHERENT LIGHT
Q. CHAMOMILE
R. SAW PALMETTO
S. SILK PROTEIN

10. Using the Across and Down clues, write the correct words in the numbered grid below.

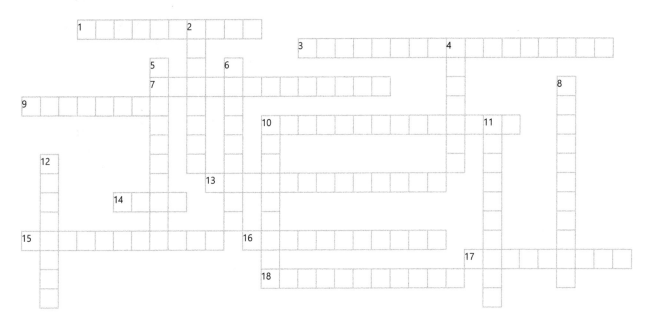

ACROSS

1. Discolored skin that should be examined and approved by a physician before hair removal.
3. These tiny blood vessels at the surface of the skin appear as streaks or blotches.
7. A rounded, thick, tightly curled hair style.
9. The greying of hair. A pigment deficiency frequently seen in middle-aged people of either sex.
10. A method of cooling the epidermis immediately prior to laser irradiation in hopes of reducing or eliminating damage to the skin's surface.
13. a type of electrical energy that travels in one direction.
14. Cleansing agent that is a sodium or potassium salt of animal or vegetable fat.
15. Causes blackheads
16. The forcing of liquids into skin from the negative to the positive pole.
17. The generic name of the brand name drug Rogaine. The first drug to be approved by the FDA for the treatment of androgenetic alopecia.
18. Active agent that allows oil to mix with water. Used in skincare products like cleansers, wetting agents, emulsifiers, solubizers, conditioning agents and foam stabilizers.

ACROSS

1. Discolored skin that should be examined and approved by a physician before hair removal.
3. These tiny blood vessels at the surface of the skin appear as streaks or blotches.
7. A rounded, thick, tightly curled hair style.
9. The greying of hair. A pigment deficiency frequently seen in middle-aged people of either sex.
10. A method of cooling the epidermis immediately prior to laser irradiation in hopes of reducing or eliminating damage to the skin's surface.
13. a type of electrical energy that travels in one direction.
14. Cleansing agent that is a sodium or potassium salt of animal or vegetable fat.
15. Causes blackheads
16. The forcing of liquids into skin from the negative to the positive pole.
17. The generic name of the brand name drug Rogaine. The first drug to be approved by the FDA for the treatment of androgenetic alopecia.
18. Active agent that allows oil to mix with water. Used in skincare products like cleansers, wetting agents, emulsifiers, solubizers, conditioning agents and foam stabilizers.

A. NEUTRALISE
B. COMEDOGENIC
C. CONTACT COOLING
D. SURFACTANTS
E. PAPILLA
F. COMEDONES
G. BASIC SHADE
H. AFRO HAIRSTYLE
I. CHAMOMILE
J. ANDROGEN
K. CATIONIC
L. BIRTHMARKS
M. CANITIES
N. BROKEN CAPILLARIES
O. DIRECT CURRENT
P. ANAPHORESIS
Q. MINOXIDIL
R. SOAP
S. AZELAIC ACID

11. Using the Across and Down clues, write the correct words in the numbered grid below.

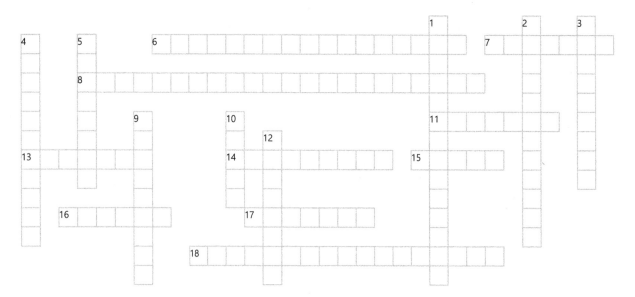

ACROSS

6. An intensive exfoliation process that rejuvenates the skin by utilizing ultra-fine aluminum oxide crystals to remove the upper layer of the stratum corneum.
7. A small fluid-filled bubble on the skin caused by heat from over treatment with certain types of hair removal.
8. A relatively rare condition in which the follicle is not straight.
11. A negative electrode in a cell or circuit.
13. A gland that affects certain types of hair growth.
14. Stops or opposes treatment.
15. Wefts are temporary hair extensions which are glued into your hair.
16. This is the growing phase of the hair cycle which lasts about seven years in a healthy person. The active stage in a hair growth cycle.
17. Term used to describe an on the scalp braid. These braids can be used to form a track for the cornrow weaving method.
18. Baldness following a nervous disorder or injury to the nervous system.

ACROSS

6. An intensive exfoliation process that rejuvenates the skin by utilizing ultra-fine aluminum oxide crystals to remove the upper layer of the stratum corneum.
7. A small fluid-filled bubble on the skin caused by heat from over treatment with certain types of hair removal.
8. A relatively rare condition in which the follicle is not straight.
11. A negative electrode in a cell or circuit.
13. A gland that affects certain types of hair growth.
14. Stops or opposes treatment.
15. Wefts are temporary hair extensions which are glued into your hair.
16. This is the growing phase of the hair cycle which lasts about seven years in a healthy person. The active stage in a hair growth cycle.
17. Term used to describe an on the scalp braid. These braids can be used to form a track for the cornrow weaving method.
18. Baldness following a nervous disorder or injury to the nervous system.

A. ANDROGEN
B. SERUM
C. ESTROGEN
D. MICRO DIFFUSE
E. MICRODERMABRASION
F. CATHODE
G. FOLLICLE SHEATH
H. BLISTER
I. WEFTS
J. CORNROW
K. PERMANENT
L. ALOPECIA NEUROTICA
M. ADRENAL
N. HAIR WEAVING
O. SPLIT ENDS
P. ANAGEN
Q. DISTORTED HAIR FOLLICLES
R. RESISTANT

34

12. Using the Across and Down clues, write the correct words in the numbered grid below.

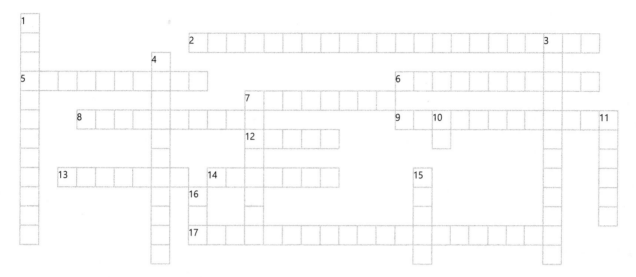

ACROSS

2. Treatments, especially IPL, where the follicle is disabled by the light energy making it unable to support any more hair growth.
5. To cancel or reduce effect.
6. A natural herb that has been shown to be an effective anti-androgen.
7. A pink ointment sometimes used to treat skin irritation
8. an extraction from the Melaleuca tree.
9. Substances used to dissolve hair above the skin's surface.
12. A medical term for swelling.
13. The medulla is a central zone of cells usually only present in large thick hairs.
14. A gland that affects certain types of hair growth.
17. Metabolising stubborn fat deposits, typically in the lower body, using methods such as Eporex mesotherapy.

ACROSS

2. Treatments, especially IPL, where the follicle is disabled by the light energy making it unable to support any more hair growth.
5. To cancel or reduce effect.
6. A natural herb that has been shown to be an effective anti-androgen.
7. A pink ointment sometimes used to treat skin irritation
8. an extraction from the Melaleuca tree.
9. Substances used to dissolve hair above the skin's surface.
12. A medical term for swelling.
13. The medulla is a central zone of cells usually only present in large thick hairs.
14. A gland that affects certain types of hair growth.
17. Metabolising stubborn fat deposits, typically in the lower body, using methods such as Eporex mesotherapy.

A. TARGETED FAT REDUCTION
C. DEPILATORIES
E. CLEARING
G. PH
I. AMINOPHENOLS
K. SAW PALMETTO
M. MEDULLA
O. TEA TREE OIL
Q. FIBROBLASTS

B. ADRENAL
D. DHT
F. PERMANENT HAIR REDUCTION
H. LASER
J. CALAMINE
L. NEUTRALISE
N. SLOUGH
P. INTERLOCKING
R. EDEMA

13. Using the Across and Down clues, write the correct words in the numbered grid below.

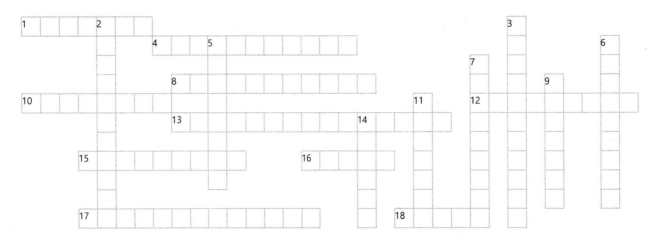

ACROSS

1. Blood or pigment based visible mark.
4. Active agent that allows oil to mix with water. Used in skincare products like cleansers, wetting agents, emulsifiers, solubizers, conditioning agents and foam stabilizers.
8. A natural water-soluble source of acid derived from liquid silk.
10. A natural polymer obtained from sea crustaceans protects the hair.
12. A medical term for blackheads.
13. A modern term used to describe hair weaving.
15. Used in many products for blonde hair to enhance color.
16. Process where water molecules are broken down by ions into smaller droplets. This then allows the hair to absorb the moisture more easily.
17. Products so labeled may still contain small amounts of fragrances to mask the fatty odor of soap or other unpleasant odors.
18. A hair weave is usually a hairpiece with layered gaps made into it.

ACROSS

1. Blood or pigment based visible mark.
4. Active agent that allows oil to mix with water. Used in skincare products like cleansers, wetting agents, emulsifiers, solubizers, conditioning agents and foam stabilizers.
8. A natural water-soluble source of acid derived from liquid silk.
10. A natural polymer obtained from sea crustaceans protects the hair.
12. A medical term for blackheads.
13. A modern term used to describe hair weaving.
15. Used in many products for blonde hair to enhance color.
16. Process where water molecules are broken down by ions into smaller droplets. This then allows the hair to absorb the moisture more easily.
17. Products so labeled may still contain small amounts of fragrances to mask the fatty odor of soap or other unpleasant odors.
18. A hair weave is usually a hairpiece with layered gaps made into it.

A. SILK PROTEIN
B. ADRENAL
C. CHROMOPHORE
D. COMEDONES
E. CHAMOMILE
F. FOLLICLE
G. MICRO FINE
H. CHITOSAN
I. HAIR INTEGRATION
J. SURFACTANTS
K. INGROWN HAIR
L. BLEMISH
M. WEAVE
N. SOLUBLE
O. IONIC
P. FRAGRANCE FREE
Q. DEVELOPER
R. AXILLA

14. Using the Across and Down clues, write the correct words in the numbered grid below.

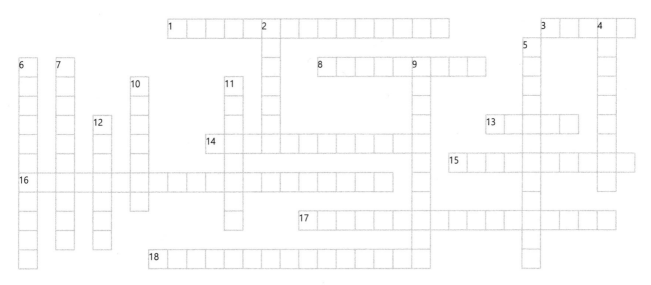

ACROSS

1. This is the complete loss of scalp hair often combined with the loss of eyebrows and eyelashes.
3. Parting or a cornrow that establishes the placement pattern of wefts or strand additions.
8. Trichoptilosis
13. A group of genetically identical cells or organisms derived from a single common cell.
14. Drugs that sometimes cause increased hair growth.
15. Is not as visible, but it's also harder to treat. Lasers have limited effects on it because of its lack of pigment, and it is difficult to see against the skin.
16. Powder or cream preparations that dissolve hair above the surface of the skin. Some find these products very irritating to the skin.
17. An over excitation of melanocytes, darkening of the skin. Can be seen as sun-induced freckles or melasma.
18. A modern term used to describe hair weaving.

ACROSS

1. This is the complete loss of scalp hair often combined with the loss of eyebrows and eyelashes.
3. Parting or a cornrow that establishes the placement pattern of wefts or strand additions.
8. Trichoptilosis
13. A group of genetically identical cells or organisms derived from a single common cell.
14. Drugs that sometimes cause increased hair growth.
15. Is not as visible, but it's also harder to treat. Lasers have limited effects on it because of its lack of pigment, and it is difficult to see against the skin.
16. Powder or cream preparations that dissolve hair above the surface of the skin. Some find these products very irritating to the skin.
17. An over excitation of melanocytes, darkening of the skin. Can be seen as sun-induced freckles or melasma.
18. A modern term used to describe hair weaving.

A. PAPILLA
B. TRACK
C. CURRENT
D. BLONDE HAIR
E. NORWOOD SCALE
F. HAIR INTEGRATION
G. NATURAL
H. CUTTING IN
I. EXFOLIATION
J. AMPHOTERIC
K. ALOPECIA TOTALIS
L. SPLIT ENDS
M. HYPERPIGMENTATION
N. CANITIES
O. CLONE
P. CHEMICAL DEPILATORIES
Q. BIRTH CONTROL
R. ACUPUNCTURE

15. Using the Across and Down clues, write the correct words in the numbered grid below.

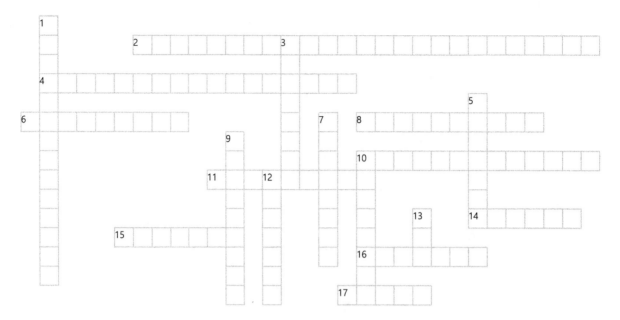

ACROSS

2. Selectively targeting dermal structures with light energy, without causing damage to surrounding tissue.
4. Baldness following a nervous disorder or injury to the nervous system.
6. The generic name of the brand name drug Rogaine. The first drug to be approved by the FDA for the treatment of androgenetic alopecia.
8. To cancel or reduce effect.
10. Produced from starch by means of enzymatic conversion and are used in a wide range of applications in food, pharmaceutical and chemical industries.
11. Refers to a product containing plants or ingredients made from plants.
14. A small temporary scab that occurs sometimes after electrolysis, especially after overtreatment.
15. The small area at the base of the hair root which provides nutrients needed for growth.
16. A chemical formed in the blood when the body uses fat instead of glucose (sugar) for energy.
17. Parting or a cornrow that establishes the placement pattern of wefts or strand additions.

ACROSS

2. Selectively targeting dermal structures with light energy, without causing damage to surrounding tissue.
4. Baldness following a nervous disorder or injury to the nervous system.
6. The generic name of the brand name drug Rogaine. The first drug to be approved by the FDA for the treatment of androgenetic alopecia.
8. To cancel or reduce effect.
10. Produced from starch by means of enzymatic conversion and are used in a wide range of applications in food, pharmaceutical and chemical industries.
11. Refers to a product containing plants or ingredients made from plants.
14. A small temporary scab that occurs sometimes after electrolysis, especially after overtreatment.
15. The small area at the base of the hair root which provides nutrients needed for growth.
16. A chemical formed in the blood when the body uses fat instead of glucose (sugar) for energy.
17. Parting or a cornrow that establishes the placement pattern of wefts or strand additions.

A. NEUTRALISE
C. ESTROGEN
E. FLUENCE
G. DHT
I. ESCHAR
K. PAPILLA
M. GLYCERIN
O. AMMONIA
Q. CYCLODEXTRINS

B. PSORIASIS
D. CLUB HAIR
F. DYNAMIC COOLING
H. SELECTIVE PHOTOTHERMOLYSIS
J. BOTANICAL
L. ALOPECIA NEUROTICA
N. MINOXIDIL
P. ACETONE
R. TRACK

16. Using the Across and Down clues, write the correct words in the numbered grid below.

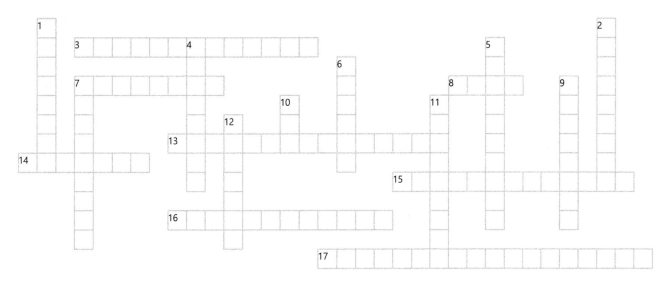

ACROSS

3. A type of electrolysis needle.
7. A protein that holds all connective tissue together under the skin.
8. An alternative to haircut, without any specific meaning to the style of the cut.
13. Variety of skin conditions mainly the result of excess melanin. Commonly known as Café au Lait stains, birthmarks, age spots and freckles.
14. A device that produces short intense bursts of energy from a laser.
15. Coarse, pigmented or non-pigmented, exist on the scalp and gain length at a rate of 1-2cm per month during a cyclical life of up to 10 years.
16. Substances used to dissolve hair above the skin's surface.
17. A treatment consisting of short pulses of light sent out through an applicator that is gently pressed against the skin.

ACROSS

3. A type of electrolysis needle.
7. A protein that holds all connective tissue together under the skin.
8. An alternative to haircut, without any specific meaning to the style of the cut.
13. Variety of skin conditions mainly the result of excess melanin. Commonly known as Café au Lait stains, birthmarks, age spots and freckles.
14. A device that produces short intense bursts of energy from a laser.
15. Coarse, pigmented or non-pigmented, exist on the scalp and gain length at a rate of 1-2cm per month during a cyclical life of up to 10 years.
16. Substances used to dissolve hair above the skin's surface.
17. A treatment consisting of short pulses of light sent out through an applicator that is gently pressed against the skin.

A. TERMINAL HAIRS
B. INTENSE PULSED LIGHT
C. CUTTING IN
D. STEAMING
E. BULBOUS NEEDLE
F. CROP
G. DONOR SITE
H. GREY HAIR
I. EMOLLIENTS
J. ALKALI
K. Q SWITCH
L. COLLAGEN
M. PIGMENTED LESION
N. CANITIES
O. ACTIVATOR
P. DEPILATORIES
Q. AMMONIA
R. DHT

17. Using the Across and Down clues, write the correct words in the numbered grid below.

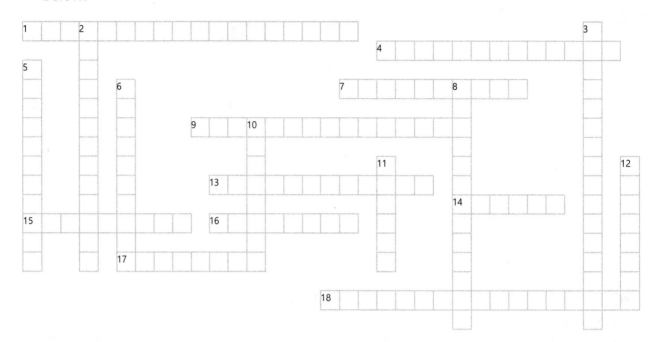

ACROSS

1. A treatment consisting of short pulses of light sent out through an applicator that is gently pressed against the skin.
4. A type of electrolysis needle.
7. The surgical removal of one or both testicles or ovaries.
9. A device that removes hair by grasping hairs above the skin's surface with an electrified tweezers.
13. A basic color with added tone.
14. A plant extract that has been used to treat swelling, soreness and bruising.
15. Means to apply directly onto the scalp.
16. A natural polymer obtained from sea crustaceans protects the hair.
17. Reducing skin discomforts from irritation, blemishes, burning skin, etc.
18. An intensive exfoliation process that rejuvenates the skin by utilizing ultra-fine aluminum oxide crystals to remove the upper layer of the stratum corneum.

ACROSS

1. A treatment consisting of short pulses of light sent out through an applicator that is gently pressed against the skin.
4. A type of electrolysis needle.
7. The surgical removal of one or both testicles or ovaries.
9. A device that removes hair by grasping hairs above the skin's surface with an electrified tweezers.
13. A basic color with added tone.
14. A plant extract that has been used to treat swelling, soreness and bruising.
15. Means to apply directly onto the scalp.
16. A natural polymer obtained from sea crustaceans protects the hair.
17. Reducing skin discomforts from irritation, blemishes, burning skin, etc.
18. An intensive exfoliation process that rejuvenates the skin by utilizing ultra-fine aluminum oxide crystals to remove the upper layer of the stratum corneum.

A. CHITOSAN
B. CRUSTING
C. ALPHA HYDROXY ACID
D. BULBOUS NEEDLE
E. SOOTHING
F. INTENSE PULSED LIGHT
G. BLACKHEADS
H. TERMINAL HAIRS
I. MICRODERMABRASION
J. ESTROGEN
K. ENERGY DENSITY
L. TOPICALLY
M. ARNICA
N. SAW PALMETTO
O. CASTRATION
P. ELECTRIC TWEEZER
Q. FASHION SHADE
R. PARFUM

18. Using the Across and Down clues, write the correct words in the numbered grid below.

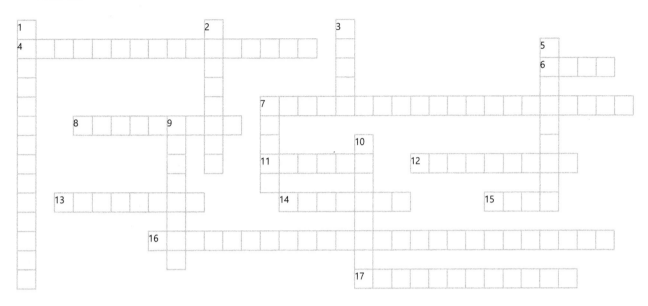

ACROSS

4. Also known as eczema.
6. An inflammation of the skin, a result of over production of oil and bacteria.
7. Metabolising stubborn fat deposits, typically in the lower body, using methods such as Eporex mesotherapy.
8. Contains superior properties to keep skin and hair soft. It is beneficial to dry hair.
11. A classification for stronger, thicker types of hair.
12. The hair follicle is the tiny blub under your scalp from which the hair grows.
13. The process of scraping or wearing hair away. Causing partial or complete absence of hair from areas.
14. To add moisture to the skin.
15. Is sometimes linked to excess hair growth, especially in the extremely obese and extremely anorexic.
16. Selectively targeting dermal structures with light energy, without causing damage to surrounding tissue.
17. Blocks the effects of androgens, normally by blocking the receptor sites.

ACROSS

4. Also known as eczema.
6. An inflammation of the skin, a result of over production of oil and bacteria.
7. Metabolising stubborn fat deposits, typically in the lower body, using methods such as Eporex mesotherapy.
8. Contains superior properties to keep skin and hair soft. It is beneficial to dry hair.
11. A classification for stronger, thicker types of hair.
12. The hair follicle is the tiny blub under your scalp from which the hair grows.
13. The process of scraping or wearing hair away. Causing partial or complete absence of hair from areas.
14. To add moisture to the skin.
15. Is sometimes linked to excess hair growth, especially in the extremely obese and extremely anorexic.
16. Selectively targeting dermal structures with light energy, without causing damage to surrounding tissue.
17. Blocks the effects of androgens, normally by blocking the receptor sites.

A. TRACK
C. COARSE
E. PATCH TEST
G. JOJOBA OIL
I. LAYERING
K. ATOPIC DERMATITIS
M. WATER RESISTANT
O. SELECTIVE PHOTOTHERMOLYSIS
Q. HYDRATE

B. ANTIANDROGEN
D. ABRASION
F. TARGETED FAT REDUCTION
H. ACNE
J. ANDROGEN
L. FOLLICLES
N. DIET
P. WEAVE
R. MELANOMA

19. Using the Across and Down clues, write the correct words in the numbered grid below.

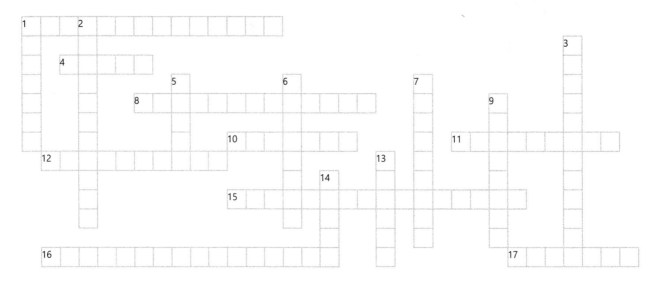

ACROSS

1. Oil producing gland in the dermis.
4. The darkness or lightness of a color.
8. Products so labeled may still contain small amounts of fragrances to mask the fatty odor of soap or other unpleasant odors.
10. A device that produces short intense bursts of energy from a laser.
11. Relating to the skin.
12. broken capillaries.
15. A treatment used on the hair. Designed to add strength and elasticity to the hair by adding protein to the cortex.
16. This refers to hair loss which occurs due to traction being placed on hair. Traction alopecia is commonly seen with braids, pony tails and other hairstyles which cause tension on the scalp.
17. Pertaining to a substance, product or drug that is not protected by trademark. It is identical in chemical composition but not necessarily equivalent in therapeutic effect.

ACROSS

1. Oil producing gland in the dermis.
4. The darkness or lightness of a color.
8. Products so labeled may still contain small amounts of fragrances to mask the fatty odor of soap or other unpleasant odors.
10. A device that produces short intense bursts of energy from a laser.
11. Relating to the skin.
12. broken capillaries.
15. A treatment used on the hair. Designed to add strength and elasticity to the hair by adding protein to the cortex.
16. This refers to hair loss which occurs due to traction being placed on hair. Traction alopecia is commonly seen with braids, pony tails and other hairstyles which cause tension on the scalp.
17. Pertaining to a substance, product or drug that is not protected by trademark. It is identical in chemical composition but not necessarily equivalent in therapeutic effect.

A. SEBACEOUS GLAND
B. FRAGRANCE FREE
C. Q SWITCH
D. GENERIC
E. CATIONIC
F. CUTANEOUS
G. PROTEIN TREATMENT
H. DEPTH
I. CILIA
J. SOLUBLE
K. MATTE
L. ALEXANDRITE
M. FASHION SHADE
N. THREAD VEIN
O. MINI GRAFT
P. DEPILATE
Q. TRACTION ALOPECIA
R. SPRITZ

20. Using the Across and Down clues, write the correct words in the numbered grid below.

ACROSS

1. The space between the eyebrows.
6. A smoothing product to stop your hair from frizzing, keeping it smooth and straight. You'll be able to find a serum that is specifically designed to your own hair type.
9. Hair passes through a series of cycles known as Anagen (growing phase), Catagen (resting phase) and Telogen (dormant phase).
10. A liquid with a pH higher than 7.
13. The body's shock absorber.
14. Hair that has lost its pigment.
15. A liquid, usually corrosive with a pH lower than 7, opposite of an alkali.
16. A product which oxidizes artificial color pigment.
17. Receptors which respond to touch, pain, pressure, heat and cold.
18. The surgical removal of one or both testicles or ovaries.
19. This is baldness due to scarring. The follicles are absent in scar tissue.

ACROSS

1. The space between the eyebrows.
6. A smoothing product to stop your hair from frizzing, keeping it smooth and straight. You'll be able to find a serum that is specifically designed to your own hair type.
9. Hair passes through a series of cycles known as Anagen (growing phase), Catagen (resting phase) and Telogen (dormant phase).
10. A liquid with a pH higher than 7.
13. The body's shock absorber.
14. Hair that has lost its pigment.
15. A liquid, usually corrosive with a pH lower than 7, opposite of an alkali.
16. A product which oxidizes artificial color pigment.
17. Receptors which respond to touch, pain, pressure, heat and cold.
18. The surgical removal of one or both testicles or ovaries.
19. This is baldness due to scarring. The follicles are absent in scar tissue.

A. WHITE HAIR
B. DEVELOPER
C. LEUCOTRICHIA
D. GREY HAIR
E. PANTHENOL
F. PIGMENT
G. HAIR GROWTH CYCLE
H. NERVE ENDINGS
I. SUBCUTANEOUS TISSUE
J. MONOFILAMENT
K. CICATRICIAL ALOPECIA
L. SERUM
M. ERYTHEMA
N. WEFTS
O. ACID
P. GLABELLA
Q. ELECTROLOGY
R. CASTRATION
S. ALKALI

21. Using the Across and Down clues, write the correct words in the numbered grid below.

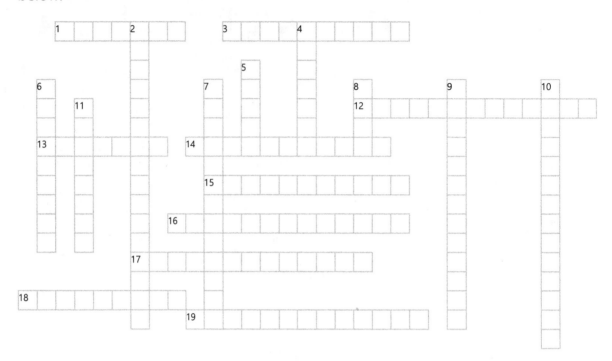

ACROSS

1. To add moisture to the skin.
3. Highly effective active anti-dandruff ingredient. Combats bacteria on the scalp.
12. Term used to measure the output energy for Lasers and Pulsed Light Sources.
13. An herbal concentrate produced by separating the essential or active part of an herb into a solvent material.
14. Causes blackheads
15. A method of relieving pain by pressing down on an area of the body.
16. a type of electrical energy that travels in one direction.
17. Overly aggressive treatment to remove hair which leads to temporary or permanent skin damage.
18. A clarifying shampoo is slightly stronger than everyday shampoos and is designed to remove products, hard water or chlorine residue that have built-up over time.
19. A doctor specializing in skin and hair conditions.

ACROSS

1. To add moisture to the skin.
3. Highly effective active anti-dandruff ingredient. Combats bacteria on the scalp.
12. Term used to measure the output energy for Lasers and Pulsed Light Sources.
13. An herbal concentrate produced by separating the essential or active part of an herb into a solvent material.
14. Causes blackheads
15. A method of relieving pain by pressing down on an area of the body.
16. a type of electrical energy that travels in one direction.
17. Overly aggressive treatment to remove hair which leads to temporary or permanent skin damage.
18. A clarifying shampoo is slightly stronger than everyday shampoos and is designed to remove products, hard water or chlorine residue that have built-up over time.
19. A doctor specializing in skin and hair conditions.

A. BONDING
B. CLARIFIER
C. COMEDOGENIC
D. DERMATOLOGIST
E. CLIMBAZOLE
F. HYDRATE
G. DIRECT CURRENT
H. REMI
I. ACUPRESSURE
J. ENERGY DENSITY
K. EXTRACT
L. AFRO HAIRSTYLE
M. ACTINIC KERATOSIS
N. CYCLODEXTRINS
O. FINISHING SPRAY
P. NUTRIENT
Q. MATTE
R. KANEKALON
S. OVERTREATMENT

22. Using the Across and Down clues, write the correct words in the numbered grid below.

ACROSS

3. Form a protective layer which covers the shaft of hair. If your hair is colored or bleached they can spread out, split or become bloated due to over processing.
4. Flaking scalp due to excessive cell production.
8. In women, a major source of female hormones. Certain conditions involving the ovaries can lead to excess hair growth, especially polycystic ovary syndrome (PCOS).
9. The type of electricity that comes from a wall outlet (AC), as opposed to direct current (DC).
11. The active stage in a hair growth cycle.
13. An organism responsible for infection.
14. Active agent that allows oil to mix with water. Used in skincare products like cleansers, wetting agents, emulsifiers, solubizers, conditioning agents and foam stabilizers.
15. Hair extensions are pieces of real or synthetic weaved close to the scalp in order to achieve greater length or fullness.
17. A natural solvent in oils and creams. It acidifies products.
18. The enzyme superoxide, catalyzes the dis-mutation of superoxide into oxygen and hydrogen peroxide.

ACROSS

3. Form a protective layer which covers the shaft of hair. If your hair is colored or bleached they can spread out, split or become bloated due to over processing.
4. Flaking scalp due to excessive cell production.
8. In women, a major source of female hormones. Certain conditions involving the ovaries can lead to excess hair growth, especially polycystic ovary syndrome (PCOS).
9. The type of electricity that comes from a wall outlet (AC), as opposed to direct current (DC).
11. The active stage in a hair growth cycle.
13. An organism responsible for infection.
14. Active agent that allows oil to mix with water. Used in skincare products like cleansers, wetting agents, emulsifiers, solubizers, conditioning agents and foam stabilizers.
15. Hair extensions are pieces of real or synthetic weaved close to the scalp in order to achieve greater length or fullness.
17. A natural solvent in oils and creams. It acidifies products.
18. The enzyme superoxide, catalyzes the dis-mutation of superoxide into oxygen and hydrogen peroxide.

A. APPLE CIDER VINEGAR
B. BARBA
C. BACTERIA
D. SUPEROXIDE DISMUTASE
E. COLLAGEN
F. A LINE BOB
G. ANAGEN CYCLE
H. OVARIES
I. EXTENSION
J. MONOFILAMENT
K. ALTERNATING CURRENT
L. OVERTREATMENT
M. DANDRUFF
N. CATAGEN
O. ERYTHEMA
P. SURFACTANTS
Q. ACCENT COLOR
R. CUTICLES
S. SEBUM

23. Using the Across and Down clues, write the correct words in the numbered grid below.

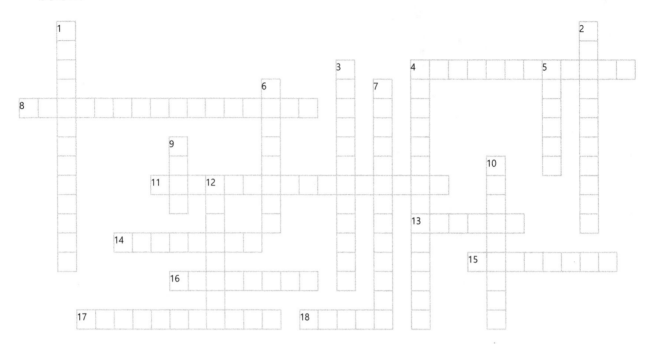

ACROSS

4. The process of converting one enzyme to another.
8. Combating the signs of ageing using the latest innovative, non-invasive treatments that give you visibly younger, healthy, radiant skin.
11. This form of hair loss is caused by pulling out one's own hair, usually without realizing it.
13. A liquid with a pH higher than 7.
14. A method of hair removal in which all hair in an area is removed at once, as opposed to thinning.
15. A recessive hereditary trait which presents as white hair due to defective melanin production thought to be caused by a mutation within genes.
16. The hair follicle houses the root of the hair. A pore in the skin from which a hair grows.
17. A bristle commonly used in natural bristle brushes.
18. A unit of energy. Describes energy output for pulsed light based systems.

ACROSS

4. The process of converting one enzyme to another.
8. Combating the signs of ageing using the latest innovative, non-invasive treatments that give you visibly younger, healthy, radiant skin.
11. This form of hair loss is caused by pulling out one's own hair, usually without realizing it.
13. A liquid with a pH higher than 7.
14. A method of hair removal in which all hair in an area is removed at once, as opposed to thinning.
15. A recessive hereditary trait which presents as white hair due to defective melanin production thought to be caused by a mutation within genes.
16. The hair follicle houses the root of the hair. A pore in the skin from which a hair grows.
17. A bristle commonly used in natural bristle brushes.
18. A unit of energy. Describes energy output for pulsed light based systems.

A. DILANTIN
B. ANAGEN
C. HAIR WEAVING
D. ALOPECIA AREATA
E. AMORTIZATION
F. CATAPHORESIS
G. CLEARING
H. CELLULITE
I. SKIN REJUVENATION
J. TERMINAL HAIRS
K. JOULE
L. BOAR BRISTLE
M. CUTICLES
N. TRICHOTILLOMANIA
O. ALBINISM
P. FRAGRANCE FREE
Q. PORE
R. FOLLICLE
S. ALKALI

24. Using the Across and Down clues, write the correct words in the numbered grid below.

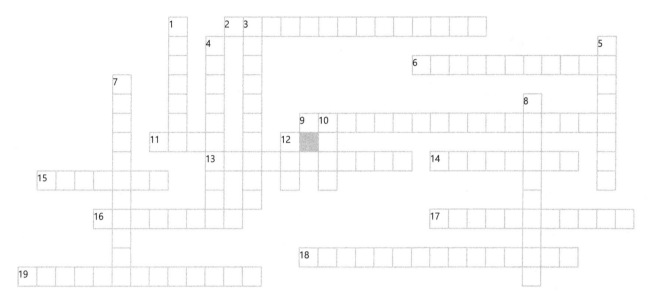

ACROSS

2. Congenital baldness or baldness at birth.
6. A disease of the skin and connective tissue that can cause hair loss over the affected areas.
9. A natural solvent in oils and creams. It acidifies products.
11. creates curls by restructuring your hair molecules with a chemical, or heat treatment and is generally a long-lasting or permanent change to your hair.
13. The forcing of liquids into skin from the negative to the positive pole.
14. Tea made by steeping an herb's leaves or flowers in hot water.
15. Color.
16. A recessive hereditary trait which presents as white hair due to defective melanin production thought to be caused by a mutation within genes.
17. Causes blackheads
18. Variety of skin conditions mainly the result of excess melanin. Commonly known as Café au Lait stains, birthmarks, age spots and freckles.
19. Produced from starch by means of enzymatic conversion and are used in a wide range of applications in food, pharmaceutical and chemical industries.

ACROSS

2. Congenital baldness or baldness at birth.
6. A disease of the skin and connective tissue that can cause hair loss over the affected areas.
9. A natural solvent in oils and creams. It acidifies products.
11. creates curls by restructuring your hair molecules with a chemical, or heat treatment and is generally a long-lasting or permanent change to your hair.
13. The forcing of liquids into skin from the negative to the positive pole.
14. Tea made by steeping an herb's leaves or flowers in hot water.
15. Color.
16. A recessive hereditary trait which presents as white hair due to defective melanin production thought to be caused by a mutation within genes.
17. Causes blackheads
18. Variety of skin conditions mainly the result of excess melanin. Commonly known as Café au Lait stains, birthmarks, age spots and freckles.
19. Produced from starch by means of enzymatic conversion and are used in a wide range of applications in food, pharmaceutical and chemical industries.

A. CATHODE
D. PERM
G. LIQUID HAIR
J. BIRTHMARKS
M. DHT
P. APPLE CIDER VINEGAR
S. PIGMENT

B. LAYERING
E. DOUBLE BLIND
H. CYCLODEXTRINS
K. INFUSION
N. ANAPHORESIS
Q. ALBINISM

C. PORE
F. ANTIBIOTIC
I. PIGMENTED LESION
L. ALOPECIA ADNATA
O. COMEDOGENIC
R. SCLERODERMA

25. Using the Across and Down clues, write the correct words in the numbered grid below.

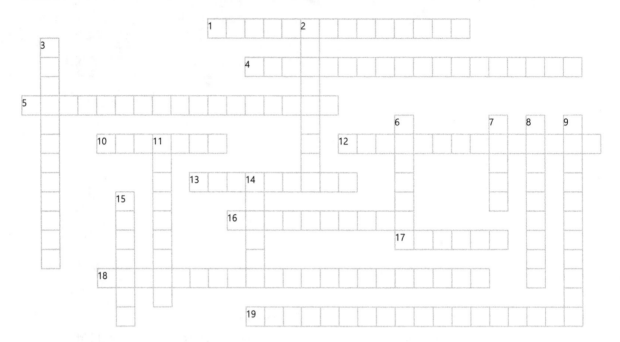

ACROSS

1. Hair loss which occurs in patches on the scalp.
4. This drug is normally used to reduce sex drive in men who have an excessive sex drive. It is also prescribed to treat hirsutism and androgenic alopecia in women.
5. The structural protein of hair.
10. Dark skin discoloration on sun-exposed areas of the face and neck. Young women with brownish skin tones are at greatest risk.
12. Groupings of hair that grow together and share the same blood supply.
13. A test performed on the skin 24 hours before its use to determine sensitivity.
16. A natural or neutral color.
17. Retinoic Acid, compound that is often used to improve the appearance and texture of the skin.
18. has been called a more extensive and severe form of dandruff.
19. The body's shock absorber.

ACROSS

1. Hair loss which occurs in patches on the scalp.
4. This drug is normally used to reduce sex drive in men who have an excessive sex drive. It is also prescribed to treat hirsutism and androgenic alopecia in women.
5. The structural protein of hair.
10. Dark skin discoloration on sun-exposed areas of the face and neck. Young women with brownish skin tones are at greatest risk.
12. Groupings of hair that grow together and share the same blood supply.
13. A test performed on the skin 24 hours before its use to determine sensitivity.
16. A natural or neutral color.
17. Retinoic Acid, compound that is often used to improve the appearance and texture of the skin.
18. has been called a more extensive and severe form of dandruff.
19. The body's shock absorber.

A. ALOPECIA AREATA
B. COARSE
C. CYPROTERONE ACETATE
D. SEBORRHOEIC DERMATITIS
E. LASER
F. SUBCUTANEOUS TISSUE
G. CURRENT
H. AUTOCLAVE
I. BASIC SHADE
J. BLISTER
K. PATCH TEST
L. RETIN-A
M. FOLLICULAR UNIT
N. HYDROLYZED KERATIN
O. FINASTERIDE
P. ACTIVATOR
Q. CORTISONE
R. CETYL ALCOHOL
S. MELASMA

26. Using the Across and Down clues, write the correct words in the numbered grid below.

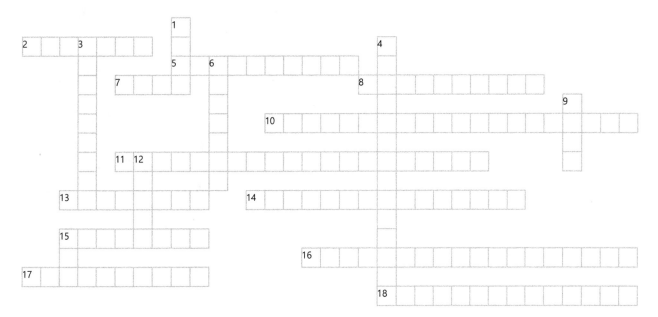

ACROSS

2. A gland that affects certain types of hair growth.
5. A hairstyle in which the hair naturally or through manipulation is encouraged to matte and form a cylindrical, rope-like pattern.
7. Commonly used laser for hair and tattoo removal.
8. A type of clogged pore in the skin with a visible black plug.
10. This is the common name for male or female pattern baldness which depends on the genetic predisposition of the hair follicles and the levels of DHT in the body.
11. Hair loss due to inflammation of hair follicles.
13. Tea made by steeping an herb's leaves or flowers in hot water.
14. Alopecia senilis is baldness due to old age.
15. Flaking scalp due to excessive cell production.
16. A treatment consisting of short pulses of light sent out through an applicator that is gently pressed against the skin.
17. The body transformation of food into energy.
18. Split ends.

ACROSS

2. A gland that affects certain types of hair growth.
5. A hairstyle in which the hair naturally or through manipulation is encouraged to matte and form a cylindrical, rope-like pattern.
7. Commonly used laser for hair and tattoo removal.
8. A type of clogged pore in the skin with a visible black plug.
10. This is the common name for male or female pattern baldness which depends on the genetic predisposition of the hair follicles and the levels of DHT in the body.
11. Hair loss due to inflammation of hair follicles.
13. Tea made by steeping an herb's leaves or flowers in hot water.
14. Alopecia senilis is baldness due to old age.
15. Flaking scalp due to excessive cell production.
16. A treatment consisting of short pulses of light sent out through an applicator that is gently pressed against the skin.
17. The body transformation of food into energy.
18. Split ends.

A. EXTRACT
B. DREADLOCKS
C. INFUSION
D. ALOPECIA ANDROGENETIC
E. METABOLISM
F. TRICHOPTILOSIS
G. DANDRUFF
H. DHT
I. ADRENAL
J. RUBY
K. BODY
L. ALOPECIA SENILIS
M. LASER
N. ALOPECIA FOLLICULARIS
O. FOLLICULAR UNIT
P. EPILATION
Q. BLACKHEADS
R. INTENSE PULSED LIGHT
S. PERM

27. Using the Across and Down clues, write the correct words in the numbered grid below.

ACROSS

3. Also known as a CO2 laser, these are commonly used to perform skin resurfacing.
7. Variety of skin conditions mainly the result of excess melanin. Commonly known as Café au Lait stains, birthmarks, age spots and freckles.
9. A term meaning how well or effectively a cosmetic device works.
10. Area at the top of the head.
12. This is the growing phase of the hair cycle which lasts about seven years in a healthy person. The active stage in a hair growth cycle.
15. The enzyme superoxide, catalyzes the dis-mutation of superoxide into oxygen and hydrogen peroxide.
16. Term for loose commercial hair. This hair is used for creating wefts or for services like fusion.
17. Used to measure acidity in cosmetic preparations.
18. A fibrous protein found in hair, nails, and skin.

ACROSS

3. Also known as a CO2 laser, these are commonly used to perform skin resurfacing.
7. Variety of skin conditions mainly the result of excess melanin. Commonly known as Café au Lait stains, birthmarks, age spots and freckles.
9. A term meaning how well or effectively a cosmetic device works.
10. Area at the top of the head.
12. This is the growing phase of the hair cycle which lasts about seven years in a healthy person. The active stage in a hair growth cycle.
15. The enzyme superoxide, catalyzes the dis-mutation of superoxide into oxygen and hydrogen peroxide.
16. Term for loose commercial hair. This hair is used for creating wefts or for services like fusion.
17. Used to measure acidity in cosmetic preparations.
18. A fibrous protein found in hair, nails, and skin.

A. PH
B. BLACKHEADS
C. EFFICACY
D. PALMITATE
E. PROPRIETARY
F. GENE THERAPY
G. CARBON DIOXIDE LASER
H. KERATIN
I. BULGE
J. LENTIGO
K. SUPEROXIDE DISMUTASE
L. LIQUID HAIR
M. COARSE
N. BULK HAIR
O. PIGMENTED LESION
P. TRACK
Q. ACCENT COLOR
R. CROWN
S. ANAGEN

28. Using the Across and Down clues, write the correct words in the numbered grid below.

ACROSS

6. The pigmented area surrounding the nipple. A very common area for hair growth.
10. The hard outer protective layer of the hair. Impart sheen to the hair.
11. Means to apply directly onto the scalp.
13. A combination of water containing alcohol and fragrant oils. Not to be confused with a concentrated perfume.
14. Removal of hair on the surface of the skin. Examples include shaving or the use of depilatory creams.
15. The darkness or lightness of a color.
16. To add moisture to the skin.
17. A Synthetic moisturizer.
18. A definition set by the American FDA that most laser and intense light source manufacturers claim to meet for hair removal.
19. Powder or cream preparations that dissolve hair above the surface of the skin. Some find these products very irritating to the skin.

ACROSS

6. The pigmented area surrounding the nipple. A very common area for hair growth.
10. The hard outer protective layer of the hair. Impart sheen to the hair.
11. Means to apply directly onto the scalp.
13. A combination of water containing alcohol and fragrant oils. Not to be confused with a concentrated perfume.
14. Removal of hair on the surface of the skin. Examples include shaving or the use of depilatory creams.
15. The darkness or lightness of a color.
16. To add moisture to the skin.
17. A Synthetic moisturizer.
18. A definition set by the American FDA that most laser and intense light source manufacturers claim to meet for hair removal.
19. Powder or cream preparations that dissolve hair above the surface of the skin. Some find these products very irritating to the skin.

A. EXTRACT
B. MOISTURIZER
C. DEPTH
D. HYDRATE
E. AREOLA
F. DOUBLE BLIND
G. CUTICLE
H. COLOGNE
I. ALKALI
J. ISOPROPYL LANOLATE
K. ECZEMA
L. CARBOMER
M. DEPILATE
N. MEDULLA
O. DIABETES
P. SILK PROTEIN
Q. TOPICALLY
R. CHEMICAL DEPILATORIES
S. PERMANENT

29. Using the Across and Down clues, write the correct words in the numbered grid below.

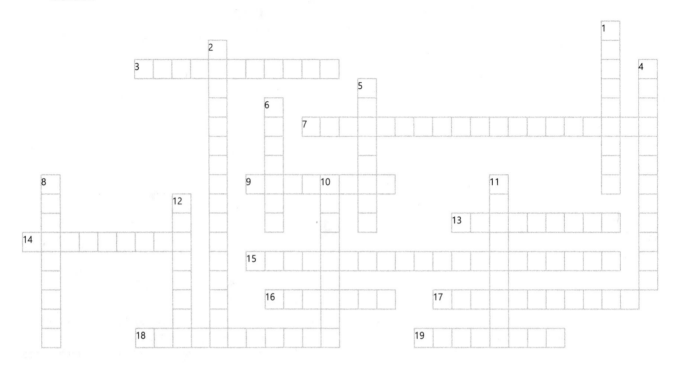

ACROSS

3. A method of relieving pain by pressing down on an area of the body.
7. The enzyme superoxide, catalyzes the dis-mutation of superoxide into oxygen and hydrogen peroxide.
9. The space between the eyebrows.
13. A small hair graft usually consisting of between three to ten hair roots.
14. A drug sometimes linked to excess hair growth.
15. Hair loss due to inflammation of hair follicles.
16. Blood or pigment based visible mark.
17. A product that works under the surface of the skin and provides the necessary ingredients for melanin production, which will accelerate the rate at which the skin tans.
18. Active agent that allows oil to mix with water. Used in skincare products like cleansers, wetting agents, emulsifiers, solubizers, conditioning agents and foam stabilizers.
19. A drug sometimes linked to excess hair growth.

ACROSS

3. A method of relieving pain by pressing down on an area of the body.
7. The enzyme superoxide, catalyzes the dis-mutation of superoxide into oxygen and hydrogen peroxide.
9. The space between the eyebrows.
13. A small hair graft usually consisting of between three to ten hair roots.
14. A drug sometimes linked to excess hair growth.
15. Hair loss due to inflammation of hair follicles.
16. Blood or pigment based visible mark.
17. A product that works under the surface of the skin and provides the necessary ingredients for melanin production, which will accelerate the rate at which the skin tans.
18. Active agent that allows oil to mix with water. Used in skincare products like cleansers, wetting agents, emulsifiers, solubizers, conditioning agents and foam stabilizers.
19. A drug sometimes linked to excess hair growth.

A. PAPILLA
B. DIAZOXIDE
C. SUNSCREEN
D. EPIDERMIS
E. ESSENTIAL OIL
F. GLABELLA
G. MINI GRAFT
H. ACUPRESSURE
I. FRECKLES
J. GREY HAIR
K. ALOPECIA FOLLICULARIS
L. DILANTIN
M. BLEMISH
N. RESISTANT
O. JOJOBA OIL
P. SURFACTANTS
Q. TRACTION ALOPECIA
R. SUPEROXIDE DISMUTASE
S. ACCELERATOR

30. Using the Across and Down clues, write the correct words in the numbered grid below.

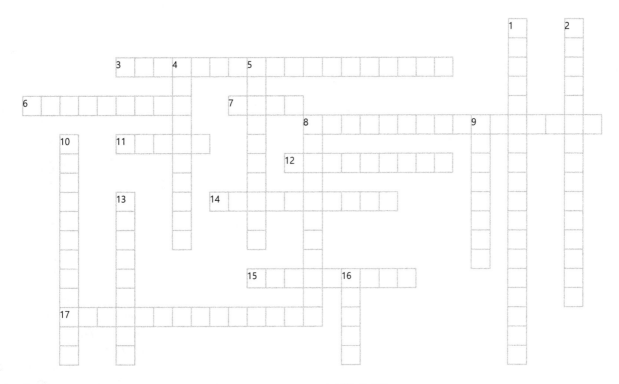

ACROSS

- 3. The body's shock absorber.
- 6. Brand name of sanitizer used to disinfect salon implements.
- 7. Commonly used laser for hair and tattoo removal.
- 8. A treatment used on the hair. Designed to add strength and elasticity to the hair by adding protein to the cortex.
- 11. A medical term for swelling.
- 12. In hair removal, a conductor through which electricity enters or leaves the body. An electrolysis needle is an electrode.
- 14. broken capillaries.
- 15. Synthetic moisturizer.
- 17. A method of epidermal cooling which cools the skin with supercooled liquid immediately before a laser pulse is applied.

ACROSS

- 3. The body's shock absorber.
- 6. Brand name of sanitizer used to disinfect salon implements.
- 7. Commonly used laser for hair and tattoo removal.
- 8. A treatment used on the hair. Designed to add strength and elasticity to the hair by adding protein to the cortex.
- 11. A medical term for swelling.
- 12. In hair removal, a conductor through which electricity enters or leaves the body. An electrolysis needle is an electrode.
- 14. broken capillaries.
- 15. Synthetic moisturizer.
- 17. A method of epidermal cooling which cools the skin with supercooled liquid immediately before a laser pulse is applied.

A. RUBY
B. ERYTHEMA
C. PROTEIN TREATMENT
D. CYPROTERONE ACETATE
E. MYRISTATE
F. HAIR INTEGRATION
G. SUBCUTANEOUS TISSUE
H. WHITE HAIR
I. TRACK
J. SPIDER VEIN
K. NEUTRALISE
L. PALM ROLLING
M. EDEMA
N. ELECTRODE
O. BARBICIDE
P. ROUGH BLOW DRY
Q. CREAM RINSE
R. DYNAMIC COOLING

1. Using the Across and Down clues, write the correct words in the numbered grid below.

ACROSS

3. Allergen is a substance that causes an allergic reaction.
4. A deep cleansing process which strips the hair lightly before a chemical service. Also known as clarifying.
6. A collection of fat cells resulting from poor lymphatic drainage, fluid retention, poor circulation, not drinking enough water, a sedentary lifestyle and hormones.
7. An antiandrogen and is used in the treatment of androgen related disorders such as female pattern baldness and hirsutism.
8. The oily secretion of the sebaceous glands of the scalp, composed of keratin, fat or cellular debris.
9. Term used to measure the output energy for Lasers and Pulsed Light Sources.
11. Surgical procedure that lifts and stretches the patient's skin to provide a firmer more youthful look.
13. A medical term for blackheads.
14. Flaking scalp due to excessive cell production.
15. The space between the eyebrows.

ACROSS

3. Allergen is a substance that causes an allergic reaction.
4. A deep cleansing process which strips the hair lightly before a chemical service. Also known as clarifying.
6. A collection of fat cells resulting from poor lymphatic drainage, fluid retention, poor circulation, not drinking enough water, a sedentary lifestyle and hormones.
7. An antiandrogen and is used in the treatment of androgen related disorders such as female pattern baldness and hirsutism.
8. The oily secretion of the sebaceous glands of the scalp, composed of keratin, fat or cellular debris.
9. Term used to measure the output energy for Lasers and Pulsed Light Sources.
11. Surgical procedure that lifts and stretches the patient's skin to provide a firmer more youthful look.
13. A medical term for blackheads.
14. Flaking scalp due to excessive cell production.
15. The space between the eyebrows.

A. FINASTERIDE
B. ESCHAR
C. ENERGY DENSITY
D. GLABELLA
E. ALLERGEN
F. FACE LIFT
G. CELLULITE
H. SPRIONOLACTONE
I. SEBUM
J. ACUPUNCTURE
K. CUTICLES
L. CHILLTIP
M. COMEDONES
N. CHELATING
O. DANDRUFF
P. T ZONE
Q. DIABETES
R. PABA

2. Using the Across and Down clues, write the correct words in the numbered grid below.

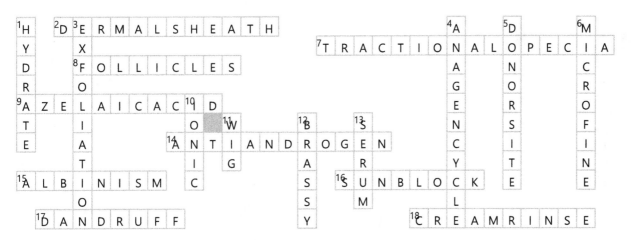

ACROSS

2. A lining around a hair.
7. This refers to hair loss which occurs due to traction being placed on hair. Traction alopecia is commonly seen with braids, pony tails and other hairstyles which cause tension on the scalp.
8. The hair follicle is the tiny blub under your scalp from which the hair grows.
9. Commonly used in the treatment of acne and other skin conditions.
14. Blocks the effects of androgens, normally by blocking the receptor sites.
15. A recessive hereditary trait which presents as white hair due to defective melanin production thought to be caused by a mutation within genes.
16. Products that reflect all the sun's rays, such as zinc oxide and titanium dioxide. They permit minimal tanning, and are a good choice for those who are sensitive to chemicals.
17. Flaking scalp due to excessive cell production.
18. A mixture of wax, thickeners, and a group of chemicals used to coat the hair shaft and detangle after shampooing.

ACROSS

2. A lining around a hair.
7. This refers to hair loss which occurs due to traction being placed on hair. Traction alopecia is commonly seen with braids, pony tails and other hairstyles which cause tension on the scalp.
8. The hair follicle is the tiny blub under your scalp from which the hair grows.
9. Commonly used in the treatment of acne and other skin conditions.
14. Blocks the effects of androgens, normally by blocking the receptor sites.
15. A recessive hereditary trait which presents as white hair due to defective melanin production thought to be caused by a mutation within genes.
16. Products that reflect all the sun's rays, such as zinc oxide and titanium dioxide. They permit minimal tanning, and are a good choice for those who are sensitive to chemicals.
17. Flaking scalp due to excessive cell production.
18. A mixture of wax, thickeners, and a group of chemicals used to coat the hair shaft and detangle after shampooing.

A. DERMAL SHEATH
B. DANDRUFF
C. IONIC
D. SUNBLOCK
E. BRASSY
F. CREAM RINSE
G. FOLLICLES
H. ALBINISM
I. ANAGEN CYCLE
J. ANTIANDROGEN
K. SERUM
L. TRACTION ALOPECIA
M. AZELAIC ACID
N. WIG
O. DONOR SITE
P. MICRO FINE
Q. EXFOLIATION
R. HYDRATE

3. Using the Across and Down clues, write the correct words in the numbered grid below.

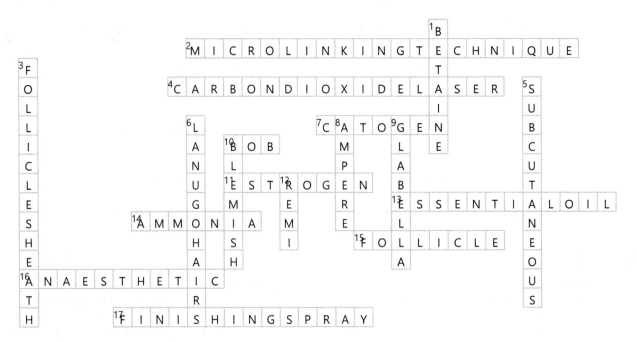

ACROSS

2. The process of attaching hair wefts without braids. The links are sewn on to the wefted hair. The user's natural hair is pulled through and locked secure.
4. Also known as a CO2 laser, these are commonly used to perform skin resurfacing.
7. The resting stage of the hair cycle.
10. The classic look of the 50s and 60s; the style was short and straight but blow-dried and curled under.
11. A female hormone sometimes linked to increased hair growth.
13. The essence of a plant, removed by compressing, steaming, dissolving or distilling.
14. An alkaline ingredient used in some permanent hair color. An ingredient that results in a chemical action that decolorizes the hair.
15. The hair follicle houses the root of the hair. A pore in the skin from which a hair grows.
16. A substance used to relieve all feeling.
17. A hairspray with medium hold used on a finished style to maintain its shape and hold.

ACROSS

2. The process of attaching hair wefts without braids. The links are sewn on to the wefted hair. The user's natural hair is pulled through and locked secure.
4. Also known as a CO2 laser, these are commonly used to perform skin resurfacing.
7. The resting stage of the hair cycle.
10. The classic look of the 50s and 60s; the style was short and straight but blow-dried and curled under.
11. A female hormone sometimes linked to increased hair growth.
13. The essence of a plant, removed by compressing, steaming, dissolving or distilling.
14. An alkaline ingredient used in some permanent hair color. An ingredient that results in a chemical action that decolorizes the hair.
15. The hair follicle houses the root of the hair. A pore in the skin from which a hair grows.
16. A substance used to relieve all feeling.
17. A hairspray with medium hold used on a finished style to maintain its shape and hold.

A. BETAINE
D. ESSENTIAL OIL
G. CARBON DIOXIDE LASER
J. MICRO LINKING TECHNIQUE
M. SUBCUTANEOUS
P. FOLLICLE

B. BLEMISH
E. GLABELLA
H. ANAESTHETIC
K. LANUGO HAIRS
N. CATOGEN
Q. AMPERE

C. BOB
F. FINISHING SPRAY
I. AMMONIA
L. REMI
O. FOLLICLE SHEATH
R. ESTROGEN

4. Using the Across and Down clues, write the correct words in the numbered grid below.

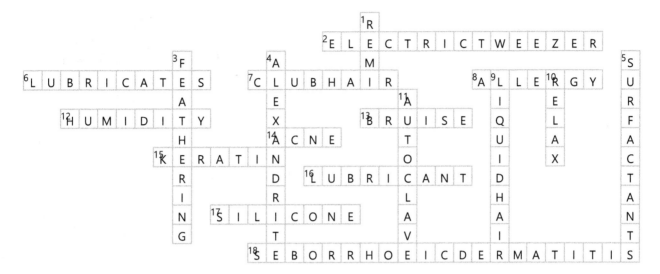

ACROSS

2. A device that removes hair by grasping hairs above the skin's surface with an electrified tweezers.
6. Makes smooth or slippery by using oil to overcome friction.
7. A non-living hair in the last stages of the hair growth cycle, it is detached from the follicle but has not yet shed.
8. A bodily reaction to an irritant. Skin allergies can be exacerbated by solutions put on the skin.
12. The amount of moisture available in the air.
13. A discoloration of skin from blood, sometimes caused by electrolysis, plucking, or waxing. Also known as Purpura.
14. An inflammation of the skin, a result of over production of oil and bacteria.
15. A fibrous protein found in hair, nails, and skin.
16. An oil or oil rich crème or lotion designed to lubricate the skin and slow moisture loss.
17. Increases wet and dry combability.
18. has been called a more extensive and severe form of dandruff.

ACROSS

2. A device that removes hair by grasping hairs above the skin's surface with an electrified tweezers.
6. Makes smooth or slippery by using oil to overcome friction.
7. A non-living hair in the last stages of the hair growth cycle, it is detached from the follicle but has not yet shed.
8. A bodily reaction to an irritant. Skin allergies can be exacerbated by solutions put on the skin.
12. The amount of moisture available in the air.
13. A discoloration of skin from blood, sometimes caused by electrolysis, plucking, or waxing. Also known as Purpura.
14. An inflammation of the skin, a result of over production of oil and bacteria.
15. A fibrous protein found in hair, nails, and skin.
16. An oil or oil rich crème or lotion designed to lubricate the skin and slow moisture loss.
17. Increases wet and dry combability.
18. has been called a more extensive and severe form of dandruff.

A. RELAX
D. KERATIN
G. ELECTRIC TWEEZER
J. SURFACTANTS
M. REMI
P. ALEXANDRITE
B. AUTOCLAVE
E. BRUISE
H. SEBORRHOEIC DERMATITIS
K. ACNE
N. HUMIDITY
Q. CLUB HAIR
C. SILICONE
F. LUBRICATES
I. FEATHERING
L. LUBRICANT
O. ALLERGY
R. LIQUID HAIR

5. Using the Across and Down clues, write the correct words in the numbered grid below.

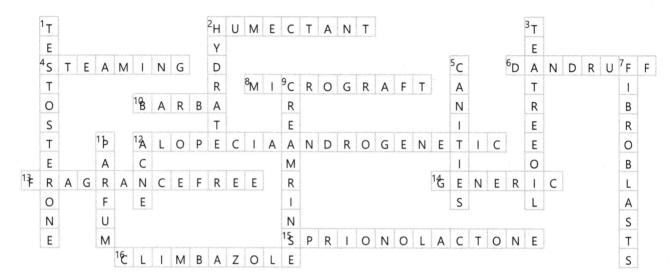

ACROSS

2. An ingredient in skin or hair products that draws moisture from the air to moisturize.
4. The process by which most synthetic fiber is curled at the factory.
6. Flaking scalp due to excessive cell production.
8. A very small hair graft usually consisting of one or two hairs.
10. Medical term for beard.
12. This is the common name for male or female pattern baldness which depends on the genetic predisposition of the hair follicles and the levels of DHT in the body.
13. Products so labeled may still contain small amounts of fragrances to mask the fatty odor of soap or other unpleasant odors.
14. Pertaining to a substance, product or drug that is not protected by trademark. It is identical in chemical composition but not necessarily equivalent in therapeutic effect.
15. An antiandrogen and is used in the treatment of androgen related disorders such as female pattern baldness and hirsutism.
16. Highly effective active anti-dandruff ingredient. Combats bacteria on the scalp.

ACROSS

2. An ingredient in skin or hair products that draws moisture from the air to moisturize.
4. The process by which most synthetic fiber is curled at the factory.
6. Flaking scalp due to excessive cell production.
8. A very small hair graft usually consisting of one or two hairs.
10. Medical term for beard.
12. This is the common name for male or female pattern baldness which depends on the genetic predisposition of the hair follicles and the levels of DHT in the body.
13. Products so labeled may still contain small amounts of fragrances to mask the fatty odor of soap or other unpleasant odors.
14. Pertaining to a substance, product or drug that is not protected by trademark. It is identical in chemical composition but not necessarily equivalent in therapeutic effect.
15. An antiandrogen and is used in the treatment of androgen related disorders such as female pattern baldness and hirsutism.
16. Highly effective active anti-dandruff ingredient. Combats bacteria on the scalp.

A. PARFUM
D. GENERIC
G. BARBA
J. MICRO GRAFT
M. HUMECTANT
P. CREAM RINSE

B. HYDRATE
E. CLIMBAZOLE
H. ACNE
K. TEA TREE OIL
N. FIBROBLASTS
Q. TESTOSTERONE

C. CANITIES
F. SPRIONOLACTONE
I. FRAGRANCE FREE
L. DANDRUFF
O. ALOPECIA ANDROGENETIC
R. STEAMING

6. Using the Across and Down clues, write the correct words in the numbered grid below.

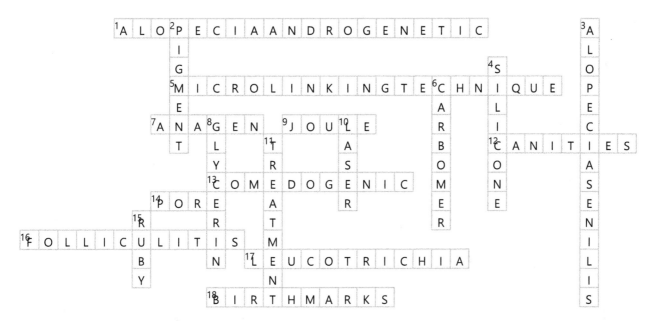

ACROSS

1. This is the common name for male or female pattern baldness which depends on the genetic predisposition of the hair follicles and the levels of DHT in the body.
5. The process of attaching hair wefts without braids. The links are sewn on to the wefted hair. The user's natural hair is pulled through and locked secure.
7. This is the growing phase of the hair cycle which lasts about seven years in a healthy person. The active stage in a hair growth cycle.
9. A unit of energy. Describes energy output for pulsed light based systems.
12. The greying of hair. A pigment deficiency frequently seen in middle-aged people of either sex.
13. Causes blackheads
14. A small opening of the sweat glands of the skin.
16. A common disorder characterized by inflammation of the hair follicle.
17. Refers to a congenital absence of pigment in a lock of hairs which will show as grey or white.
18. Discolored skin that should be examined and approved by a physician before hair removal.

ACROSS

1. This is the common name for male or female pattern baldness which depends on the genetic predisposition of the hair follicles and the levels of DHT in the body.
5. The process of attaching hair wefts without braids. The links are sewn on to the wefted hair. The user's natural hair is pulled through and locked secure.
7. This is the growing phase of the hair cycle which lasts about seven years in a healthy person. The active stage in a hair growth cycle.
9. A unit of energy. Describes energy output for pulsed light based systems.
12. The greying of hair. A pigment deficiency frequently seen in middle-aged people of either sex.
13. Causes blackheads
14. A small opening of the sweat glands of the skin.
16. A common disorder characterized by inflammation of the hair follicle.
17. Refers to a congenital absence of pigment in a lock of hairs which will show as grey or white.
18. Discolored skin that should be examined and approved by a physician before hair removal.

A. GLYCERIN
D. TREATMENT
G. COMEDOGENIC
J. MICRO LINKING TECHNIQUE
M. BIRTHMARKS
P. JOULE

B. ANAGEN
E. CANITIES
H. PIGMENT
K. PORE
N. FOLLICULITIS
Q. CARBOMER

C. LASER
F. ALOPECIA SENILIS
I. SILICONE
L. LEUCOTRICHIA
O. RUBY
R. ALOPECIA ANDROGENETIC

7. Using the Across and Down clues, write the correct words in the numbered grid below.

```
                                    ¹T
                              ²B     R          ³A
    ⁴A    ⁵T                  ⁶E F F I C A C Y  N     ⁷S L O U G H
    N     O         ⁸A        R     N          T     C
    A     U    ⁹A C T I V A T O R   S          I     R         ¹⁰S
    G     R         I         T     L          A     U         E
    E     M         D    ¹¹P A R F U M         N     N         B
    N     A         M              A           D     C    ¹²S  A
    C     L    ¹³A C C E L E R A T O R         R     H    A    C
    Y     I         N              E      ¹⁴N  O R W O O D S A L E
    ¹⁵C O N T A C T C O O L I N G  K      T         G     R    O
    L     E         L                                E     Y    U
    E          ¹⁶D E P I L A T I O N       ¹⁷C L O N E          S
```

ACROSS

6. A term meaning how well or effectively a cosmetic device works.
7. To become shed or cast off.
9. A chemical ingredients that is specifically added to hair bleach to speed up the action of the bleach without unnecessarily damaging the hair.
11. The most concentrated and most fragrant scent and therefore the most expensive.
13. A product that works under the surface of the skin and provides the necessary ingredients for melanin production, which will accelerate the rate at which the skin tans.
14. The most commonly used scale for the classification of hair loss.
15. A method of cooling the epidermis immediately prior to laser irradiation in hopes of reducing or eliminating damage to the skin's surface.
16. The temporary removal of hair.
17. A group of genetically identical cells or organisms derived from a single common cell.

ACROSS

6. A term meaning how well or effectively a cosmetic device works.
7. To become shed or cast off.
9. A chemical ingredients that is specifically added to hair bleach to speed up the action of the bleach without unnecessarily damaging the hair.
11. The most concentrated and most fragrant scent and therefore the most expensive.
13. A product that works under the surface of the skin and provides the necessary ingredients for melanin production, which will accelerate the rate at which the skin tans.
14. The most commonly used scale for the classification of hair loss.
15. A method of cooling the epidermis immediately prior to laser irradiation in hopes of reducing or eliminating damage to the skin's surface.
16. The temporary removal of hair.
17. A group of genetically identical cells or organisms derived from a single common cell.

A. DEPILATION	B. CONTACT COOLING	C. ACCELERATOR	D. SLOUGH
E. ACTIVATOR	F. ANAGEN CYCLE	G. EFFICACY	H. PARFUM
I. CLONE	J. ACID MANTLE	K. NORWOOD SCALE	L. ANTIANDROGEN
M. BIRTHMARKS	N. SEBACEOUS	O. SACRUM	P. SCRUNCH DRY
Q. TRANSLUCENT	R. TOURMALINE		

8. Using the Across and Down clues, write the correct words in the numbered grid below.

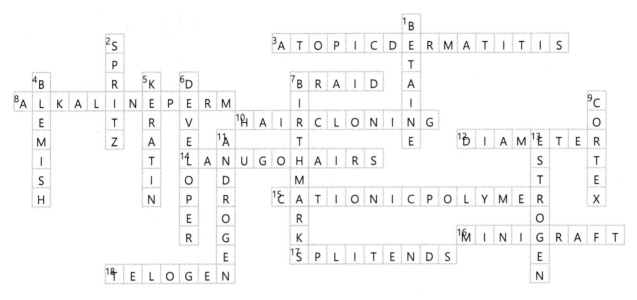

ACROSS

3. Also known as eczema.
7. To weave strands of hair together. On the scalp braiding is used to form a base or track to sew on a commercial weft.
8. A chemically based permanent waving product that has a pH from 7.5 to 9.5. Stronger than acid perms, alkaline perms are designed to produce tight, firm, springy curls.
10. A technique under development which could make an unlimited crop of donor hair available for transplanting.
12. A measurement across the width of the hair.
14. Are usually shed during the 7th month of fetal life following primary folliculo-genesis.
15. Positively charges the hair to provide manageability and reduces static.
16. A small hair graft usually consisting of between three to ten hair roots.
17. Trichoptilosis
18. The resting phase in the hair cycle.

ACROSS

3. Also known as eczema.
7. To weave strands of hair together. On the scalp braiding is used to form a base or track to sew on a commercial weft.
8. A chemically based permanent waving product that has a pH from 7.5 to 9.5. Stronger than acid perms, alkaline perms are designed to produce tight, firm, springy curls.
10. A technique under development which could make an unlimited crop of donor hair available for transplanting.
12. A measurement across the width of the hair.
14. Are usually shed during the 7th month of fetal life following primary folliculo-genesis.
15. Positively charges the hair to provide manageability and reduces static.
16. A small hair graft usually consisting of between three to ten hair roots.
17. Trichoptilosis
18. The resting phase in the hair cycle.

A. CORTEX
B. BLEMISH
C. SPLIT ENDS
D. ANDROGEN
E. ESTROGEN
F. CATIONIC POLYMER
G. ALKALINE PERM
H. DEVELOPER
I. TELOGEN
J. KERATIN
K. HAIR CLONING
L. LANUGO HAIRS
M. BIRTHMARKS
N. BETAINE
O. SPRITZ
P. DIAMETER
Q. ATOPIC DERMATITIS
R. MINI GRAFT
S. BRAID

61

9. Using the Across and Down clues, write the correct words in the numbered grid below.

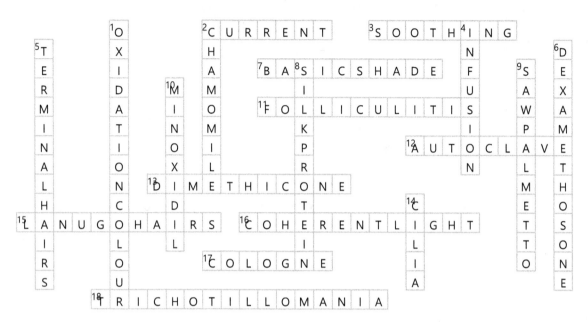

ACROSS

2. The flow of electricity.
3. Reducing skin discomforts from irritation, blemishes, burning skin, etc.
7. A natural or neutral color.
11. A common disorder characterized by inflammation of the hair follicle.
12. A machine used to sterilize medical utensils and some hair removal devices.
13. Detangling aid which conditions, protects against humidity, and adds shine.
15. Are usually shed during the 7th month of fetal life following primary folliculo-genesis.
16. Light that stays focused, a property of lasers.
17. A combination of water containing alcohol and fragrant oils. Not to be confused with a concentrated perfume.
18. This form of hair loss is caused by pulling out one's own hair, usually without realizing it.

ACROSS

2. The flow of electricity.
3. Reducing skin discomforts from irritation, blemishes, burning skin, etc.
7. A natural or neutral color.
11. A common disorder characterized by inflammation of the hair follicle.
12. A machine used to sterilize medical utensils and some hair removal devices.
13. Detangling aid which conditions, protects against humidity, and adds shine.
15. Are usually shed during the 7th month of fetal life following primary folliculo-genesis.
16. Light that stays focused, a property of lasers.
17. A combination of water containing alcohol and fragrant oils. Not to be confused with a concentrated perfume.
18. This form of hair loss is caused by pulling out one's own hair, usually without realizing it.

A. TERMINAL HAIRS
B. BASIC SHADE
C. DEXAMETHOSONE
D. INFUSION
E. FOLLICULITIS
F. COLOGNE
G. OXIDATION COLOUR
H. DIMETHICONE
I. MINOXIDIL
J. TRICHOTILLOMANIA
K. LANUGO HAIRS
L. SOOTHING
M. CURRENT
N. CILIA
O. AUTOCLAVE
P. COHERENT LIGHT
Q. CHAMOMILE
R. SAW PALMETTO
S. SILK PROTEIN

10. Using the Across and Down clues, write the correct words in the numbered grid below.

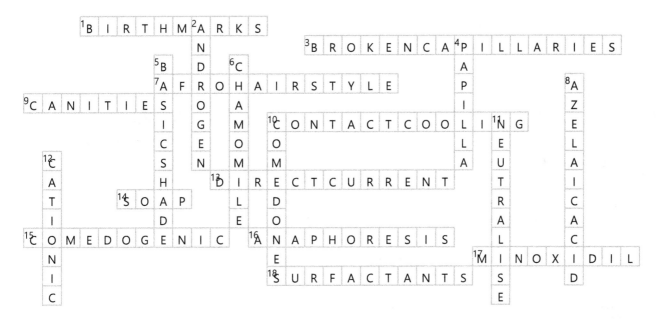

ACROSS

1. Discolored skin that should be examined and approved by a physician before hair removal.
3. These tiny blood vessels at the surface of the skin appear as streaks or blotches.
7. A rounded, thick, tightly curled hair style.
9. The greying of hair. A pigment deficiency frequently seen in middle-aged people of either sex.
10. A method of cooling the epidermis immediately prior to laser irradiation in hopes of reducing or eliminating damage to the skin's surface.
13. a type of electrical energy that travels in one direction.
14. Cleansing agent that is a sodium or potassium salt of animal or vegetable fat.
15. Causes blackheads
16. The forcing of liquids into skin from the negative to the positive pole.
17. The generic name of the brand name drug Rogaine. The first drug to be approved by the FDA for the treatment of androgenetic alopecia.
18. Active agent that allows oil to mix with water. Used in skincare products like cleansers, wetting agents, emulsifiers, solubizers, conditioning agents and foam stabilizers.

ACROSS

1. Discolored skin that should be examined and approved by a physician before hair removal.
3. These tiny blood vessels at the surface of the skin appear as streaks or blotches.
7. A rounded, thick, tightly curled hair style.
9. The greying of hair. A pigment deficiency frequently seen in middle-aged people of either sex.
10. A method of cooling the epidermis immediately prior to laser irradiation in hopes of reducing or eliminating damage to the skin's surface.
13. a type of electrical energy that travels in one direction.
14. Cleansing agent that is a sodium or potassium salt of animal or vegetable fat.
15. Causes blackheads
16. The forcing of liquids into skin from the negative to the positive pole.
17. The generic name of the brand name drug Rogaine. The first drug to be approved by the FDA for the treatment of androgenetic alopecia.
18. Active agent that allows oil to mix with water. Used in skincare products like cleansers, wetting agents, emulsifiers, solubizers, conditioning agents and foam stabilizers.

A. NEUTRALISE
B. COMEDOGENIC
C. CONTACT COOLING
D. SURFACTANTS
E. PAPILLA
F. COMEDONES
G. BASIC SHADE
H. AFRO HAIRSTYLE
I. CHAMOMILE
J. ANDROGEN
K. CATIONIC
L. BIRTHMARKS
M. CANITIES
N. BROKEN CAPILLARIES
O. DIRECT CURRENT
P. ANAPHORESIS
Q. MINOXIDIL
R. SOAP
S. AZELAIC ACID

11. Using the Across and Down clues, write the correct words in the numbered grid below.

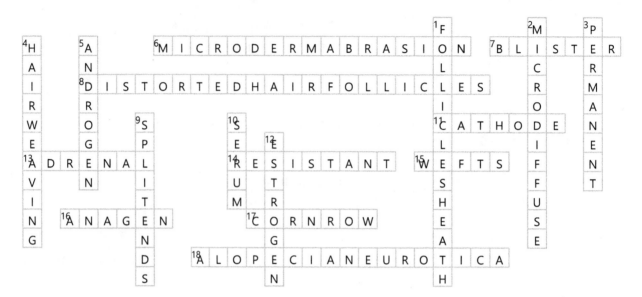

ACROSS

6. An intensive exfoliation process that rejuvenates the skin by utilizing ultra-fine aluminum oxide crystals to remove the upper layer of the stratum corneum.
7. A small fluid-filled bubble on the skin caused by heat from over treatment with certain types of hair removal.
8. A relatively rare condition in which the follicle is not straight.
11. A negative electrode in a cell or circuit.
13. A gland that affects certain types of hair growth.
14. Stops or opposes treatment.
15. Wefts are temporary hair extensions which are glued into your hair.
16. This is the growing phase of the hair cycle which lasts about seven years in a healthy person. The active stage in a hair growth cycle.
17. Term used to describe an on the scalp braid. These braids can be used to form a track for the cornrow weaving method.
18. Baldness following a nervous disorder or injury to the nervous system.

ACROSS

6. An intensive exfoliation process that rejuvenates the skin by utilizing ultra-fine aluminum oxide crystals to remove the upper layer of the stratum corneum.
7. A small fluid-filled bubble on the skin caused by heat from over treatment with certain types of hair removal.
8. A relatively rare condition in which the follicle is not straight.
11. A negative electrode in a cell or circuit.
13. A gland that affects certain types of hair growth.
14. Stops or opposes treatment.
15. Wefts are temporary hair extensions which are glued into your hair.
16. This is the growing phase of the hair cycle which lasts about seven years in a healthy person. The active stage in a hair growth cycle.
17. Term used to describe an on the scalp braid. These braids can be used to form a track for the cornrow weaving method.
18. Baldness following a nervous disorder or injury to the nervous system.

A. ANDROGEN
B. SERUM
C. ESTROGEN
D. MICRO DIFFUSE
E. MICRODERMABRASION
F. CATHODE
G. FOLLICLE SHEATH
H. BLISTER
I. WEFTS
J. CORNROW
K. PERMANENT
L. ALOPECIA NEUROTICA
M. ADRENAL
N. HAIR WEAVING
O. SPLIT ENDS
P. ANAGEN
Q. DISTORTED HAIR FOLLICLES
R. RESISTANT

12. Using the Across and Down clues, write the correct words in the numbered grid below.

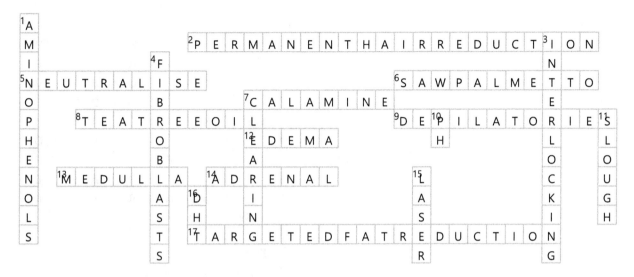

ACROSS

2. Treatments, especially IPL, where the follicle is disabled by the light energy making it unable to support any more hair growth.
5. To cancel or reduce effect.
6. A natural herb that has been shown to be an effective anti-androgen.
7. A pink ointment sometimes used to treat skin irritation
8. an extraction from the Melaleuca tree.
9. Substances used to dissolve hair above the skin's surface.
12. A medical term for swelling.
13. The medulla is a central zone of cells usually only present in large thick hairs.
14. A gland that affects certain types of hair growth.
17. Metabolising stubborn fat deposits, typically in the lower body, using methods such as Eporex mesotherapy.

ACROSS

2. Treatments, especially IPL, where the follicle is disabled by the light energy making it unable to support any more hair growth.
5. To cancel or reduce effect.
6. A natural herb that has been shown to be an effective anti-androgen.
7. A pink ointment sometimes used to treat skin irritation
8. an extraction from the Melaleuca tree.
9. Substances used to dissolve hair above the skin's surface.
12. A medical term for swelling.
13. The medulla is a central zone of cells usually only present in large thick hairs.
14. A gland that affects certain types of hair growth.
17. Metabolising stubborn fat deposits, typically in the lower body, using methods such as Eporex mesotherapy.

A. TARGETED FAT REDUCTION
C. DEPILATORIES
E. CLEARING
G. PH
I. AMINOPHENOLS
K. SAW PALMETTO
M. MEDULLA
O. TEA TREE OIL
Q. FIBROBLASTS

B. ADRENAL
D. DHT
F. PERMANENT HAIR REDUCTION
H. LASER
J. CALAMINE
L. NEUTRALISE
N. SLOUGH
P. INTERLOCKING
R. EDEMA

13. Using the Across and Down clues, write the correct words in the numbered grid below.

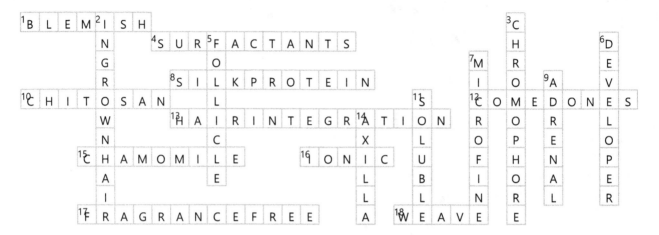

ACROSS

1. Blood or pigment based visible mark.
4. Active agent that allows oil to mix with water. Used in skincare products like cleansers, wetting agents, emulsifiers, solubizers, conditioning agents and foam stabilizers.
8. A natural water-soluble source of acid derived from liquid silk.
10. A natural polymer obtained from sea crustaceans protects the hair.
12. A medical term for blackheads.
13. A modern term used to describe hair weaving.
15. Used in many products for blonde hair to enhance color.
16. Process where water molecules are broken down by ions into smaller droplets. This then allows the hair to absorb the moisture more easily.
17. Products so labeled may still contain small amounts of fragrances to mask the fatty odor of soap or other unpleasant odors.
18. A hair weave is usually a hairpiece with layered gaps made into it.

ACROSS

1. Blood or pigment based visible mark.
4. Active agent that allows oil to mix with water. Used in skincare products like cleansers, wetting agents, emulsifiers, solubizers, conditioning agents and foam stabilizers.
8. A natural water-soluble source of acid derived from liquid silk.
10. A natural polymer obtained from sea crustaceans protects the hair.
12. A medical term for blackheads.
13. A modern term used to describe hair weaving.
15. Used in many products for blonde hair to enhance color.
16. Process where water molecules are broken down by ions into smaller droplets. This then allows the hair to absorb the moisture more easily.
17. Products so labeled may still contain small amounts of fragrances to mask the fatty odor of soap or other unpleasant odors.
18. A hair weave is usually a hairpiece with layered gaps made into it.

A. SILK PROTEIN   B. ADRENAL   C. CHROMOPHORE   D. COMEDONES
E. CHAMOMILE   F. FOLLICLE   G. MICRO FINE   H. CHITOSAN
I. HAIR INTEGRATION J. SURFACTANTS   K. INGROWN HAIR   L. BLEMISH
M. WEAVE   N. SOLUBLE   O. IONIC   P. FRAGRANCE FREE
Q. DEVELOPER   R. AXILLA

66

14. Using the Across and Down clues, write the correct words in the numbered grid below.

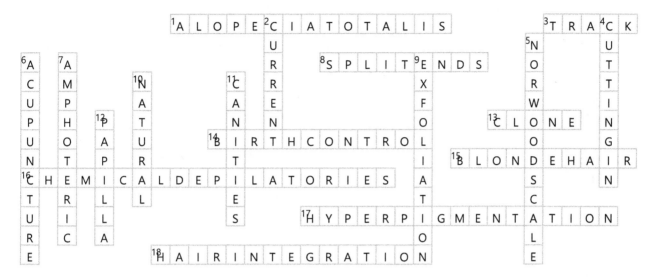

ACROSS

1. This is the complete loss of scalp hair often combined with the loss of eyebrows and eyelashes.
3. Parting or a cornrow that establishes the placement pattern of wefts or strand additions.
8. Trichoptilosis
13. A group of genetically identical cells or organisms derived from a single common cell.
14. Drugs that sometimes cause increased hair growth.
15. Is not as visible, but it's also harder to treat. Lasers have limited effects on it because of its lack of pigment, and it is difficult to see against the skin.
16. Powder or cream preparations that dissolve hair above the surface of the skin. Some find these products very irritating to the skin.
17. An over excitation of melanocytes, darkening of the skin. Can be seen as sun-induced freckles or melasma.
18. A modern term used to describe hair weaving.

ACROSS

1. This is the complete loss of scalp hair often combined with the loss of eyebrows and eyelashes.
3. Parting or a cornrow that establishes the placement pattern of wefts or strand additions.
8. Trichoptilosis
13. A group of genetically identical cells or organisms derived from a single common cell.
14. Drugs that sometimes cause increased hair growth.
15. Is not as visible, but it's also harder to treat. Lasers have limited effects on it because of its lack of pigment, and it is difficult to see against the skin.
16. Powder or cream preparations that dissolve hair above the surface of the skin. Some find these products very irritating to the skin.
17. An over excitation of melanocytes, darkening of the skin. Can be seen as sun-induced freckles or melasma.
18. A modern term used to describe hair weaving.

A. PAPILLA
D. BLONDE HAIR
G. NATURAL
J. AMPHOTERIC
M. HYPERPIGMENTATION
P. CHEMICAL DEPILATORIES

B. TRACK
E. NORWOOD SCALE
H. CUTTING IN
K. ALOPECIA TOTALIS
N. CANITIES
Q. BIRTH CONTROL

C. CURRENT
F. HAIR INTEGRATION
I. EXFOLIATION
L. SPLIT ENDS
O. CLONE
R. ACUPUNCTURE

15. Using the Across and Down clues, write the correct words in the numbered grid below.

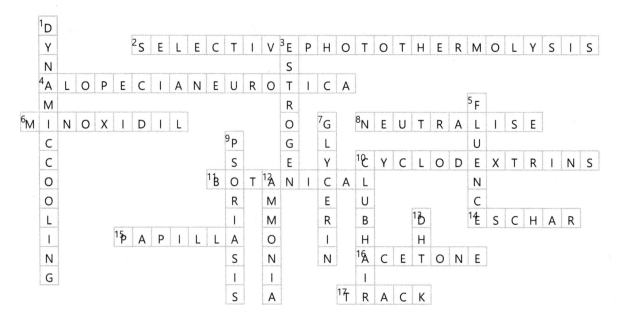

ACROSS

2. Selectively targeting dermal structures with light energy, without causing damage to surrounding tissue.
4. Baldness following a nervous disorder or injury to the nervous system.
6. The generic name of the brand name drug Rogaine. The first drug to be approved by the FDA for the treatment of androgenetic alopecia.
8. To cancel or reduce effect.
10. Produced from starch by means of enzymatic conversion and are used in a wide range of applications in food, pharmaceutical and chemical industries.
11. Refers to a product containing plants or ingredients made from plants.
14. A small temporary scab that occurs sometimes after electrolysis, especially after overtreatment.
15. The small area at the base of the hair root which provides nutrients needed for growth.
16. A chemical formed in the blood when the body uses fat instead of glucose (sugar) for energy.
17. Parting or a cornrow that establishes the placement pattern of wefts or strand additions.

ACROSS

2. Selectively targeting dermal structures with light energy, without causing damage to surrounding tissue.
4. Baldness following a nervous disorder or injury to the nervous system.
6. The generic name of the brand name drug Rogaine. The first drug to be approved by the FDA for the treatment of androgenetic alopecia.
8. To cancel or reduce effect.
10. Produced from starch by means of enzymatic conversion and are used in a wide range of applications in food, pharmaceutical and chemical industries.
11. Refers to a product containing plants or ingredients made from plants.
14. A small temporary scab that occurs sometimes after electrolysis, especially after overtreatment.
15. The small area at the base of the hair root which provides nutrients needed for growth.
16. A chemical formed in the blood when the body uses fat instead of glucose (sugar) for energy.
17. Parting or a cornrow that establishes the placement pattern of wefts or strand additions.

A. NEUTRALISE
C. ESTROGEN
E. FLUENCE
G. DHT
I. ESCHAR
K. PAPILLA
M. GLYCERIN
O. AMMONIA
Q. CYCLODEXTRINS

B. PSORIASIS
D. CLUB HAIR
F. DYNAMIC COOLING
H. SELECTIVE PHOTOTHERMOLYSIS
J. BOTANICAL
L. ALOPECIA NEUROTICA
N. MINOXIDIL
P. ACETONE
R. TRACK

16. Using the Across and Down clues, write the correct words in the numbered grid below.

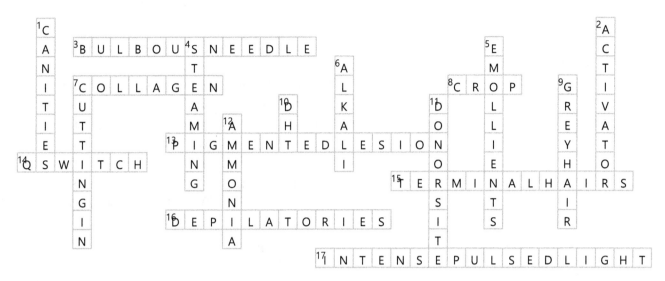

ACROSS

3. A type of electrolysis needle.
7. A protein that holds all connective tissue together under the skin.
8. An alternative to haircut, without any specific meaning to the style of the cut.
13. Variety of skin conditions mainly the result of excess melanin. Commonly known as Café au Lait stains, birthmarks, age spots and freckles.
14. A device that produces short intense bursts of energy from a laser.
15. Coarse, pigmented or non-pigmented, exist on the scalp and gain length at a rate of 1-2cm per month during a cyclical life of up to 10 years.
16. Substances used to dissolve hair above the skin's surface.
17. A treatment consisting of short pulses of light sent out through an applicator that is gently pressed against the skin.

ACROSS

3. A type of electrolysis needle.
7. A protein that holds all connective tissue together under the skin.
8. An alternative to haircut, without any specific meaning to the style of the cut.
13. Variety of skin conditions mainly the result of excess melanin. Commonly known as Café au Lait stains, birthmarks, age spots and freckles.
14. A device that produces short intense bursts of energy from a laser.
15. Coarse, pigmented or non-pigmented, exist on the scalp and gain length at a rate of 1-2cm per month during a cyclical life of up to 10 years.
16. Substances used to dissolve hair above the skin's surface.
17. A treatment consisting of short pulses of light sent out through an applicator that is gently pressed against the skin.

A. TERMINAL HAIRS
B. INTENSE PULSED LIGHT
C. CUTTING IN
D. STEAMING
E. BULBOUS NEEDLE
F. CROP
G. DONOR SITE
H. GREY HAIR
I. EMOLLIENTS
J. ALKALI
K. Q SWITCH
L. COLLAGEN
M. PIGMENTED LESION
N. CANITIES
O. ACTIVATOR
P. DEPILATORIES
Q. AMMONIA
R. DHT

17. Using the Across and Down clues, write the correct words in the numbered grid below.

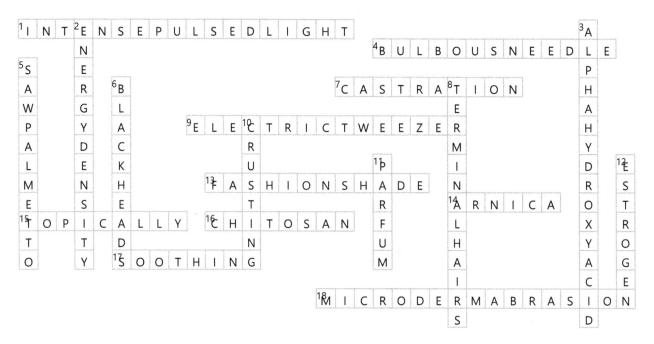

ACROSS

1. A treatment consisting of short pulses of light sent out through an applicator that is gently pressed against the skin.
4. A type of electrolysis needle.
7. The surgical removal of one or both testicles or ovaries.
9. A device that removes hair by grasping hairs above the skin's surface with an electrified tweezers.
13. A basic color with added tone.
14. A plant extract that has been used to treat swelling, soreness and bruising.
15. Means to apply directly onto the scalp.
16. A natural polymer obtained from sea crustaceans protects the hair.
17. Reducing skin discomforts from irritation, blemishes, burning skin, etc.
18. An intensive exfoliation process that rejuvenates the skin by utilizing ultra-fine aluminum oxide crystals to remove the upper layer of the stratum corneum.

ACROSS

1. A treatment consisting of short pulses of light sent out through an applicator that is gently pressed against the skin.
4. A type of electrolysis needle.
7. The surgical removal of one or both testicles or ovaries.
9. A device that removes hair by grasping hairs above the skin's surface with an electrified tweezers.
13. A basic color with added tone.
14. A plant extract that has been used to treat swelling, soreness and bruising.
15. Means to apply directly onto the scalp.
16. A natural polymer obtained from sea crustaceans protects the hair.
17. Reducing skin discomforts from irritation, blemishes, burning skin, etc.
18. An intensive exfoliation process that rejuvenates the skin by utilizing ultra-fine aluminum oxide crystals to remove the upper layer of the stratum corneum.

A. CHITOSAN
D. BULBOUS NEEDLE
G. BLACKHEADS
J. ESTROGEN
M. ARNICA
P. ELECTRIC TWEEZER

B. CRUSTING
E. SOOTHING
H. TERMINAL HAIRS
K. ENERGY DENSITY
N. SAW PALMETTO
Q. FASHION SHADE

C. ALPHA HYDROXY ACID
F. INTENSE PULSED LIGHT
I. MICRODERMABRASION
L. TOPICALLY
O. CASTRATION
R. PARFUM

18. Using the Across and Down clues, write the correct words in the numbered grid below.

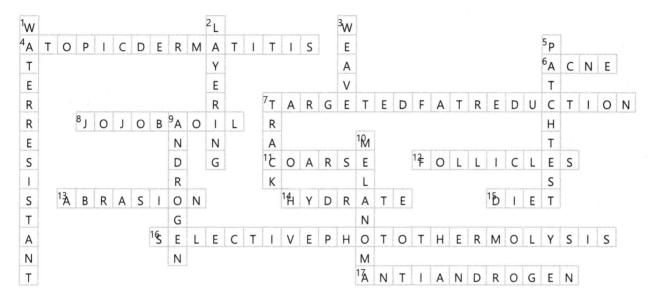

ACROSS

4. Also known as eczema.
6. An inflammation of the skin, a result of over production of oil and bacteria.
7. Metabolising stubborn fat deposits, typically in the lower body, using methods such as Eporex mesotherapy.
8. Contains superior properties to keep skin and hair soft. It is beneficial to dry hair.
11. A classification for stronger, thicker types of hair.
12. The hair follicle is the tiny blub under your scalp from which the hair grows.
13. The process of scraping or wearing hair away. Causing partial or complete absence of hair from areas.
14. To add moisture to the skin.
15. Is sometimes linked to excess hair growth, especially in the extremely obese and extremely anorexic.
16. Selectively targeting dermal structures with light energy, without causing damage to surrounding tissue.
17. Blocks the effects of androgens, normally by blocking the receptor sites.

ACROSS

4. Also known as eczema.
6. An inflammation of the skin, a result of over production of oil and bacteria.
7. Metabolising stubborn fat deposits, typically in the lower body, using methods such as Eporex mesotherapy.
8. Contains superior properties to keep skin and hair soft. It is beneficial to dry hair.
11. A classification for stronger, thicker types of hair.
12. The hair follicle is the tiny blub under your scalp from which the hair grows.
13. The process of scraping or wearing hair away. Causing partial or complete absence of hair from areas.
14. To add moisture to the skin.
15. Is sometimes linked to excess hair growth, especially in the extremely obese and extremely anorexic.
16. Selectively targeting dermal structures with light energy, without causing damage to surrounding tissue.
17. Blocks the effects of androgens, normally by blocking the receptor sites.

A. TRACK
C. COARSE
E. PATCH TEST
G. JOJOBA OIL
I. LAYERING
K. ATOPIC DERMATITIS
M. WATER RESISTANT
O. SELECTIVE PHOTOTHERMOLYSIS
Q. HYDRATE

B. ANTIANDROGEN
D. ABRASION
F. TARGETED FAT REDUCTION
H. ACNE
J. ANDROGEN
L. FOLLICLES
N. DIET
P. WEAVE
R. MELANOMA

19. Using the Across and Down clues, write the correct words in the numbered grid below.

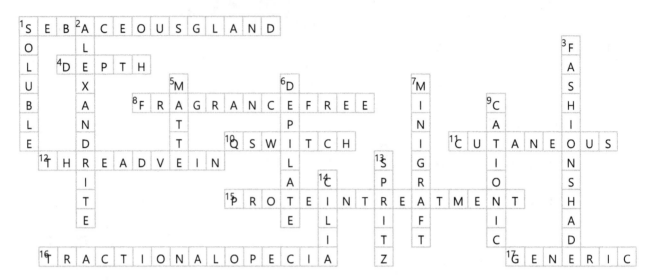

ACROSS

1. Oil producing gland in the dermis.
4. The darkness or lightness of a color.
8. Products so labeled may still contain small amounts of fragrances to mask the fatty odor of soap or other unpleasant odors.
10. A device that produces short intense bursts of energy from a laser.
11. Relating to the skin.
12. broken capillaries.
15. A treatment used on the hair. Designed to add strength and elasticity to the hair by adding protein to the cortex.
16. This refers to hair loss which occurs due to traction being placed on hair. Traction alopecia is commonly seen with braids, pony tails and other hairstyles which cause tension on the scalp.
17. Pertaining to a substance, product or drug that is not protected by trademark. It is identical in chemical composition but not necessarily equivalent in therapeutic effect.

ACROSS

1. Oil producing gland in the dermis.
4. The darkness or lightness of a color.
8. Products so labeled may still contain small amounts of fragrances to mask the fatty odor of soap or other unpleasant odors.
10. A device that produces short intense bursts of energy from a laser.
11. Relating to the skin.
12. broken capillaries.
15. A treatment used on the hair. Designed to add strength and elasticity to the hair by adding protein to the cortex.
16. This refers to hair loss which occurs due to traction being placed on hair. Traction alopecia is commonly seen with braids, pony tails and other hairstyles which cause tension on the scalp.
17. Pertaining to a substance, product or drug that is not protected by trademark. It is identical in chemical composition but not necessarily equivalent in therapeutic effect.

A. SEBACEOUS GLAND   B. FRAGRANCE FREE   C. Q SWITCH
D. GENERIC   E. CATIONIC   F. CUTANEOUS
G. PROTEIN TREATMENT   H. DEPTH   I. CILIA
J. SOLUBLE   K. MATTE   L. ALEXANDRITE
M. FASHION SHADE   N. THREAD VEIN   O. MINI GRAFT
P. DEPILATE   Q. TRACTION ALOPECIA   R. SPRITZ

20. Using the Across and Down clues, write the correct words in the numbered grid below.

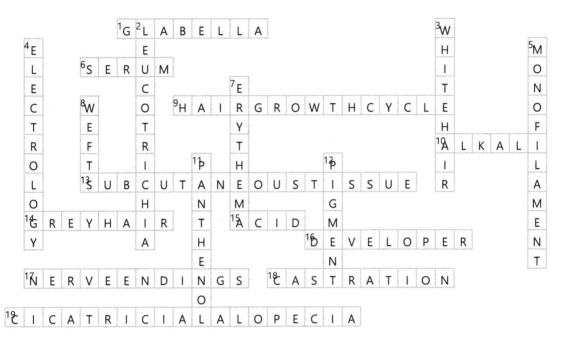

ACROSS

1. The space between the eyebrows.
6. A smoothing product to stop your hair from frizzing, keeping it smooth and straight. You'll be able to find a serum that is specifically designed to your own hair type.
9. Hair passes through a series of cycles known as Anagen (growing phase), Catagen (resting phase) and Telogen (dormant phase).
10. A liquid with a pH higher than 7.
13. The body's shock absorber.
14. Hair that has lost its pigment.
15. A liquid, usually corrosive with a pH lower than 7, opposite of an alkali.
16. A product which oxidizes artificial color pigment.
17. Receptors which respond to touch, pain, pressure, heat and cold.
18. The surgical removal of one or both testicles or ovaries.
19. This is baldness due to scarring. The follicles are absent in scar tissue.

ACROSS

1. The space between the eyebrows.
6. A smoothing product to stop your hair from frizzing, keeping it smooth and straight. You'll be able to find a serum that is specifically designed to your own hair type.
9. Hair passes through a series of cycles known as Anagen (growing phase), Catagen (resting phase) and Telogen (dormant phase).
10. A liquid with a pH higher than 7.
13. The body's shock absorber.
14. Hair that has lost its pigment.
15. A liquid, usually corrosive with a pH lower than 7, opposite of an alkali.
16. A product which oxidizes artificial color pigment.
17. Receptors which respond to touch, pain, pressure, heat and cold.
18. The surgical removal of one or both testicles or ovaries.
19. This is baldness due to scarring. The follicles are absent in scar tissue.

A. WHITE HAIR
B. DEVELOPER
C. LEUCOTRICHIA
D. GREY HAIR
E. PANTHENOL
F. PIGMENT
G. HAIR GROWTH CYCLE
H. NERVE ENDINGS
I. SUBCUTANEOUS TISSUE
J. MONOFILAMENT
K. CICATRICIAL ALOPECIA
L. SERUM
M. ERYTHEMA
N. WEFTS
O. ACID
P. GLABELLA
Q. ELECTROLOGY
R. CASTRATION
S. ALKALI

21. Using the Across and Down clues, write the correct words in the numbered grid below.

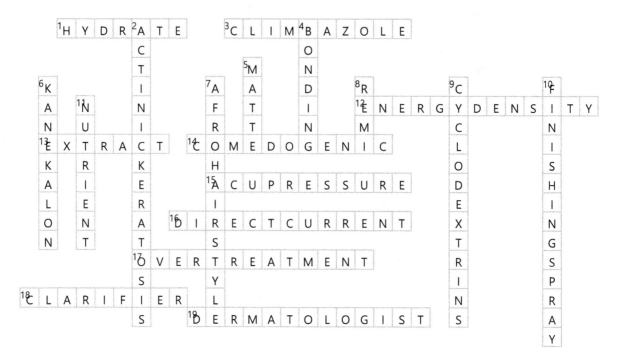

ACROSS

1. To add moisture to the skin.
3. Highly effective active anti-dandruff ingredient. Combats bacteria on the scalp.
12. Term used to measure the output energy for Lasers and Pulsed Light Sources.
13. An herbal concentrate produced by separating the essential or active part of an herb into a solvent material.
14. Causes blackheads
15. A method of relieving pain by pressing down on an area of the body.
16. a type of electrical energy that travels in one direction.
17. Overly aggressive treatment to remove hair which leads to temporary or permanent skin damage.
18. A clarifying shampoo is slightly stronger than everyday shampoos and is designed to remove products, hard water or chlorine residue that have built-up over time.
19. A doctor specializing in skin and hair conditions.

ACROSS

1. To add moisture to the skin.
3. Highly effective active anti-dandruff ingredient. Combats bacteria on the scalp.
12. Term used to measure the output energy for Lasers and Pulsed Light Sources.
13. An herbal concentrate produced by separating the essential or active part of an herb into a solvent material.
14. Causes blackheads
15. A method of relieving pain by pressing down on an area of the body.
16. a type of electrical energy that travels in one direction.
17. Overly aggressive treatment to remove hair which leads to temporary or permanent skin damage.
18. A clarifying shampoo is slightly stronger than everyday shampoos and is designed to remove products, hard water or chlorine residue that have built-up over time.
19. A doctor specializing in skin and hair conditions.

A. BONDING B. CLARIFIER C. COMEDOGENIC D. DERMATOLOGIST
E. CLIMBAZOLE F. HYDRATE G. DIRECT CURRENT H. REMI
I. ACUPRESSURE J. ENERGY DENSITY K. EXTRACT L. AFRO HAIRSTYLE
M. ACTINIC KERATOSIS N. CYCLODEXTRINS O. FINISHING SPRAY P. NUTRIENT
Q. MATTE R. KANEKALON S. OVERTREATMENT

22. Using the Across and Down clues, write the correct words in the numbered grid below.

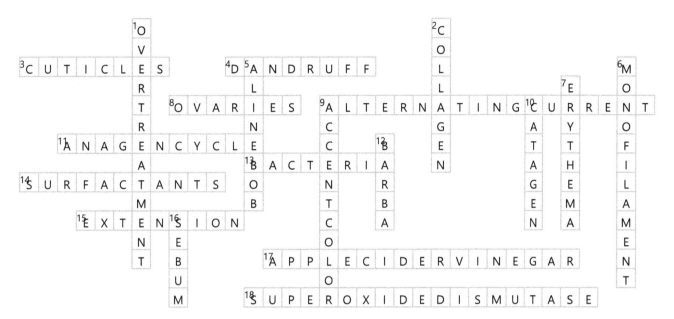

ACROSS

3. Form a protective layer which covers the shaft of hair. If your hair is colored or bleached they can spread out, split or become bloated due to over processing.
4. Flaking scalp due to excessive cell production.
8. In women, a major source of female hormones. Certain conditions involving the ovaries can lead to excess hair growth, especially polycystic ovary syndrome (PCOS).
9. The type of electricity that comes from a wall outlet (AC), as opposed to direct current (DC).
11. The active stage in a hair growth cycle.
13. An organism responsible for infection.
14. Active agent that allows oil to mix with water. Used in skincare products like cleansers, wetting agents, emulsifiers, solubizers, conditioning agents and foam stabilizers.
15. Hair extensions are pieces of real or synthetic weaved close to the scalp in order to achieve greater length or fullness.
17. A natural solvent in oils and creams. It acidifies products.
18. The enzyme superoxide, catalyzes the dis-mutation of superoxide into oxygen and hydrogen peroxide.

ACROSS

3. Form a protective layer which covers the shaft of hair. If your hair is colored or bleached they can spread out, split or become bloated due to over processing.
4. Flaking scalp due to excessive cell production.
8. In women, a major source of female hormones. Certain conditions involving the ovaries can lead to excess hair growth, especially polycystic ovary syndrome (PCOS).
9. The type of electricity that comes from a wall outlet (AC), as opposed to direct current (DC).
11. The active stage in a hair growth cycle.
13. An organism responsible for infection.
14. Active agent that allows oil to mix with water. Used in skincare products like cleansers, wetting agents, emulsifiers, solubizers, conditioning agents and foam stabilizers.
15. Hair extensions are pieces of real or synthetic weaved close to the scalp in order to achieve greater length or fullness.
17. A natural solvent in oils and creams. It acidifies products.
18. The enzyme superoxide, catalyzes the dis-mutation of superoxide into oxygen and hydrogen peroxide.

A. APPLE CIDER VINEGAR
B. BARBA
C. BACTERIA
D. SUPEROXIDE DISMUTASE
E. COLLAGEN
F. A LINE BOB
G. ANAGEN CYCLE
H. OVARIES
I. EXTENSION
J. MONOFILAMENT
K. ALTERNATING CURRENT
L. OVERTREATMENT
M. DANDRUFF
N. CATAGEN
O. ERYTHEMA
P. SURFACTANTS
Q. ACCENT COLOR
R. CUTICLES
S. SEBUM

23. Using the Across and Down clues, write the correct words in the numbered grid below.

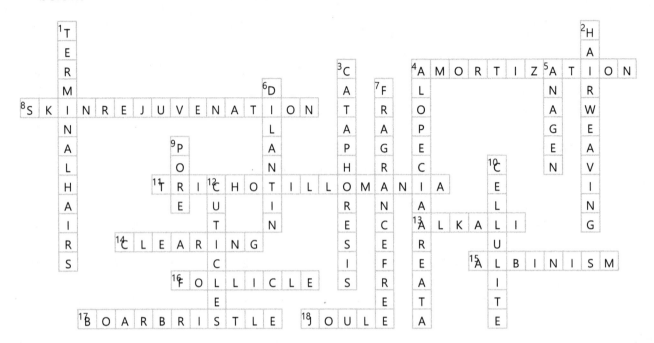

ACROSS

4. The process of converting one enzyme to another.
8. Combating the signs of ageing using the latest innovative, non-invasive treatments that give you visibly younger, healthy, radiant skin.
11. This form of hair loss is caused by pulling out one's own hair, usually without realizing it.
13. A liquid with a pH higher than 7.
14. A method of hair removal in which all hair in an area is removed at once, as opposed to thinning.
15. A recessive hereditary trait which presents as white hair due to defective melanin production thought to be caused by a mutation within genes.
16. The hair follicle houses the root of the hair. A pore in the skin from which a hair grows.
17. A bristle commonly used in natural bristle brushes.
18. A unit of energy. Describes energy output for pulsed light based systems.

ACROSS

4. The process of converting one enzyme to another.
8. Combating the signs of ageing using the latest innovative, non-invasive treatments that give you visibly younger, healthy, radiant skin.
11. This form of hair loss is caused by pulling out one's own hair, usually without realizing it.
13. A liquid with a pH higher than 7.
14. A method of hair removal in which all hair in an area is removed at once, as opposed to thinning.
15. A recessive hereditary trait which presents as white hair due to defective melanin production thought to be caused by a mutation within genes.
16. The hair follicle houses the root of the hair. A pore in the skin from which a hair grows.
17. A bristle commonly used in natural bristle brushes.
18. A unit of energy. Describes energy output for pulsed light based systems.

A. DILANTIN
B. ANAGEN
C. HAIR WEAVING
D. ALOPECIA AREATA
E. AMORTIZATION
F. CATAPHORESIS
G. CLEARING
H. CELLULITE
I. SKIN REJUVENATION
J. TERMINAL HAIRS
K. JOULE
L. BOAR BRISTLE
M. CUTICLES
N. TRICHOTILLOMANIA
O. ALBINISM
P. FRAGRANCE FREE
Q. PORE
R. FOLLICLE
S. ALKALI

24. Using the Across and Down clues, write the correct words in the numbered grid below.

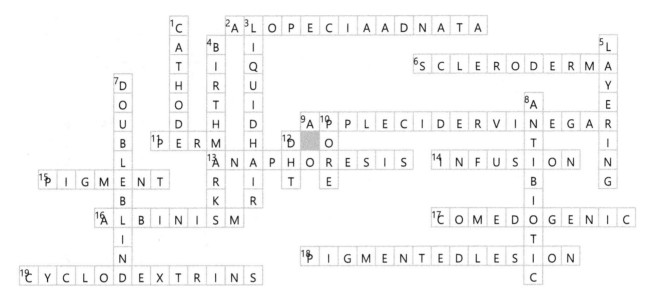

ACROSS

2. Congenital baldness or baldness at birth.
6. A disease of the skin and connective tissue that can cause hair loss over the affected areas.
9. A natural solvent in oils and creams. It acidifies products.
11. creates curls by restructuring your hair molecules with a chemical, or heat treatment and is generally a long-lasting or permanent change to your hair.
13. The forcing of liquids into skin from the negative to the positive pole.
14. Tea made by steeping an herb's leaves or flowers in hot water.
15. Color.
16. A recessive hereditary trait which presents as white hair due to defective melanin production thought to be caused by a mutation within genes.
17. Causes blackheads
18. Variety of skin conditions mainly the result of excess melanin. Commonly known as Café au Lait stains, birthmarks, age spots and freckles.
19. Produced from starch by means of enzymatic conversion and are used in a wide range of applications in food, pharmaceutical and chemical industries.

ACROSS

2. Congenital baldness or baldness at birth.
6. A disease of the skin and connective tissue that can cause hair loss over the affected areas.
9. A natural solvent in oils and creams. It acidifies products.
11. creates curls by restructuring your hair molecules with a chemical, or heat treatment and is generally a long-lasting or permanent change to your hair.
13. The forcing of liquids into skin from the negative to the positive pole.
14. Tea made by steeping an herb's leaves or flowers in hot water.
15. Color.
16. A recessive hereditary trait which presents as white hair due to defective melanin production thought to be caused by a mutation within genes.
17. Causes blackheads
18. Variety of skin conditions mainly the result of excess melanin. Commonly known as Café au Lait stains, birthmarks, age spots and freckles.
19. Produced from starch by means of enzymatic conversion and are used in a wide range of applications in food, pharmaceutical and chemical industries.

A. CATHODE
D. PERM
G. LIQUID HAIR
J. BIRTHMARKS
M. DHT
P. APPLE CIDER VINEGAR
S. PIGMENT

B. LAYERING
E. DOUBLE BLIND
H. CYCLODEXTRINS
K. INFUSION
N. ANAPHORESIS
Q. ALBINISM

C. PORE
F. ANTIBIOTIC
I. PIGMENTED LESION
L. ALOPECIA ADNATA
O. COMEDOGENIC
R. SCLERODERMA

25. Using the Across and Down clues, write the correct words in the numbered grid below.

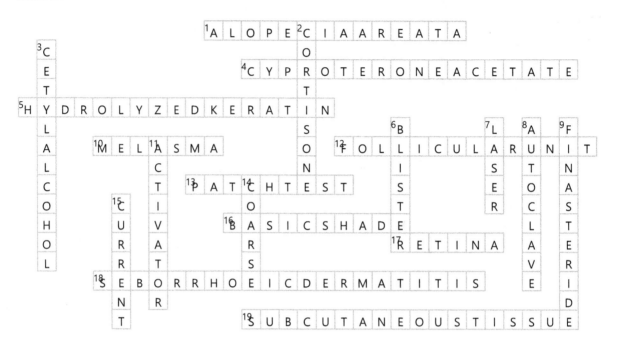

ACROSS

1. Hair loss which occurs in patches on the scalp.
4. This drug is normally used to reduce sex drive in men who have an excessive sex drive. It is also prescribed to treat hirsutism and androgenic alopecia in women.
5. The structural protein of hair.
10. Dark skin discoloration on sun-exposed areas of the face and neck. Young women with brownish skin tones are at greatest risk.
12. Groupings of hair that grow together and share the same blood supply.
13. A test performed on the skin 24 hours before its use to determine sensitivity.
16. A natural or neutral color.
17. Retinoic Acid, compound that is often used to improve the appearance and texture of the skin.
18. has been called a more extensive and severe form of dandruff.
19. The body's shock absorber.

ACROSS

1. Hair loss which occurs in patches on the scalp.
4. This drug is normally used to reduce sex drive in men who have an excessive sex drive. It is also prescribed to treat hirsutism and androgenic alopecia in women.
5. The structural protein of hair.
10. Dark skin discoloration on sun-exposed areas of the face and neck. Young women with brownish skin tones are at greatest risk.
12. Groupings of hair that grow together and share the same blood supply.
13. A test performed on the skin 24 hours before its use to determine sensitivity.
16. A natural or neutral color.
17. Retinoic Acid, compound that is often used to improve the appearance and texture of the skin.
18. has been called a more extensive and severe form of dandruff.
19. The body's shock absorber.

A. ALOPECIA AREATA
D. SEBORRHOEIC DERMATITIS
G. CURRENT
J. BLISTER
M. FOLLICULAR UNIT
P. ACTIVATOR
S. MELASMA

B. COARSE
E. LASER
H. AUTOCLAVE
K. PATCH TEST
N. HYDROLYZED KERATIN
Q. CORTISONE

C. CYPROTERONE ACETATE
F. SUBCUTANEOUS TISSUE
I. BASIC SHADE
L. RETIN-A
O. FINASTERIDE
R. CETYL ALCOHOL

26. Using the Across and Down clues, write the correct words in the numbered grid below.

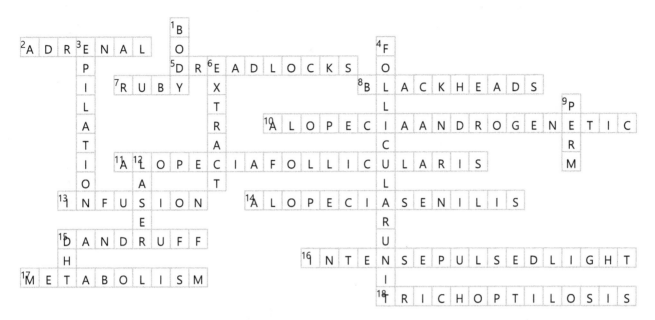

ACROSS

2. A gland that affects certain types of hair growth.
5. A hairstyle in which the hair naturally or through manipulation is encouraged to matte and form a cylindrical, rope-like pattern.
7. Commonly used laser for hair and tattoo removal.
8. A type of clogged pore in the skin with a visible black plug.
10. This is the common name for male or female pattern baldness which depends on the genetic predisposition of the hair follicles and the levels of DHT in the body.
11. Hair loss due to inflammation of hair follicles.
13. Tea made by steeping an herb's leaves or flowers in hot water.
14. Alopecia senilis is baldness due to old age.
15. Flaking scalp due to excessive cell production.
16. A treatment consisting of short pulses of light sent out through an applicator that is gently pressed against the skin.
17. The body transformation of food into energy.
18. Split ends.

ACROSS

2. A gland that affects certain types of hair growth.
5. A hairstyle in which the hair naturally or through manipulation is encouraged to matte and form a cylindrical, rope-like pattern.
7. Commonly used laser for hair and tattoo removal.
8. A type of clogged pore in the skin with a visible black plug.
10. This is the common name for male or female pattern baldness which depends on the genetic predisposition of the hair follicles and the levels of DHT in the body.
11. Hair loss due to inflammation of hair follicles.
13. Tea made by steeping an herb's leaves or flowers in hot water.
14. Alopecia senilis is baldness due to old age.
15. Flaking scalp due to excessive cell production.
16. A treatment consisting of short pulses of light sent out through an applicator that is gently pressed against the skin.
17. The body transformation of food into energy.
18. Split ends.

A. EXTRACT
D. ALOPECIA ANDROGENETIC
G. DANDRUFF
J. RUBY
M. LASER
P. EPILATION
S. PERM

B. DREADLOCKS
E. METABOLISM
H. DHT
K. BODY
N. ALOPECIA FOLLICULARIS
Q. BLACKHEADS

C. INFUSION
F. TRICHOPTILOSIS
I. ADRENAL
L. ALOPECIA SENILIS
O. FOLLICULAR UNIT
R. INTENSE PULSED LIGHT

27. Using the Across and Down clues, write the correct words in the numbered grid below.

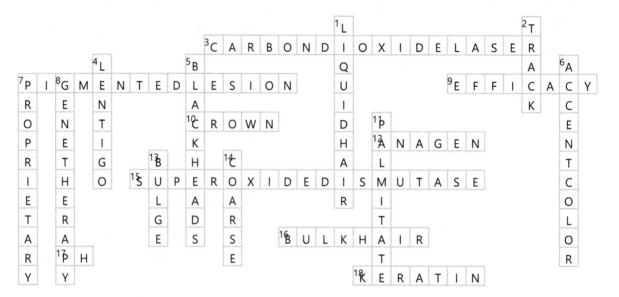

ACROSS

3. Also known as a CO2 laser, these are commonly used to perform skin resurfacing.
7. Variety of skin conditions mainly the result of excess melanin. Commonly known as Café au Lait stains, birthmarks, age spots and freckles.
9. A term meaning how well or effectively a cosmetic device works.
10. Area at the top of the head.
12. This is the growing phase of the hair cycle which lasts about seven years in a healthy person. The active stage in a hair growth cycle.
15. The enzyme superoxide, catalyzes the dis-mutation of superoxide into oxygen and hydrogen peroxide.
16. Term for loose commercial hair. This hair is used for creating wefts or for services like fusion.
17. Used to measure acidity in cosmetic preparations.
18. A fibrous protein found in hair, nails, and skin.

ACROSS

3. Also known as a CO2 laser, these are commonly used to perform skin resurfacing.
7. Variety of skin conditions mainly the result of excess melanin. Commonly known as Café au Lait stains, birthmarks, age spots and freckles.
9. A term meaning how well or effectively a cosmetic device works.
10. Area at the top of the head.
12. This is the growing phase of the hair cycle which lasts about seven years in a healthy person. The active stage in a hair growth cycle.
15. The enzyme superoxide, catalyzes the dis-mutation of superoxide into oxygen and hydrogen peroxide.
16. Term for loose commercial hair. This hair is used for creating wefts or for services like fusion.
17. Used to measure acidity in cosmetic preparations.
18. A fibrous protein found in hair, nails, and skin.

A. PH
B. BLACKHEADS
C. EFFICACY
D. PALMITATE
E. PROPRIETARY
F. GENE THERAPY
G. CARBON DIOXIDE LASER
H. KERATIN
I. BULGE
J. LENTIGO
K. SUPEROXIDE DISMUTASE
L. LIQUID HAIR
M. COARSE
N. BULK HAIR
O. PIGMENTED LESION
P. TRACK
Q. ACCENT COLOR
R. CROWN
S. ANAGEN

28. Using the Across and Down clues, write the correct words in the numbered grid below.

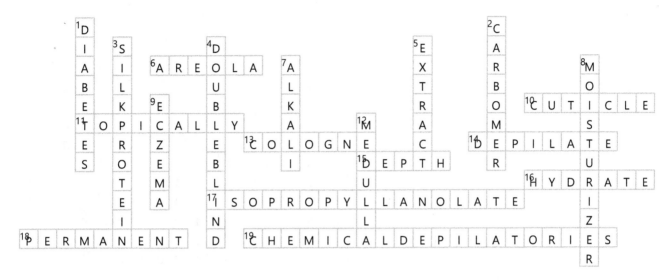

ACROSS

6. The pigmented area surrounding the nipple. A very common area for hair growth.
10. The hard outer protective layer of the hair. Impart sheen to the hair.
11. Means to apply directly onto the scalp.
13. A combination of water containing alcohol and fragrant oils. Not to be confused with a concentrated perfume.
14. Removal of hair on the surface of the skin. Examples include shaving or the use of depilatory creams.
15. The darkness or lightness of a color.
16. To add moisture to the skin.
17. A Synthetic moisturizer.
18. A definition set by the American FDA that most laser and intense light source manufacturers claim to meet for hair removal.
19. Powder or cream preparations that dissolve hair above the surface of the skin. Some find these products very irritating to the skin.

ACROSS

6. The pigmented area surrounding the nipple. A very common area for hair growth.
10. The hard outer protective layer of the hair. Impart sheen to the hair.
11. Means to apply directly onto the scalp.
13. A combination of water containing alcohol and fragrant oils. Not to be confused with a concentrated perfume.
14. Removal of hair on the surface of the skin. Examples include shaving or the use of depilatory creams.
15. The darkness or lightness of a color.
16. To add moisture to the skin.
17. A Synthetic moisturizer.
18. A definition set by the American FDA that most laser and intense light source manufacturers claim to meet for hair removal.
19. Powder or cream preparations that dissolve hair above the surface of the skin. Some find these products very irritating to the skin.

A. EXTRACT
D. HYDRATE
G. CUTICLE
J. ISOPROPYL LANOLATE
M. DEPILATE
P. SILK PROTEIN
S. PERMANENT

B. MOISTURIZER
E. AREOLA
H. COLOGNE
K. ECZEMA
N. MEDULLA
Q. TOPICALLY

C. DEPTH
F. DOUBLE BLIND
I. ALKALI
L. CARBOMER
O. DIABETES
R. CHEMICAL DEPILATORIES

29. Using the Across and Down clues, write the correct words in the numbered grid below.

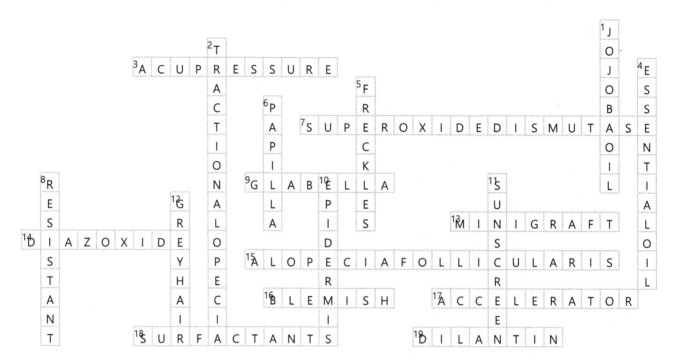

ACROSS

3. A method of relieving pain by pressing down on an area of the body.
7. The enzyme superoxide, catalyzes the dis-mutation of superoxide into oxygen and hydrogen peroxide.
9. The space between the eyebrows.
13. A small hair graft usually consisting of between three to ten hair roots.
14. A drug sometimes linked to excess hair growth.
15. Hair loss due to inflammation of hair follicles.
16. Blood or pigment based visible mark.
17. A product that works under the surface of the skin and provides the necessary ingredients for melanin production, which will accelerate the rate at which the skin tans.
18. Active agent that allows oil to mix with water. Used in skincare products like cleansers, wetting agents, emulsifiers, solubizers, conditioning agents and foam stabilizers.
19. A drug sometimes linked to excess hair growth.

ACROSS

3. A method of relieving pain by pressing down on an area of the body.
7. The enzyme superoxide, catalyzes the dis-mutation of superoxide into oxygen and hydrogen peroxide.
9. The space between the eyebrows.
13. A small hair graft usually consisting of between three to ten hair roots.
14. A drug sometimes linked to excess hair growth.
15. Hair loss due to inflammation of hair follicles.
16. Blood or pigment based visible mark.
17. A product that works under the surface of the skin and provides the necessary ingredients for melanin production, which will accelerate the rate at which the skin tans.
18. Active agent that allows oil to mix with water. Used in skincare products like cleansers, wetting agents, emulsifiers, solubizers, conditioning agents and foam stabilizers.
19. A drug sometimes linked to excess hair growth.

A. PAPILLA
D. EPIDERMIS
G. MINI GRAFT
J. GREY HAIR
M. BLEMISH
P. SURFACTANTS
S. ACCELERATOR

B. DIAZOXIDE
E. ESSENTIAL OIL
H. ACUPRESSURE
K. ALOPECIA FOLLICULARIS
N. RESISTANT
Q. TRACTION ALOPECIA

C. SUNSCREEN
F. GLABELLA
I. FRECKLES
L. DILANTIN
O. JOJOBA OIL
R. SUPEROXIDE DISMUTASE

30. Using the Across and Down clues, write the correct words in the numbered grid below.

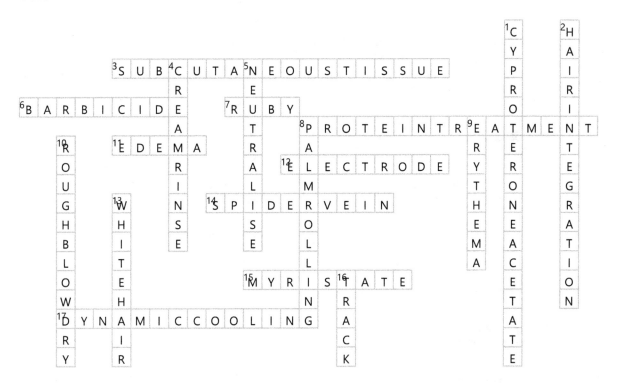

ACROSS

3. The body's shock absorber.
6. Brand name of sanitizer used to disinfect salon implements.
7. Commonly used laser for hair and tattoo removal.
8. A treatment used on the hair. Designed to add strength and elasticity to the hair by adding protein to the cortex.
11. A medical term for swelling.
12. In hair removal, a conductor through which electricity enters or leaves the body. An electrolysis needle is an electrode.
14. broken capillaries.
15. Synthetic moisturizer.
17. A method of epidermal cooling which cools the skin with supercooled liquid immediately before a laser pulse is applied.

ACROSS

3. The body's shock absorber.
6. Brand name of sanitizer used to disinfect salon implements.
7. Commonly used laser for hair and tattoo removal.
8. A treatment used on the hair. Designed to add strength and elasticity to the hair by adding protein to the cortex.
11. A medical term for swelling.
12. In hair removal, a conductor through which electricity enters or leaves the body. An electrolysis needle is an electrode.
14. broken capillaries.
15. Synthetic moisturizer.
17. A method of epidermal cooling which cools the skin with supercooled liquid immediately before a laser pulse is applied.

A. RUBY
B. ERYTHEMA
C. PROTEIN TREATMENT
D. CYPROTERONE ACETATE
E. MYRISTATE
F. HAIR INTEGRATION
G. SUBCUTANEOUS TISSUE
H. WHITE HAIR
I. TRACK
J. SPIDER VEIN
K. NEUTRALISE
L. PALM ROLLING
M. EDEMA
N. ELECTRODE
O. BARBICIDE
P. ROUGH BLOW DRY
Q. CREAM RINSE
R. DYNAMIC COOLING

Multiple Choice

From the words provided for each clue, provide the letter of the word which best matches the clue.

1. ___ Synthetic moisturizer.
   A. ESTROGEN   B. PALMITATE   C. LAYERING   D. DANAZOL

2. ___ This is the common name for male or female pattern baldness which depends on the genetic predisposition of the hair follicles and the levels of DHT in the body.
   A. CONDITIONER   B. ALOPECIA ANDROGENETIC   C. LAYERING   D. DOUBLE BLIND

3. ___ An herbal concentrate produced by separating the essential or active part of an herb into a solvent material.
   A. LENTIGO   B. ANDROGEN   C. EXTRACT   D. ALLERGEN

4. ___ Blood or pigment based visible mark.
   A. PABA   B. HAIR INTEGRATION   C. FOLLICLES   D. BLEMISH

5. ___ A common disorder characterized by inflammation of the hair follicle.
   A. AXILLA   B. LUBRICATES   C. FOLLICULITIS   D. LUVIMER

6. ___ Trichoptilosis
   A. SPLIT ENDS   B. DERMAL SHEATH   C. CASTRATION   D. ANAGEN

7. ___ The pigmented area surrounding the nipple. A very common area for hair growth.
   A. CALCIUM THIOGLYCOLATE   B. TRACK   C. TARGETED FAT REDUCTION   D. AREOLA

8. ___ Treatments, especially IPL, where the follicle is disabled by the light energy making it unable to support any more hair growth.
   A. CALCIUM THIOGLYCOLATE   B. CASTRATION   C. WEFT   D. PERMANENT HAIR REDUCTION

9. ___ The body transformation of food into energy.
   A. METABOLISM   B. FASHION SHADE   C. COAGULATION   D. CLIMBAZOLE

10. ___ A small fluid-filled bubble on the skin caused by heat from over treatment with certain types of hair removal.
    A. DIET   B. BLISTER   C. APPLE CIDER VINEGAR   D. CROWN

11. ___ A fibrous protein found in hair, nails, and skin.
    A. KERATIN   B. DIET   C. SEMI PERMANENT   D. CONDITIONER

12. ___ A combination of water containing alcohol and fragrant oils. Not to be confused with a concentrated perfume.
    A. OXIDATION COLOUR   B. AXILLA   C. HAIR INTEGRATION   D. COLOGNE

13. ___ The surgical removal of one or both testicles or ovaries.
    A. CLIMBAZOLE   B. SECTIONING   C. SCLERODERMA   D. CASTRATION

14. ___ The process by which most synthetic fiber is curled at the factory.
    A. TAN   B. ELECTROLOGY   C. ORGANIC   D. STEAMING

15. ___ Dried fluid that seeps from skin in some clients following hair removal such as laser, electrolysis, and depilatories.
    A. SELECTIVE PHOTOTHERMOLYSIS   B. CRUSTING   C. ELECTRIC TWEEZER   D. CUSHING SYNDROME

16. ___ Is sometimes linked to excess hair growth, especially in the extremely obese and extremely anorexic.
    A. WEFTS   B. ECZEMA   C. DIET   D. ANDROGEN

17. Any natural or synthetic substance or substances use solely to impart a sweet or pleasant smell (odor) to a cosmetic product.
A. KELOIDS B. BULK HAIR C. AZELAIC ACID D. FRAGRANCE

18. A medical term for blackheads.
A. EDEMA B. TESTOSTERONE C. COMEDONES D. AMMONIUM THIOGLYCOLATE

19. When your skin is damaged by exposure to the UVA and UVB rays of the sun, its reaction is to produce more melanin as an attempt to protect itself against further damage.
A. PROPRIETARY B. METABOLISM C. TAN D. DEPTH

20. Positively charges the hair to provide manageability and reduces static.
A. CATIONIC POLYMER B. WEFTS C. ACCENT COLOR D. SECTIONING

21. A smoothing product to stop your hair from frizzing, keeping it smooth and straight. You'll be able to find a serum that is specifically designed to your own hair type.
A. ACNE B. SERUM C. LUBRICATES D. WIG

22. A condition that is hereditary. Excess hair often runs in the family.
A. ALOPECIA ADNATA B. CONGENITAL C. SCLERODERMA D. TESTOSTERONE

23. A discoloration of skin from blood, sometimes caused by electrolysis, plucking, or waxing. Also known as Purpura.
A. DERMAL SHEATH B. BRUISE C. FOLLICLES D. SEBORRHOEIC DERMATITIS

24. Term used to measure the output energy, for Lasers and Pulsed Light Sources that is delivered to tissue.
A. KERATIN B. FLUENCE C. DIODE D. CUSHING SYNDROME

25. a light mist or spray, which when used as verb means to lightly spray your hair.
A. SPRITZ B. METABOLISM C. MELANIN D. SECTIONING

26. A modern term used to describe hair weaving.
A. SEBACEOUS B. HAIR INTEGRATION C. MICRO GRAFT D. DEPILATION

27. A substance used to relieve pain.
A. SEBACEOUS B. ANALGESIC C. DIODE D. NERVE ENDINGS

28. Contact dermatitis, it's a mild inflammation of the skin.
A. DEPILATION B. MICRO GRAFT C. SERUM D. ECZEMA

29. allows you to only pay attention to a particular area or panel of hair.
A. REMI B. SECTIONING C. BARBA D. INDENTATION

30. Relating to the skin.
A. ACCENT COLOR B. FOLLICULITIS C. DEPILATORIES D. CUTANEOUS

31. A water gel-like substance that is known for its ability to soothe irritated skin, especially sunburned skin.
A. MEDULLA B. SPRITZ C. STEAMING D. ALOE VERA

32. This is the end of the active growth period, and is marked by changes occurring in the follicle.
A. CATAGEN B. ELECTRIC TWEEZER C. FREEZING SPRAY D. DIAZOXIDE

33. A process of removing the top dead skin layers to reveal healthier, newer skin underneath.
A. SPLIT ENDS B. BLANCHING C. DEVELOPER D. EXFOLIATING

34. A natural water-soluble source of acid derived from liquid silk.
A. FLUENCE   B. SILK PROTEIN   C. COAGULATION   D. DIMETHICONE

35. A drug sometimes linked to excess hair growth.
A. PORE   B. PIGMENT   C. DANAZOL   D. CAPILLARIES

36. Pertaining to carbon - based compounds produced by living plants, animals or by synthetic processes.
A. BETAINE   B. ORGANIC   C. HYDROLYZED KERATIN   D. ALOE VERA

37. Discolored skin that should be examined and approved by a physician before hair removal.
A. ALOPECIA ADNATA   B. AZELAIC ACID   C. LENTIGO   D. BIRTHMARKS

38. A semi-conductive material which mainly lets energy travel one direction and not the other.
A. FOLLICLES   B. BLEMISH   C. DIODE   D. T ZONE

39. a crystal silicate mineral compounded with elements such as aluminum, iron, magnesium, sodium, lithium, or potassium.
A. SPLIT ENDS   B. ANAGEN CYCLE   C. APPLE CIDER VINEGAR   D. TOURMALINE

40. The structural protein of hair.
A. SEMI PERMANENT   B. ALOPECIA ADNATA   C. DHT   D. HYDROLYZED KERATIN

41. Site where hair roots are taken from during transplant surgery.
A. ELECTROLOGY   B. BLEMISH   C. LAYERING   D. DONOR SITE

42. Allergen is a substance that causes an allergic reaction.
A. DEPTH   B. ALOE VERA   C. ALLERGEN   D. ADRENAL

43. A color which lasts from 6 - 8 shampoos.
A. FLY-AWAY HAIR   B. ACID   C. SEMI PERMANENT   D. PERMANENT HAIR REDUCTION

44. The medical term for armpit, a common place for gonadal hair after puberty.
A. AXILLA   B. LIPID LAYER   C. HYDROGEN PEROXIDE   D. INDENTATION

45. A mixture of wax, thickeners, and a group of chemicals used to coat the hair shaft and detangle after shampooing.
A. CATAGEN   B. CREAM RINSE   C. EDEMA   D. CLIMBAZOLE

46. A disease of the skin and connective tissue that can cause hair loss over the affected areas.
A. KELOIDS   B. PALMITATE   C. ALKALINE   D. SCLERODERMA

47. Detangling aid which conditions, protects against humidity, and adds shine.
A. CLARIFIER   B. SCRUNCH DRY   C. DIMETHICONE   D. ALOPECIA UNIVERSALIS

48. Clinic based method of reducing the appearance of cellulite.
A. BETAINE   B. CLARIFIER   C. CELLULITE REDUCTION   D. ACTIVATOR

49. Commonly used in the treatment of acne and other skin conditions.
A. ANODE   B. DIMETHICONE   C. AZELAIC ACID   D. SEBORRHOEIC DERMATITIS

50. Usually a sharp, intense color used as a contrast or pickup for color scheme. It is used to add excitement to an overall effect
A. FRAGRANCE FREE   B. HAIR INTEGRATION   C. RELAX   D. ACCENT COLOR

51. Medical term for beard.
A. BARBA   B. ALCOHOL   C. NATURAL   D. CLARIFIER

52. Coarse, pigmented or non-pigmented, exist on the scalp and gain length at a rate of 1-2cm per month during a cyclical life of up to 10 years.
A. CREAM RINSE   B. TERMINAL HAIRS   C. WATER RESISTANT   D. ENDOCRINE SYSTEM

53. The volume or springiness of hair.
A. BODY   B. COHERENT LIGHT   C. FRAGRANCE FREE   D. ACID MANTLE

54. Natural substance that gives color (pigment) to hair and skin.
A. ANODE   B. CAPILLARIES   C. CONTACT COOLING   D. MELANIN

55. A product which oxidizes artificial color pigment.
A. LUVIMER   B. RELAX   C. DEVELOPER   D. OXIDATION COLOUR

56. The process of scraping or wearing hair away. Causing partial or complete absence of hair from areas.
A. JOJOBA OIL   B. ABRASION   C. COMEDONES   D. CATIONIC POLYMER

57. A female hormone sometimes linked to increased hair growth.
A. ESTROGEN   B. HYDRATE   C. ECZEMA   D. SCLERODERMA

58. a male hormone that is suggested to be the main cause for the miniaturization of the hair follicle and for hair loss.
A. TONE   B. BETAINE   C. CHAMOMILE   D. DHT

59. A device that removes hair by grasping hairs above the skin's surface with an electrified tweezers.
A. SCRUNCH DRY   B. AMPERE   C. BLEACH   D. ELECTRIC TWEEZER

60. To add moisture to the skin.
A. EDEMA   B. HYDRATE   C. BARBA   D. WIG

61. Groupings of hair that grow together and share the same blood supply.
A. SEMI PERMANENT   B. FOLLICULAR UNIT   C. IONIC   D. NORWOOD SCALE

62. Hormone that causes masculine characteristics and affects hair growth.
A. BLANCHING   B. COUTURE CUT   C. BARBICIDE   D. ANDROGEN

63. Term for loose commercial hair. This hair is used for creating wefts or for services like fusion.
A. MELASMA   B. BULK HAIR   C. JOJOBA OIL   D. FOLLICULITIS

64. Used in many products for blonde hair to enhance color.
A. CHAMOMILE   B. ACNE   C. FASHION SHADE   D. ARNICA

65. Makes smooth or slippery by using oil to overcome friction.
A. LUBRICATES   B. LEUCOTRICHIA   C. KELOIDS   D. HAIR WEAVING

66. A classification for stronger, thicker types of hair.
A. KERATIN   B. CONGENITAL   C. COARSE   D. STEAMING

67. A whitening of the skin sometimes caused by some types of hair removal.
A. BLANCHING   B. WEFTS   C. CATHODE   D. TERMINAL HAIRS

68. A clinical testing method in which neither patient nor doctor know what medication or procedure is being used.
A. CARBOMER   B. EPIDERMIS   C. PH   D. DOUBLE BLIND

69. used in between Shampoo and Conditioner to put protein back into the hair.
A. HYDROLYZED KERATIN   B. SEBACEOUS   C. SPLIT ENDS   D. TREATMENT

70. The main structure of the hair shaft. The cortex determines the color and texture of the hair. The largest section of a single hair, containing the main bulk of the hair.
A. ELECTROLYSIS B. APPLE CIDER VINEGAR C. SILK PROTEIN D. CORTEX

71. A point midway up the hair follicle which researchers suspect must be damaged to induce permanent hair removal
A. HENNA B. BULGE C. PERMANENTLY D. NERVE ENDINGS

72. A technique for drying your hair which creates a style at the same time.
A. COUTURE CUT B. KELOIDS C. TOPICALLY D. SCRUNCH DRY

73. A negative electrode in a cell or circuit.
A. CATHODE B. HAIR WEAVING C. CHILLTIP D. DERMAL SHEATH

74. A group of glands which maintain the body's internal environment through the production of hormones.
A. SPRITZ B. ENDOCRINE SYSTEM C. COAGULATION D. ACTIVATOR

75. The temporary removal of hair.
A. INFUSION B. T ZONE C. DERMATITIS D. DEPILATION

76. Ingredients extracted directly from plants, earth minerals, or animal products as opposed to being produced synthetically.
A. BLEACH B. NATURAL C. T ZONE D. DOUBLE BLIND

77. In women, a major source of female hormones. Certain conditions involving the ovaries can lead to excess hair growth, especially polycystic ovary syndrome (PCOS).
A. SEBACEOUS GLAND B. DEVELOPER C. OVARIES D. SPLIT ENDS

78. Refers to a congenital absence of pigment in a lock of hairs which will show as grey or white.
A. AXILLA B. TOURMALINE C. APPLE CIDER VINEGAR D. LEUCOTRICHIA

79. The hair follicle is the tiny blub under your scalp from which the hair grows.
A. ANODE B. DERMABRASION C. FOLLICLES D. T ZONE

80. Oil producing gland in the dermis.
A. CATHODE B. ELECTRIC TWEEZER C. SEBACEOUS GLAND D. ALEXANDRITE

81. A method used to disguise (not remove) hair by lightening its color.
A. BLEACH B. COUTURE CUT C. EDEMA D. OVARIES

82. Flexible resin.
A. ALCOHOL B. HENNA C. LUVIMER D. COAGULATION

83. Increases wet and dry combability.
A. SELECTIVE PHOTOTHERMOLYSIS B. AMMONIUM THIOGLYCOLATE C. SILICONE D. BLEMISH

84. A geometric bob with a straight fringe, so called because of the resemblance to the capital A, with it's horizontal line, the fringe and its legs the hair passing your ears.
A. SOAP B. CONTACT COOLING C. ALOPECIA UNIVERSALIS D. A LINE BOB

85. Receptors which respond to touch, pain, pressure, heat and cold.
A. ALEXANDRITE B. CARBOMER C. NERVE ENDINGS D. PIGMENT

86. In hair removal, the practice of epilation with electrified needles.
A. TRACK B. ELECTROLYSIS C. TREATMENT D. LAYERING

87. Contains superior properties to keep skin and hair soft. It is beneficial to dry hair.
A. AXILLA   B. ACNE   C. JOJOBA OIL   D. BULK HAIR

88. To chemically straighten the hair to gently smooth out curl, reduce frizz, or create a straight style.
A. CREAM RINSE   B. HENNA   C. BULK HAIR   D. RELAX

89. A gland that affects certain types of hair growth.
A. WATER RESISTANT   B. MEDULLA   C. SEBACEOUS GLAND   D. ADRENAL

90. Small blood vessels which connect the arteries and veins that feed the hair.
A. COHERENT LIGHT   B. CAPILLARIES   C. CATAPHORESIS   D. DHT

91. Pertaining to a drug that is produced for profit.
A. ESTROGEN   B. SOAP   C. ACCENT COLOR   D. PROPRIETARY

92. Used to oxidize (expand) artificial color molecules. Can also lighten natural color pigment.
A. PIGMENT   B. HYDROGEN PEROXIDE   C. BLEND   D. BASIC SHADE

93. A type of raised darkened scar, more common with dark skin. Due to a defect in the healing process.
A. COCAMIDE DEA   B. HAIR WEAVING   C. LUVIMER   D. KELOIDS

94. The term used to describe any hairpiece with a full cap which covers the hair on the head, or the entire area where hair normally grows, as a substitute for hair.
A. HYDROGEN PEROXIDE   B. ALEXANDRITE   C. ACID MANTLE   D. WIG

95. A very small hair graft usually consisting of one or two hairs.
A. TAN   B. DIODE   C. DIET   D. MICRO GRAFT

96. Area at the top of the head.
A. CROWN   B. COHERENT LIGHT   C. EXFOLIATING   D. FRAGRANCE FREE

97. Selectively targeting dermal structures with light energy, without causing damage to surrounding tissue.
A. JOJOBA OIL   B. COARSE   C. CRUSTING   D. SELECTIVE PHOTOTHERMOLYSIS

98. A medical term for swelling.
A. AMPERE   B. DANAZOL   C. EDEMA   D. CHILLTIP

99. The medulla is a central zone of cells usually only present in large thick hairs.
A. COUTURE CUT   B. MEDULLA   C. TRACK   D. ALOPECIA UNIVERSALIS

100. Metabolising stubborn fat deposits, typically in the lower body, using methods such as Eporex mesotherapy.
A. EPIDERMIS   B. TARGETED FAT REDUCTION   C. KERATIN   D. ANDROGEN

From the words provided for each clue, provide the letter of the word which best matches the clue.

101. Process where water molecules are broken down by ions into smaller droplets. This then allows the hair to absorb the moisture more easily.
A. TERMINAL HAIRS   B. THREAD VEIN   C. HYPOPIGMENTATION   D. IONIC

102. To weave strands of hair together. On the scalp braiding is used to form a base or track to sew on a commercial weft.
A. WEAVE   B. CURRENT   C. BRAID   D. DIODE

103. A protein that holds all connective tissue together under the skin.
A. SILICONE B. CHIGNON C. COLLAGEN D. ABDOMEN

104. The removal of dead skin cells to reveal softer skin underneath.
A. BARBICIDE B. EXFOLIATION C. SILICONE D. PUNCH GRAFT

105. The pigmented area surrounding the nipple. A very common area for hair growth.
A. HAIR INTEGRATION B. COAGULATION C. AREOLA D. LUBRICANT

106. Pertains to the skin.
A. PIGMENTED LESION B. SUBCUTANEOUS C. Q SWITCH D. CHEMICAL DEPILATORIES

107. The substructure that is responsible for the spectral selective absorption of electromagnetic radiation.
A. CARBOMER B. ALOPECIA UNIVERSALIS C. FINISHING SPRAY D. CHROMOPHORE

108. The small area at the base of the hair root which provides nutrients needed for growth.
A. ANODE B. PAPILLA C. CLUB HAIR D. MICRO LINKING TECHNIQUE

109. This drug is normally used to reduce sex drive in men who have an excessive sex drive. It is also prescribed to treat hirsutism and androgenic alopecia in women.
A. DERMABRASION B. LUBRICANT C. CYPROTERONE ACETATE D. PROPECIA

110. Hair extensions are pieces of real or synthetic weaved close to the scalp in order to achieve greater length or fullness.
A. ANTI ANDROGEN B. EXTENSION C. PERM D. BETAINE

111. This is the complete loss of scalp hair often combined with the loss of eyebrows and eyelashes.
A. ALOPECIA TOTALIS B. OVARIES C. MICRO LINKING TECHNIQUE D. DIODE

112. Congenital baldness or baldness at birth.
A. TRICHOTILLOMANIA B. SPRIONOLACTONE C. ALOPECIA ADNATA D. SEBACEOUS

113. A flat, discolored area of skin similar to a freckle.
A. SEBACEOUS GLAND B. LENTIGO C. TARGETED FAT REDUCTION D. PAPILLA

114. The body's shock absorber.
A. BULBOUS NEEDLE B. TRICHOTILLOMANIA C. SUBCUTANEOUS TISSUE D. PH

115. Powder or cream preparations that dissolve hair above the surface of the skin. Some find these products very irritating to the skin.
A. SEBACEOUS B. GENERIC C. CHEMICAL DEPILATORIES D. ESCHAR

116. A discoloration of skin from blood, sometimes caused by electrolysis, plucking, or waxing. Also known as Purpura.
A. DISCOMFORT B. BRUISE C. SPRIONOLACTONE D. LUBRICATES

117. Hormone that causes masculine characteristics and affects hair growth.
A. A LINE BOB B. ANDROGEN C. ANTIANDROGEN D. DONOR SITE

118. In hair removal, the practice of epilation with electrified needles.
A. DERMATITIS B. ELECTROLYSIS C. BARBICIDE D. CHIGNON

119. Flexible resin.
A. ALOE VERA B. DOUBLE BLIND C. T ZONE D. LUVIMER

120. A chemical substance found in plants and animals. The building blocks of hair.
A. DERMATITIS   B. AMINO ACID   C. PUNCH GRAFT   D. BOB

121. A sun tanning product that contains DHA, which reacts with amino acids in the top layer of skin, causing it to temporarily darken (2-4 days).
A. SELF TANNER   B. TEXTURIZER   C. BASIC SHADE   D. SILK PROTEIN

122. A smoothing product to stop your hair from frizzing, keeping it smooth and straight. You'll be able to find a serum that is specifically designed to your own hair type.
A. EPILATION   B. ISOPROPYL LANOLATE   C. SERUM   D. IONIC

123. Laser at 755nm used for hair removal.
A. LUBRICANT   B. ECCRINE GLAND   C. TRICHOPTILOSIS   D. ALEXANDRITE

124. a light mist or spray, which when used as verb means to lightly spray your hair.
A. ANAGEN CYCLE   B. SPRITZ   C. BLACK SKIN   D. ARRECTOR PILI

125. A test performed on the skin 24 hours before its use to determine sensitivity.
A. CHEMICAL DEPILATORIES   B. CLONE   C. DISTORTED HAIR FOLLICLES   D. PATCH TEST

126. A method used to disguise (not remove) hair by lightening its color.
A. MONOFILAMENT   B. KELOIDS   C. BLEACH   D. ANDROGEN

127. A device that produces short intense bursts of energy from a laser.
A. CURRENT   B. Q SWITCH   C. CHEMICAL DEPILATORIES   D. CYPROTERONE ACETATE

128. Also called vitamin B5 (a B vitamin), is a water-soluble vitamin required to sustain life (essential nutrient).
A. ELECTROLYSIS   B. PERMANENT   C. PANTOTHENIC ACID   D. ALLERGEN

129. Fine, transparent nylon or silk mesh with hairs individually hand-knotted into the mesh. Allows the hair to fall naturally and gives more versatility in styling.
A. MONOFILAMENT   B. SKIN REJUVENATION   C. ANTIBIOTIC   D. LEUCOTRICHIA

130. A group of genetically identical cells or organisms derived from a single common cell.
A. DERMIS   B. SLOUGH   C. CLONE   D. BETAINE

131. The brand name for finestaride. The only drug approved by the FDA to treat hair loss.
A. PROPECIA   B. FOLLICLES   C. EMOLLIENTS   D. CETYL ALCOHOL

132. Contains superior properties to keep skin and hair soft. It is beneficial to dry hair.
A. ELECTROLOGY   B. JOJOBA OIL   C. FINASTERIDE   D. LIPID LAYER

133. A geometric bob with a straight fringe, so called because of the resemblance to the capital A, with it's horizontal line, the fringe and its legs the hair passing your ears.
A. ALLERGEN   B. MONOFILAMENT   C. A LINE BOB   D. SLOUGH

134. Completely changing the natural color of the hair.
A. PERMANENTLY   B. DERMATITIS   C. ENERGY DENSITY   D. CARBON DIOXIDE LASER

135. The body transformation of food into energy.
A. AMMONIUM THIOGLYCOLATE   B. METABOLISM   C. LIPID LAYER   D. ARRECTOR PILI

136. Creamy hair product meant to be used after shampoo. Moisturizes and detangles hair.
A. ENERGY DENSITY   B. TERMINAL HAIRS   C. ELECTROCOAGULATION   D. CONDITIONER

137. ___ The practice of hair removal through the use of electrified needles, invented in the 1870's.
A. BIOPSY   B. ELECTROLOGY   C. IONIC   D. FOLLICLES

138. ___ Optimum hold without overload.
A. TOURMALINE   B. ACNE   C. MICRO DIFFUSE   D. DISTORTED HAIR FOLLICLES

139. ___ The invisible spectrum of solar radiation. It is divided into three regions with increasing danger to the skin.
A. TOURMALINE   B. NORWOOD SCALE   C. UV   D. HYPOPIGMENTATION

140. ___ a crystal silicate mineral compounded with elements such as aluminum, iron, magnesium, sodium, lithium, or potassium.
A. ENERGY DENSITY   B. FLY-AWAY HAIR   C. Q SWITCH   D. TOURMALINE

141. ___ Is sometimes linked to excess hair growth, especially in the extremely obese and extremely anorexic.
A. GENERIC   B. ISOPROPYL LANOLATE   C. ARNICA   D. DIET

142. ___ The active stage in a hair growth cycle.
A. CORTISONE   B. ANAGEN CYCLE   C. SPRIONOLACTONE   D. CLUB HAIR

143. ___ Combating the signs of ageing using the latest innovative, non-invasive treatments that give you visibly younger, healthy, radiant skin.
A. ELECTRIC TWEEZER   B. TREATMENT   C. BLACKHEADS   D. SKIN REJUVENATION

144. ___ A color which lasts from 6 - 8 shampoos.
A. PERMANENTLY   B. SEMI PERMANENT   C. ISOPROPYL LANOLATE   D. ESCHAR

145. ___ Tiny hair-like blood vessels, some of which carry nutrient to the hair growth matrix.
A. FINISHING SPRAY   B. CAPILLARIES   C. ALLERGEN   D. DIODE

146. ___ A medical term for swelling.
A. EFFICACY   B. EDEMA   C. REMI   D. DERMATITIS

147. ___ The hair follicle is the tiny blub under your scalp from which the hair grows.
A. SILICONE   B. EPILATION   C. SOLUBLE   D. FOLLICLES

148. ___ Ingredients extracted directly from plants, earth minerals, or animal products as opposed to being produced synthetically.
A. ACNE   B. NATURAL   C. BLISTER   D. DISCOMFORT

149. ___ A color which requires oxygen to make it work.
A. OXIDATION COLOUR   B. ALOPECIA TOTALIS   C. EXTRACT   D. TELOGEN

150. ___ Substances used to dissolve hair above the skin's surface.
A. CARBOMER   B. ESCHAR   C. AMINOPHENOLS   D. DEPILATORIES

151. ___ allows you to only pay attention to a particular area or panel of hair.
A. PERMANENTLY   B. CREAM RINSE   C. SECTIONING   D. DERMABRASION

152. ___ Procedures that do not involve tools that break the skin or physically enter the body.
A. AMINO ACID   B. CONDITIONER   C. NON INVASIVE   D. BROKEN CAPILLARIES

153. ___ Refers to a congenital absence of pigment in a lock of hairs which will show as grey or white.
A. ENERGY DENSITY   B. ABDOMEN   C. LEUCOTRICHIA   D. ESCHAR

154. ___ A bodily reaction to an irritant. Skin allergies can be exacerbated by solutions put on the skin.
A. ALLERGY   B. Q SWITCH   C. CHELATING   D. ALCOHOL

155. An inflammation of the skin, a result of over production of oil and bacteria.
A. AMINOPHENOLS B. ACNE C. FLY-AWAY HAIR D. INTENSE PULSED LIGHT

156. Produced from starch by means of enzymatic conversion and are used in a wide range of applications in food, pharmaceutical and chemical industries.
A. DERMATITIS B. DEPILATE C. CYCLODEXTRINS D. FOLLICLE SHEATH

157. part of the structure of the hair and also form a protective barrier. They are composed of EFA's amongst other complicated scientific things.
A. DERMABRASION B. PH C. TARGETED FAT REDUCTION D. LIPID LAYER

158. A type of raised darkened scar, more common with dark skin. Due to a defect in the healing process.
A. CORTISONE B. Q SWITCH C. DISCOMFORT D. KELOIDS

159. Used to measure acidity in cosmetic preparations.
A. ACNE B. ESCHAR C. ACTINIC KERATOSIS D. PH

160. Creates "Goose Bumps" when stimulated.
A. ARRECTOR PILI B. PROTEIN TREATMENT C. ALLERGEN D. PSORIASIS

161. A hair weave is usually a hairpiece with layered gaps made into it.
A. WEAVE B. OUTER ROOT SHEATH C. EXFOLIATION D. BARBA

162. Allergen is a substance that causes an allergic reaction.
A. ANAGEN CYCLE B. LIPID LAYER C. HYPERPIGMENTATION D. ALLERGEN

163. A natural water-soluble source of acid derived from liquid silk.
A. ALEXANDRITE B. FOLLICLES C. HAIR INTEGRATION D. SILK PROTEIN

164. The term for hair loss which occurs over the entire body.
A. THREAD VEIN B. WEAVE C. ALOPECIA UNIVERSALIS D. EMOLLIENTS

165. Variety of skin conditions mainly the result of excess melanin. Commonly known as Café au Lait stains, birthmarks, age spots and freckles.
A. EPILATION B. ANTI ANDROGEN C. PIGMENTED LESION D. AMINOPHENOLS

166. Allows some light to pass through.
A. BROKEN CAPILLARIES B. TRANSLUCENT C. SPRITZ D. EPILATION

167. The soft area between the rib cage and the pubic area. A common area for excess hair, often in a line from the belly button to the pubic hair.
A. ABDOMEN B. ALLERGY C. SPLIT ENDS D. CUTTING IN

168. An anti-inflammatory sometimes linked to hair growth when taken internally.
A. HAIR INTEGRATION B. CYPROTERONE ACETATE C. DOUBLE BLIND D. CORTISONE

169. The removal of hair below the skin's surface.
A. INDENTATION B. SILK PROTEIN C. ALCOHOL D. EPILATION

170. Products so labeled may still contain small amounts of fragrances to mask the fatty odor of soap or other unpleasant odors.
A. BOTANICAL B. DERMABRASION C. SPRITZ D. FRAGRANCE FREE

171. A clinical testing method in which neither patient nor doctor know what medication or procedure is being used.
A. NORWOOD SCALE B. SELF TANNER C. DOUBLE BLIND D. BROKEN CAPILLARIES

172. _____ This form of hair loss is caused by pulling out one's own hair, usually without realizing it.
A. MICRO DIFFUSE   B. HYPERPIGMENTATION   C. ESTROGEN   D. TRICHOTILLOMANIA

173. _____ Split ends.
A. HYPERPIGMENTATION   B. TRANSLUCENT   C. TRICHOPTILOSIS   D. BULB

174. _____ A machine used to sterilize medical utensils and some hair removal devices.
A. HYPOPIGMENTATION   B. BLEACH   C. CYCLODEXTRINS   D. AUTOCLAVE

175. _____ creates curls by restructuring your hair molecules with a chemical, or heat treatment and is generally a long-lasting or permanent change to your hair.
A. CARBON DIOXIDE LASER   B. TRICHOTILLOMANIA   C. PERM   D. PUNCH GRAFT

176. _____ The resting phase in the hair cycle.
A. FOLLICLES   B. DIET   C. TELOGEN   D. DERMIS

177. _____ The thin outer layer of skin, on top of the thicker and deeper dermis.
A. EPIDERMIS   B. CURRENT   C. TRICHOPTILOSIS   D. SEMI PERMANENT

178. _____ A definition set by the American FDA that most laser and intense light source manufacturers claim to meet for hair removal.
A. BIOPSY   B. AZELAIC ACID   C. PERMANENT   D. SUBCUTANEOUS

179. _____ Atopic Dermatitis is also known as Eczema. Contact Dermatitis is an inflammation of the skin caused by direct contact with an irritating substance.
A. SOLUBLE   B. DERMATITIS   C. MELASMA   D. SCHIZOTRICHIA

180. _____ The process by which most synthetic fiber is curled at the factory.
A. ACNE   B. SURFACTANTS   C. BRAID   D. STEAMING

181. _____ The use of heat generated by electricity to change tissue from a fluid to a semi-solid, similar to cooking an egg.
A. MICRO LINKING TECHNIQUE   B. BLEACH   C. BASIC SHADE   D. ELECTROCOAGULATION

182. _____ A common ingredient in chemical depilatories.
A. SCHIZOTRICHIA   B. ALOPECIA TOTALIS   C. AMMONIUM THIOGLYCOLATE   D. ACUPRESSURE

183. _____ used in between Shampoo and Conditioner to put protein back into the hair.
A. SCHIZOTRICHIA   B. THREAD VEIN   C. MICRODERMABRASION   D. TREATMENT

184. _____ Possessing a positive electrical charge. Cationic detergents are often used in shampoos because they reduce static electricity and leave the hair manageable.
A. DERMABRASION   B. OUTER ROOT SHEATH   C. CATIONIC   D. CHROMOPHORE

185. _____ A soft thin layer surrounding the lower two-thirds of a hair.
A. BASIC SHADE   B. SUNSCREEN   C. DERMATITIS   D. OUTER ROOT SHEATH

186. _____ Refers to a product containing plants or ingredients made from plants.
A. COLLAGEN   B. FLY-AWAY HAIR   C. AMMONIUM THIOGLYCOLATE   D. BOTANICAL

187. _____ A medical term for sweat gland. These tiny pores do not contain hair follicles.
A. ANTIBIOTIC   B. DIODE   C. BOTANICAL   D. ECCRINE GLAND

188. _____ A plant extract that has been used to treat swelling, soreness and bruising.
A. EPIDERMIS   B. BARBA   C. ARNICA   D. HUMECTANT

189. Products with ingredients that absorb UVA and UVB rays.
A. BOB   B. TREATMENT   C. SUNSCREEN   D. ANODE

190. The volume or springiness of hair.
A. BODY   B. ANODE   C. AREOLA   D. IONIC

191. In hair removal, a conductor through which electricity enters or leaves the body. An electrolysis needle is an electrode.
A. TEXTURIZER   B. ELECTRODE   C. BLACK SKIN   D. SECTIONING

192. Caused by an absence of melanocytes, whitening of the skin. Vitiligo is a common medical complaint.
A. HYPOPIGMENTATION   B. HYPERPIGMENTATION   C. ALPHA HYDROXY ACID   D. PATCH TEST

193. Small clumps of coagulated melanin.
A. CUTICLE   B. PUNCH GRAFT   C. FRECKLES   D. ALPHA HYDROXY ACID

194. Phenol derivatives used in combination with other chemicals in permanent (two step) hair dyes.
A. AMINOPHENOLS   B. SEBACEOUS   C. HYPOPIGMENTATION   D. SKIN REJUVENATION

195. A Synthetic moisturizer.
A. PERMANENTLY   B. EFFICACY   C. ISOPROPYL LANOLATE   D. ALOPECIA UNIVERSALIS

196. A hairspray with medium hold used on a finished style to maintain its shape and hold.
A. MICRO LINKING TECHNIQUE   B. HYPERPIGMENTATION   C. PUNCH GRAFT   D. FINISHING SPRAY

197. A type of electrolysis needle.
A. SILK PROTEIN   B. BULBOUS NEEDLE   C. NON INVASIVE   D. FLY-AWAY HAIR

198. A technique used by hairdressers to change the thickness of the hair, creating either a thinning or thicker appearance.
A. T ZONE   B. THREAD VEIN   C. LAYERING   D. CATAGEN

199. The process by which blood clots, and can be induced by heat or chemicals.
A. REMI   B. LUVIMER   C. CUTICLE   D. COAGULATION

200. Causes blackheads
A. CUTICLE   B. UV   C. ALPHA HYDROXY ACID   D. COMEDOGENIC

From the words provided for each clue, provide the letter of the word which best matches the clue.

201. Hair that has lost its pigment.
A. BOAR BRISTLE   B. GREY HAIR   C. BLEACH   D. TREATMENT

202. An oil or oil rich crème or lotion designed to lubricate the skin and slow moisture loss.
A. TRANSLUCENT   B. ACUPUNCTURE   C. CHITOSAN   D. LUBRICANT

203. Commonly used in the treatment of acne and other skin conditions.
A. SPIDER VEIN   B. BULBOUS NEEDLE   C. AZELAIC ACID   D. HYPERPIGMENTATION

204. A term meaning how well or effectively a cosmetic device works.
A. EFFICACY   B. BULK HAIR   C. AMORTIZATION   D. SELECTIVE PHOTOTHERMOLYSIS

205. Increases wet and dry combability.
A. BOAR BRISTLE   B. INDENTATION   C. ELECTRIC TWEEZER   D. SILICONE

206. A small rough spot on skin chronically exposed to the sun, occurs most frequently in fair skinned people.
A. SEBUM   B. BETAINE   C. ACTINIC KERATOSIS   D. ALOPECIA AREATA

207. The oily secretion of the sebaceous glands of the scalp, composed of keratin, fat or cellular debris.
A. FUSION   B. SEBUM   C. CATIONIC   D. SOLUBLE

208. A drug or product that limited the effects of androgens (male hormones).
A. HYDRATE   B. ANTI ANDROGEN   C. ALOPECIA SENILIS   D. ACTIVE INGREDIENT

209. A medical term for blackheads.
A. CATIONIC   B. BETAINE   C. SELF TANNER   D. COMEDONES

210. Synthetic moisturizer.
A. PALMITATE   B. ALOPECIA ADNATA   C. ACTIVE INGREDIENT   D. NORWOOD SCALE

211. Used to remove the moisture from wet hair.
A. BASIC SHADE   B. CORNROW   C. ROUGH BLOW DRY   D. PALMITATE

212. a male hormone that is suggested to be the main cause for the miniaturization of the hair follicle and for hair loss.
A. ALOPECIA TOTALIS   B. DHT   C. BLACKHEADS   D. EMLA

213. Drugs that sometimes cause increased hair growth.
A. DEPILATORIES   B. APPLE CIDER VINEGAR   C. TELOGEN   D. BIRTH CONTROL

214. The thin outer layer of skin, on top of the thicker and deeper dermis.
A. ANTIANDROGEN   B. EMLA   C. EPIDERMIS   D. SELECTIVE PHOTOTHERMOLYSIS

215. Either made synthetically or derived from the kernel of the coconut, it gives lather and cleans skin and hair.
A. ALOPECIA TOTALIS   B. COCAMIDE DEA   C. SOOTHING   D. CYST

216. A bristle commonly used in natural bristle brushes.
A. GLYCERIN   B. CORTEX   C. BOAR BRISTLE   D. AMORTIZATION

217. Refers to a congenital absence of pigment in a lock of hairs which will show as grey or white.
A. ADRENAL   B. LEUCOTRICHIA   C. MYRISTATE   D. DEPILATION

218. Selectively targeting dermal structures with light energy, without causing damage to surrounding tissue.
A. ACUPUNCTURE   B. CELLULITE REDUCTION   C. SELECTIVE PHOTOTHERMOLYSIS   D. CHELATING

219. A relatively rare condition in which the follicle is not straight.
A. FASHION SHADE   B. ALOPECIA SENILIS   C. GLYCERIN   D. DISTORTED HAIR FOLLICLES

220. The process of converting one enzyme to another.
A. DERMABRASION   B. HYPERPIGMENTATION   C. FUSION   D. AMORTIZATION

221. Thin hair that is charged by static and is a particular problem with straight looks as the hair just won't lie properly and can spoil your look.
A. MEDULLA   B. FUSION   C. FLY-AWAY HAIR   D. CONTACT COOLING

222. A group of genetically identical cells or organisms derived from a single common cell.
A. ALOPECIA TOTALIS   B. HAIR GROWTH CYCLE   C. ANTIANDROGEN   D. CLONE

223. To cancel or reduce effect.
A. NEUTRALISE   B. ELASTICITY   C. HYDROLYZED KERATIN   D. PALMITATE

224. A basic color with added tone.
A. FASHION SHADE   B. METABOLISM   C. ARRECTOR PILI   D. DERMIS

225. A method in which hair is maintained or tightened using a tool.
A. INTERLOCKING   B. ALOPECIA   C. RUBY   D. AMPHOTERIC

226. Ability to absorb moisture.
A. POROSITY   B. PANTOTHENIC ACID   C. ACNE   D. ALOPECIA ANDROGENETIC

227. A technique used by hairdressers to change the thickness of the hair, creating either a thinning or thicker appearance.
A. POROSITY   B. DEXAMETHOSONE   C. LAYERING   D. ROUGH BLOW DRY

228. Receptors which respond to touch, pain, pressure, heat and cold.
A. BACTERIA   B. NERVE ENDINGS   C. TEMPORARY COLOR   D. CELLULITE REDUCTION

229. In women, a major source of female hormones. Certain conditions involving the ovaries can lead to excess hair growth, especially polycystic ovary syndrome (PCOS).
A. DISTORTED HAIR FOLLICLES   B. FRAGRANCE   C. ABDOMEN   D. OVARIES

230. Used to oxidize (expand) artificial color molecules. Can also lighten natural color pigment.
A. NORWOOD SCALE   B. BIRTH CONTROL   C. CILIA   D. HYDROGEN PEROXIDE

231. The hair's ability to stretch without breaking and then return to its original shape.
A. BLEACH   B. ELASTICITY   C. NORWOOD SCALE   D. LASER

232. A mild nonirritating surfactant often used in shampoos; leaves hair manageable and is gentle enough for chemically treated hair.
A. ACNE   B. NEUTRALISE   C. DERMABRASION   D. AMPHOTERIC

233. A drug sometimes linked to excess hair growth.
A. NERVE ENDINGS   B. ALOPECIA AREATA   C. APPLE CIDER VINEGAR   D. DILANTIN

234. Products that reflect all the sun's rays, such as zinc oxide and titanium dioxide. They permit minimal tanning, and are a good choice for those who are sensitive to chemicals.
A. HEATCLAMPS   B. SUNBLOCK   C. SOLUBLE   D. SCLERODERMA

235. The enzyme superoxide, catalyzes the dis-mutation of superoxide into oxygen and hydrogen peroxide.
A. CHELATING   B. CORTEX   C. EFFICACY   D. SUPEROXIDE DISMUTASE

236. Contains superior properties to keep skin and hair soft. It is beneficial to dry hair.
A. HYPERPIGMENTATION   B. JOJOBA OIL   C. LUVIMER   D. HYDROLYZED KERATIN

237. Small clumps of coagulated melanin.
A. INTERLOCKING   B. FRECKLES   C. CORTEX   D. ACCELERATOR

238. has been called a more extensive and severe form of dandruff.
A. BIRTH CONTROL   B. DIATHERMY   C. SEBORRHOEIC DERMATITIS   D. CORTEX

239. A condition that is hereditary. Excess hair often runs in the family.
A. LUBRICANT   B. HAIR GROWTH CYCLE   C. CONGENITAL   D. HUMIDITY

240. The body's shock absorber.
A. COCAMIDE DEA   B. SUBCUTANEOUS TISSUE   C. ROUGH BLOW DRY   D. ANAESTHETIC

241. Used to measure acidity in cosmetic preparations.
A. PH B. COARSE C. DEPILATION D. DEXAMETHOSONE

242. Is sometimes linked to excess hair growth, especially in the extremely obese and extremely anorexic.
A. GLYCERIN B. SILICONE C. TRICLOSAN D. DIET

243. Split ends.
A. HAIR EXTENSIONS B. ARNICA C. CASTRATION D. TRICHOPTILOSIS

244. Refers to unflattering warm tones in hair color created by chemicals or damage.
A. HEATCLAMPS B. AZELAIC ACID C. BRASSY D. ACTIVATOR

245. Blocks the effects of androgens, normally by blocking the receptor sites.
A. SERUM B. ANTIANDROGEN C. FASHION SHADE D. MELANOMA

246. An alkaline ingredient used in some permanent hair color. An ingredient that results in a chemical action that decolorizes the hair.
A. UV B. AMMONIA C. DEXAMETHOSONE D. OVARIES

247. To add moisture to the skin.
A. ADRENAL B. HYDRATE C. DEPILATORIES D. TESTOSTERONE

248. Probably the most difficult type of skin from which to remove hair.
A. BLACK SKIN B. TELOGEN C. TRICHOPTILOSIS D. FLY-AWAY HAIR

249. Small blood vessels which connect the arteries and veins that feed the hair.
A. SACRUM B. SEBUM C. CARBOMER D. CAPILLARIES

250. Is effective against most bacteria occurring on the skin.
A. NERVE ENDINGS B. TRICLOSAN C. ALOPECIA AREATA D. BLEACH

251. This is the complete loss of scalp hair often combined with the loss of eyebrows and eyelashes.
A. ALOPECIA TOTALIS B. DRUG TREATMENT C. ARRECTOR PILI D. AZELAIC ACID

252. Commonly used laser for hair and tattoo removal.
A. MICRO DIFFUSE B. HYDRATE C. CARBOMER D. RUBY

253. A device that removes hair by grasping hairs above the skin's surface with an electrified tweezers.
A. CICATRICIAL ALOPECIA B. ELECTRIC TWEEZER C. ALKALI D. CAPILLARIES

254. A form of skin cancer.
A. DHT B. DIABETES C. MELANOMA D. SUPEROXIDE DISMUTASE

255. A hair color formula that lasts only until you shampoo your hair.
A. TOPICALLY B. TEMPORARY COLOR C. ABDOMEN D. TRICHOPTILOSIS

256. The active dissolving ingredient in many cream depilatories
A. CALCIUM THIOGLYCOLATE B. ACCELERATOR C. TEA TREE OIL D. ALOPECIA ADNATA

257. Detangling aid which conditions, protects against humidity, and adds shine.
A. DIMETHICONE B. PANTOTHENIC ACID C. PH D. BRAID

258. A small opening of the sweat glands of the skin.
A. PORE B. SERUM C. FUSION D. ALOPECIA SENILIS

259. A type of electrolysis needle.
A. CAPILLARIES   B. DERMIS   C. CLEARING   D. BULBOUS NEEDLE

260. Loss of hair, especially from the head, which either happens naturally or is caused by disease
A. MELANOMA   B. ALOPECIA   C. OVARIES   D. DIMETHICONE

261. Being able to dissolve into, or being compatible with, another substance.
A. SOLUBLE   B. SPIDER VEIN   C. ACTIVATOR   D. DISTORTED HAIR FOLLICLES

262. Clinic based method of reducing the appearance of cellulite.
A. HYDRATE   B. CELLULITE REDUCTION   C. ALOPECIA   D. NEUTRALISE

263. A type of clogged pore in the skin with a visible black plug.
A. SUNBLOCK   B. BLACKHEADS   C. SCLERODERMA   D. MEDULLA

264. To attach wefted hair to the natural hair with a latex or surgical type adhesive.
A. DEPILATE   B. FOLLICLE SHEATH   C. ACTIVATOR   D. BONDING

265. A method of hair removal in which all hair in an area is removed at once, as opposed to thinning.
A. JOJOBA OIL   B. NEUTRALISE   C. FUSION   D. CLEARING

266. A trademark for a Japanese-made synthetic fiber which is used extensively in the manufacture of wigs and hairpieces
A. AMORTIZATION   B. NORWOOD SCALE   C. COMEDOGENIC   D. KANEKALON

267. A chemically based permanent waving product that has a pH from 7.5 to 9.5. Stronger than acid perms, alkaline perms are designed to produce tight, firm, springy curls.
A. PATCH TEST   B. ACTIVATOR   C. ALKALINE PERM   D. NERVE ENDINGS

268. Another name for thermolysis.
A. BLEACH   B. BONDING   C. DIATHERMY   D. INFUSION

269. A method used to disguise (not remove) hair by lightening its color.
A. CONGENITAL   B. SPLIT ENDS   C. BLEACH   D. DHT

270. Term for loose commercial hair. This hair is used for creating wefts or for services like fusion.
A. SELF TANNER   B. DEPILATORIES   C. RELAX   D. BULK HAIR

271. The deepest layers of the skin, where blood vessels, lymph channels, nerve endings, sweat glands, sebaceous glands, fat cells, hair follicles and muscles are located.
A. CILIA   B. DERMIS   C. BIRTH CONTROL   D. SUPEROXIDE DISMUTASE

272. Tiny hair-like blood vessels, some of which carry nutrient to the hair growth matrix.
A. ROUGH BLOW DRY   B. SERUM   C. CAPILLARIES   D. HEATCLAMPS

273. A natural or neutral color.
A. CATAPHORESIS   B. POROSITY   C. BASIC SHADE   D. GLYCERIN

274. A doctor specializing in skin and hair conditions.
A. DIABETES   B. BLEACH   C. DERMATOLOGIST   D. PANTHENOL

275. Aids detangling. Provides volume, control and shine.
A. CATAGEN   B. PANTHENOL   C. CASTRATION   D. EMLA

276. Products so labeled may still contain small amounts of fragrances to mask the fatty odor of soap or other unpleasant odors.
A. PANTHENOL B. FRAGRANCE FREE C. PATCH TEST D. DEPILATE

277. Reducing skin discomforts from irritation, blemishes, burning skin, etc.
A. FACE LIFT B. SOOTHING C. DIMETHICONE D. ROUGH BLOW DRY

278. When your skin is damaged by exposure to the UVA and UVB rays of the sun, its reaction is to produce more melanin as an attempt to protect itself against further damage.
A. CAPILLARIES B. FACE LIFT C. TAN D. ALOPECIA ADNATA

279. Also known as eczema.
A. CLARIFIER B. ANTISEPTIC C. ATOPIC DERMATITIS D. DILANTIN

280. In hair removal, a conductor through which electricity enters or leaves the body. An electrolysis needle is an electrode.
A. PORE B. CORTEX C. DISCOMFORT D. ELECTRODE

281. A small temporary scab that occurs sometimes after electrolysis, especially after overtreatment.
A. INFUSION B. PANTHENOL C. ESCHAR D. HYDRATE

282. The invisible spectrum of solar radiation. It is divided into three regions with increasing danger to the skin.
A. UV B. TRANSLUCENT C. CELLULITE REDUCTION D. DISCOMFORT

283. A chemical ingredients that is specifically added to hair bleach to speed up the action of the bleach without unnecessarily damaging the hair.
A. CHITOSAN B. BULBOUS NEEDLE C. ACTIVATOR D. FOLLICULITIS

284. A substance used to relieve all feeling.
A. JOJOBA OIL B. DIMETHICONE C. ANAESTHETIC D. DIATHERMY

285. Trichoptilosis
A. APPLE CIDER VINEGAR B. SPLIT ENDS C. EXTRACT D. HYPERPIGMENTATION

286. An herbal concentrate produced by separating the essential or active part of an herb into a solvent material.
A. EXTRACT B. FRAGRANCE FREE C. HAIR EXTENSIONS D. ADRENAL

287. A non- shiny surface that absorbs light; a dead or dull finish.
A. DEPILATORIES B. FRECKLES C. MATTE D. LUBRICANT

288. An organism responsible for infection.
A. BETAINE B. CALAMINE C. BACTERIA D. EMLA

289. A natural conditioning substance for example: from molasses or sugar beet.
A. ROUGH BLOW DRY B. WEFTS C. BETAINE D. FRECKLES

290. An over excitation of melanocytes, darkening of the skin. Can be seen as sun-induced freckles or melasma.
A. HYPERPIGMENTATION B. CORNROW C. CALCIUM THIOGLYCOLATE D. INTERLOCKING

291. This is the common name for male or female pattern baldness which depends on the genetic predisposition of the hair follicles and the levels of DHT in the body.
A. HYDROGEN PEROXIDE B. SACRUM C. ELASTICITY D. ALOPECIA ANDROGENETIC

292. A natural solvent in oils and creams. It acidifies products.
A. APPLE CIDER VINEGAR B. BIRTH CONTROL C. BARBICIDE D. LASER

293. Excessive development of the male breasts.
A. ALOPECIA AREATA B. ALOPECIA SENILIS C. GYNECOMASTIA D. CONGENITAL

294. The process of attaching small pieces of human hair with a special adhesive and a thermal gun.
A. ELASTICITY B. ARNICA C. FUSION D. ELECTRIC TWEEZER

295. Synthetic moisturizer.
A. DEPILATE B. BARBICIDE C. POROSITY D. MYRISTATE

296. A common disorder characterized by inflammation of the hair follicle.
A. GLABELLA B. FOLLICULITIS C. NERVE ENDINGS D. OVARIES

297. Medical term for eyelashes. Ingrown eyelashes should never be removed except under the supervision of a trained medical specialist
A. FACE LIFT B. CHELATING C. CILIA D. CORNROW

298. A liquid with a pH higher than 7.
A. ALKALI B. HAIR EXTENSIONS C. DEXAMETHOSONE D. CONGENITAL

299. Causes blackheads
A. BACTERIA B. BULBOUS NEEDLE C. COMEDOGENIC D. CORNROW

300. Proteins that catalyze (i.e. accelerate) and control the rates of chemical reactions.
A. ELECTRIC TWEEZER B. ENZYME C. CORNROW D. ACNE

From the words provided for each clue, provide the letter of the word which best matches the clue.

301. A hollow or pocket in the skin.
A. INDENTATION B. SPRITZ C. DISCOMFORT D. PALM ROLLING

302. The use of heat generated by electricity to change tissue from a fluid to a semi-solid, similar to cooking an egg.
A. BIOPSY B. TEA TREE OIL C. BULGE D. ELECTROCOAGULATION

303. Temporarily straightening the hair with a heated iron.
A. DOUBLE BLIND B. LASER C. COHERENT LIGHT D. THERMAL PROCESS

304. This is the complete loss of scalp hair often combined with the loss of eyebrows and eyelashes.
A. ELECTROCOAGULATION B. ALOPECIA TOTALIS C. ANAGEN D. ANTI ANDROGEN

305. The main structure of the hair shaft. The cortex determines the color and texture of the hair. The largest section of a single hair, containing the main bulk of the hair.
A. ACUPRESSURE B. BETAINE C. CORTEX D. ALLERGY

306. A basic color with added tone.
A. FASHION SHADE B. ROSACEA C. TOURMALINE D. DIAZOXIDE

307. A hair weave is usually a hairpiece with layered gaps made into it.
A. WEAVE B. DIAMETER C. EXFOLIATING D. DHT

308. A relatively rare condition in which the follicle is not straight.
A. SCLERODERMA B. FOLLICULITIS C. DISTORTED HAIR FOLLICLES D. PARFUM

309. Refers to unflattering warm tones in hair color created by chemicals or damage.
A. CLUB HAIR B. SUPEROXIDE DISMUTASE C. ACCENT COLOR D. BRASSY

310. Loss of hair, especially from the head, which either happens naturally or is caused by disease
A. ELECTRIC TWEEZER B. ALOPECIA C. STEAMING D. DIAZOXIDE

311. A whitening of the skin sometimes caused by some types of hair removal.
A. BLANCHING B. DILANTIN C. CONDITIONER D. BULGE

312. Caused by an absence of melanocytes, whitening of the skin. Vitiligo is a common medical complaint.
A. BIOPSY B. HYPOPIGMENTATION C. BETAINE D. BRUISE

313. Removal of hair on the surface of the skin. Examples include shaving or the use of depilatory creams.
A. TOPICALLY B. BIOPSY C. TRICHOPTILOSIS D. DEPILATE

314. A common ingredient in chemical depilatories.
A. TEA TREE OIL B. CHIGNON C. WEFTS D. AMMONIUM THIOGLYCOLATE

315. An over excitation of melanocytes, darkening of the skin. Can be seen as sun-induced freckles or melasma.
A. EFFICACY B. ALOPECIA NEUROTICA C. MEDULLA D. HYPERPIGMENTATION

316. The greying of hair. A pigment deficiency frequently seen in middle-aged people of either sex.
A. ANODE B. CANITIES C. INGROWN HAIR D. HUMECTANT

317. The combination of sweat and sebum that provides the skin's protective coating.
A. ACID MANTLE B. CHEMICAL DEPILATORIES C. LUVIMER D. WEFT

318. a light mist or spray, which when used as verb means to lightly spray your hair.
A. MEDULLA B. COHERENT LIGHT C. CICATRICIAL ALOPECIA D. SPRITZ

319. Products that reflect all the sun's rays, such as zinc oxide and titanium dioxide. They permit minimal tanning, and are a good choice for those who are sensitive to chemicals.
A. MEDULLA B. SUNBLOCK C. WHITE HAIR D. HUMIDITY

320. A device that removes hair by grasping hairs above the skin's surface with an electrified tweezers.
A. CATHODE B. GYNECOMASTIA C. ELECTRIC TWEEZER D. BARBA

321. Varies greatly by individual and body area. Electrolysis is generally considered most painful, followed by laser, plucking, waxing and finally pulse light sources.
A. TEMPORARY COLOR B. SUPEROXIDE DISMUTASE C. HYPERPIGMENTATION D. DISCOMFORT

322. An antiandrogen and is used in the treatment of androgen related disorders such as female pattern baldness and hirsutism.
A. PANTOTHENIC ACID B. SPRIONOLACTONE C. LASER D. ERYTHEMA

323. A disease of the skin and connective tissue that can cause hair loss over the affected areas.
A. CANITIES B. SELF TANNER C. EXFOLIATION D. SCLERODERMA

324. Baldness following a nervous disorder or injury to the nervous system.
A. Q SWITCH B. BLONDE HAIR C. ALOPECIA NEUROTICA D. WEAVE

325. A drug sometimes linked to excess hair growth.
A. EXFOLIATING B. ACETONE C. DIAZOXIDE D. CLARIFIER

326. The process of converting one enzyme to another.
A. COHERENT LIGHT B. HUMECTANT C. AMORTIZATION D. DEPILATORIES

327. The deepest layers of the skin, where blood vessels, lymph channels, nerve endings, sweat glands, sebaceous glands, fat cells, hair follicles and muscles are located.
A. ANTI ANDROGEN   B. FASHION SHADE   C. BRUISE   D. DERMIS

328. A form of skin cancer.
A. NORWOOD SCALE   B. PUNCH GRAFT   C. MELANOMA   D. A LINE BOB

329. Dark skin discoloration on sun-exposed areas of the face and neck. Young women with brownish skin tones are at greatest risk.
A. DISTORTED HAIR FOLLICLES   B. EXFOLIATING   C. MELASMA   D. DIAZOXIDE

330. Protects the hair during its growth stage.
A. SPRITZ   B. FASHION SHADE   C. FOLLICLE SHEATH   D. PARFUM

331. has been called a more extensive and severe form of dandruff.
A. CAPILLARIES   B. ACUPUNCTURE   C. SEBORRHOEIC DERMATITIS   D. EXFOLIATING

332. Distribution of ashen and warm pigments, visual effect of gold or ash in the hair.
A. FOLLICULITIS   B. ANTI ANDROGEN   C. COHERENT LIGHT   D. TONE

333. One of a group of hormonal steroid compounds that promote the development of female secondary sex characteristics.
A. BARBICIDE   B. ESTROGEN   C. EXFOLIATING   D. FASHION SHADE

334. A common disorder characterized by inflammation of the hair follicle.
A. ALCOHOL   B. FOLLICULITIS   C. DEPILATE   D. SERUM

335. The medical term for armpit, a common place for gonadal hair after puberty.
A. COHERENT LIGHT   B. LANUGO HAIRS   C. Q SWITCH   D. AXILLA

336. A hair that does not break the surface of the skin, and grows back inward. Can be severe and cause inflammation, soreness and infection.
A. NORWOOD SCALE   B. BRASSY   C. INGROWN HAIR   D. BRUISE

337. A clinical testing method in which neither patient nor doctor know what medication or procedure is being used.
A. ALOPECIA UNIVERSALIS   B. DOUBLE BLIND   C. WHITE HAIR   D. INFUSION

338. Excessive development of the male breasts.
A. BLISTER   B. ACID PERM   C. EXFOLIATION   D. GYNECOMASTIA

339. Usually a sharp, intense color used as a contrast or pickup for color scheme. It is used to add excitement to an overall effect
A. CATOGEN   B. ACCENT COLOR   C. OVERTREATMENT   D. CATHODE

340. A drug sometimes linked to excess hair growth.
A. WEFTS   B. FLY-AWAY HAIR   C. SPRITZ   D. DANAZOL

341. The space between the eyebrows.
A. HAIR GROWTH CYCLE   B. ALLERGY   C. SERUM   D. GLABELLA

342. Hair loss which occurs in patches on the scalp.
A. NATURAL   B. ALOPECIA AREATA   C. ESTROGEN   D. ALKALI

343. Excess hair can be increased or decreased by certain drugs. These drugs often affect hormonal levels.
A. EXFOLIATING   B. ARRECTOR PILI   C. DRUG TREATMENT   D. CATHODE

344. A polymer on the basis of acrylic acid. Provides a thickening, gelling action and consistency regulator for cosmetic products.
A. CARBOMER B. CAPILLARIES C. INDENTATION D. WEFT

345. Tea made by steeping an herb's leaves or flowers in hot water.
A. ALOPECIA ANDROGENETIC B. INFUSION C. SUPEROXIDE DISMUTASE D. GLYCERIN

346. Laser at 755nm used for hair removal.
A. SELF TANNER B. JOULE C. ALEXANDRITE D. AMMONIUM THIOGLYCOLATE

347. Color.
A. PIGMENT B. AXILLA C. RELAXER D. AMPERE

348. Repels moisture or water; not readily removed with water.
A. ANDROGEN B. WATER RESISTANT C. CLUB HAIR D. CHILLTIP

349. The medulla is a central zone of cells usually only present in large thick hairs.
A. CARBOMER B. MEDULLA C. ANTISEPTIC D. FUSION

350. Thin hair that is charged by static and is a particular problem with straight looks as the hair just won't lie properly and can spoil your look.
A. FLY-AWAY HAIR B. SEMI PERMANENT C. PARFUM D. PERMANENT HAIR REDUCTION

351. Proteins that catalyze (i.e. accelerate) and control the rates of chemical reactions.
A. ENZYME B. PARFUM C. DISTORTED HAIR FOLLICLES D. BULGE

352. Having no pigment. Possible causes: Genetic. Vitamin B deficiency. Drugs for treatment of arthritis. Other health factors.
A. LUVIMER B. CLARIFIER C. ENERGY DENSITY D. WHITE HAIR

353. Natural substance that gives color (pigment) to hair and skin.
A. SEBACEOUS B. BULK HAIR C. MELANIN D. BRUISE

354. A unit of energy. Describes energy output for pulsed light based systems.
A. COLD SORE B. DHT C. TEA TREE OIL D. JOULE

355. Overly aggressive treatment to remove hair which leads to temporary or permanent skin damage.
A. ANODE B. TOPICALLY C. OVERTREATMENT D. EFFICACY

356. A drug sometimes linked to excess hair growth.
A. CHIGNON B. DILANTIN C. COLOGNE D. LASER

357. The resting stage of the hair cycle.
A. BULGE B. AXILLA C. CATOGEN D. CROWN

358. A point midway up the hair follicle which researchers suspect must be damaged to induce permanent hair removal
A. BULGE B. BLEND C. TELOGEN D. GLABELLA

359. To become shed or cast off.
A. ACUPUNCTURE B. RUBY C. ANTIBIOTIC D. SLOUGH

360. an extraction from the Melaleuca tree.
A. TERMINAL HAIRS B. FOLLICLES C. HIGHLIGHTS D. TEA TREE OIL

361. This is the growing phase of the hair cycle which lasts about seven years in a healthy person. The active stage in a hair growth cycle.
A. ACID PERM B. SCLERODERMA C. ANAGEN D. REMI

362. The subtle lifting of color in specific sections of hair.
A. HAIR INTEGRATION B. HIGHLIGHTS C. DIODE D. SCLERODERMA

363. A combination of water containing alcohol and fragrant oils. Not to be confused with a concentrated perfume.
A. HIRSUTISM B. DIAZOXIDE C. SPRIONOLACTONE D. COLOGNE

364. A clarifying shampoo is slightly stronger than everyday shampoos and is designed to remove products, hard water or chlorine residue that have built-up over time.
A. ANTI ANDROGEN B. BARBA C. CHIGNON D. CLARIFIER

365. Products so labeled may still contain small amounts of fragrances to mask the fatty odor of soap or other unpleasant odors.
A. CILIA B. DANAZOL C. FRAGRANCE FREE D. GREY HAIR

366. Commonly used laser for hair and tattoo removal.
A. EYELASHES B. AMPERE C. BLEND D. RUBY

367. A chemical process by which the hair is permanently straightened. New-growth areas have to be maintained via 'touch-ups' to continue the straightened pattern.
A. HAIR GROWTH CYCLE B. OVARIES C. RELAXER D. MELASMA

368. A recessive hereditary trait which presents as white hair due to defective melanin production thought to be caused by a mutation within genes.
A. FOLLICULITIS B. REMI C. ACCENT COLOR D. ALBINISM

369. A fibrous protein found in hair, nails, and skin.
A. GLABELLA B. MEDULLA C. SELF TANNER D. KERATIN

370. Flexible resin.
A. LUVIMER B. ANTIBIOTIC C. HUMECTANT D. OVERTREATMENT

371. Split ends.
A. CICATRICIAL ALOPECIA B. DEPILATORIES C. TRICHOPTILOSIS D. HAIR GROWTH CYCLE

372. Aids detangling. Provides volume, control and shine.
A. MELANOMA B. ACUPUNCTURE C. HAIR EXTENSIONS D. PANTHENOL

373. This drug is normally used to reduce sex drive in men who have an excessive sex drive. It is also prescribed to treat hirsutism and androgenic alopecia in women.
A. BETAINE B. LASER C. CYPROTERONE ACETATE D. ACCENT COLOR

374. Powder or cream preparations that dissolve hair above the surface of the skin. Some find these products very irritating to the skin.
A. SPRIONOLACTONE B. HAIR INTEGRATION C. CHEMICAL DEPILATORIES D. CARBOMER

375. Means to apply directly onto the scalp.
A. CICATRICIAL ALOPECIA B. NORWOOD SCALE C. OVERTREATMENT D. TOPICALLY

376. Produces permanent hair waves with curls that are actually softer than an alkaline perm. It also has a pH from 6.5 to 8.0.
A. AMPHOTERIC B. ACID PERM C. ANALGESIC D. ALOPECIA ANDROGENETIC

377. Creates "Goose Bumps" when stimulated.
A. CLARIFIER   B. PERMANENT HAIR REDUCTION   C. HIGHLIGHTS   D. ARRECTOR PILI

378. Wefts are temporary hair extensions which are glued into your hair.
A. FACE LIFT   B. WEFTS   C. ANTISEPTIC   D. AXILLA

379. Increases wet and dry combability.
A. SLOUGH   B. SILICONE   C. DHT   D. CALAMINE

380. A semi-conductive material which mainly lets energy travel one direction and not the other.
A. ALOPECIA ADNATA   B. ANDROGEN   C. BULGE   D. DIODE

381. The process by which most synthetic fiber is curled at the factory.
A. CATOGEN   B. STEAMING   C. LASER   D. SLOUGH

382. A method of hair removal in which all hair in an area is removed at once, as opposed to thinning.
A. CHEMICAL DEPILATORIES   B. CLUB HAIR   C. CLEARING   D. ACID MANTLE

383. A disorder involving chronic inflammation of the cheeks, nose, chin, forehead or eyelids. It may cause redness, vascularity, swelling or hyperplasia.
A. CLUB HAIR   B. ELECTROCOAGULATION   C. ROSACEA   D. TRACK

384. Creamy hair product meant to be used after shampoo. Moisturizes and detangles hair.
A. ENERGY DENSITY   B. TELOGEN   C. CONDITIONER   D. ACETONE

385. A treatment consisting of short pulses of light sent out through an applicator that is gently pressed against the skin.
A. INTENSE PULSED LIGHT   B. FOLLICLES   C. EYELASHES   D. ANDROGENS

386. A pink ointment sometimes used to treat skin irritation
A. CALAMINE   B. EFFICACY   C. INDENTATION   D. SPLIT ENDS

387. Congenital baldness or baldness at birth.
A. PALM ROLLING   B. ACID PERM   C. ALOPECIA ADNATA   D. ALOPECIA AREATA

388. A mild nonirritating surfactant often used in shampoos; leaves hair manageable and is gentle enough for chemically treated hair.
A. CALAMINE   B. BLONDE HAIR   C. WEAVE   D. AMPHOTERIC

389. A modality of electrolysis which uses both thermolysis and galvanic methods.
A. TEXTURIZER   B. BLEND   C. ANALGESIC   D. CARBOMER

390. A chemical formed in the blood when the body uses fat instead of glucose (sugar) for energy.
A. AXILLA   B. PIGMENT   C. ACETONE   D. BRUISE

391. An amount of hair or fiber which is doubled over and MACHINE-SEWN along the top to create a long strand of hair.
A. ARRECTOR PILI   B. EYELASHES   C. WEFT   D. AMPHOTERIC

392. The most concentrated and most fragrant scent and therefore the most expensive.
A. CATHODE   B. DRUG TREATMENT   C. PARFUM   D. BARBA

393. Hair passes through a series of cycles known as Anagen (growing phase), Catagen (resting phase) and Telogen (dormant phase).
A. HAIR GROWTH CYCLE   B. ANTIBIOTIC   C. WATER RESISTANT   D. CHILLTIP

394. Coarse, pigmented or non-pigmented, exist on the scalp and gain length at a rate of 1-2cm per month during a cyclical life of up to 10 years.
A. HENNA B. EFFICACY C. CATOGEN D. TERMINAL HAIRS

395. The temporary removal of hair.
A. CALAMINE B. CATHODE C. ALOPECIA ANDROGENETIC D. DEPILATION

396. A drug or preparation used to prevent and treat infection.
A. CLEARING B. ANDROGEN C. ANTIBIOTIC D. ACID MANTLE

397. Term used to measure the output energy for Lasers and Pulsed Light Sources.
A. SUNBLOCK B. ENERGY DENSITY C. CROWN D. INGROWN HAIR

398. A bodily reaction to an irritant. Skin allergies can be exacerbated by solutions put on the skin.
A. AUTOCLAVE B. TERMINAL HAIRS C. CHILLTIP D. ALLERGY

399. A positive electrode.
A. RUBY B. ANODE C. WEFT D. SILICONE

400. A negative electrode in a cell or circuit.
A. DISTORTED HAIR FOLLICLES B. BLANCHING C. LUVIMER D. CATHODE

From the words provided for each clue, provide the letter of the word which best matches the clue.

1. __B__ Synthetic moisturizer.
   A. ESTROGEN B. PALMITATE C. LAYERING D. DANAZOL

2. __B__ This is the common name for male or female pattern baldness which depends on the genetic predisposition of the hair follicles and the levels of DHT in the body.
   A. CONDITIONER B. ALOPECIA ANDROGENETIC C. LAYERING D. DOUBLE BLIND

3. __C__ An herbal concentrate produced by separating the essential or active part of an herb into a solvent material.
   A. LENTIGO B. ANDROGEN C. EXTRACT D. ALLERGEN

4. __D__ Blood or pigment based visible mark.
   A. PABA B. HAIR INTEGRATION C. FOLLICLES D. BLEMISH

5. __C__ A common disorder characterized by inflammation of the hair follicle.
   A. AXILLA B. LUBRICATES C. FOLLICULITIS D. LUVIMER

6. __A__ Trichoptilosis
   A. SPLIT ENDS B. DERMAL SHEATH C. CASTRATION D. ANAGEN

7. __D__ The pigmented area surrounding the nipple. A very common area for hair growth.
   A. CALCIUM THIOGLYCOLATE B. TRACK C. TARGETED FAT REDUCTION D. AREOLA

8. __D__ Treatments, especially IPL, where the follicle is disabled by the light energy making it unable to support any more hair growth.
   A. CALCIUM THIOGLYCOLATE B. CASTRATION C. WEFT D. PERMANENT HAIR REDUCTION

9. __A__ The body transformation of food into energy.
   A. METABOLISM B. FASHION SHADE C. COAGULATION D. CLIMBAZOLE

10. __B__ A small fluid-filled bubble on the skin caused by heat from over treatment with certain types of hair removal.
    A. DIET B. BLISTER C. APPLE CIDER VINEGAR D. CROWN

11. __A__ A fibrous protein found in hair, nails, and skin.
    A. KERATIN B. DIET C. SEMI PERMANENT D. CONDITIONER

12. __D__ A combination of water containing alcohol and fragrant oils. Not to be confused with a concentrated perfume.
    A. OXIDATION COLOUR B. AXILLA C. HAIR INTEGRATION D. COLOGNE

13. __D__ The surgical removal of one or both testicles or ovaries.
    A. CLIMBAZOLE B. SECTIONING C. SCLERODERMA D. CASTRATION

14. __D__ The process by which most synthetic fiber is curled at the factory.
    A. TAN B. ELECTROLOGY C. ORGANIC D. STEAMING

15. __B__ Dried fluid that seeps from skin in some clients following hair removal such as laser, electrolysis, and depilatories.
    A. SELECTIVE PHOTOTHERMOLYSIS B. CRUSTING C. ELECTRIC TWEEZER D. CUSHING SYNDROME

16. __C__ Is sometimes linked to excess hair growth, especially in the extremely obese and extremely anorexic.
    A. WEFTS B. ECZEMA C. DIET D. ANDROGEN

17. **D** — Any natural or synthetic substance or substances use solely to impart a sweet or pleasant smell (odor) to a cosmetic product.
A. KELOIDS B. BULK HAIR C. AZELAIC ACID D. FRAGRANCE

18. **C** — A medical term for blackheads.
A. EDEMA B. TESTOSTERONE C. COMEDONES D. AMMONIUM THIOGLYCOLATE

19. **C** — When your skin is damaged by exposure to the UVA and UVB rays of the sun, its reaction is to produce more melanin as an attempt to protect itself against further damage.
A. PROPRIETARY B. METABOLISM C. TAN D. DEPTH

20. **A** — Positively charges the hair to provide manageability and reduces static.
A. CATIONIC POLYMER B. WEFTS C. ACCENT COLOR D. SECTIONING

21. **B** — A smoothing product to stop your hair from frizzing, keeping it smooth and straight. You'll be able to find a serum that is specifically designed to your own hair type.
A. ACNE B. SERUM C. LUBRICATES D. WIG

22. **B** — A condition that is hereditary. Excess hair often runs in the family.
A. ALOPECIA ADNATA B. CONGENITAL C. SCLERODERMA D. TESTOSTERONE

23. **B** — A discoloration of skin from blood, sometimes caused by electrolysis, plucking, or waxing. Also known as Purpura.
A. DERMAL SHEATH B. BRUISE C. FOLLICLES D. SEBORRHOEIC DERMATITIS

24. **B** — Term used to measure the output energy, for Lasers and Pulsed Light Sources that is delivered to tissue.
A. KERATIN B. FLUENCE C. DIODE D. CUSHING SYNDROME

25. **A** — a light mist or spray, which when used as verb means to lightly spray your hair.
A. SPRITZ B. METABOLISM C. MELANIN D. SECTIONING

26. **B** — A modern term used to describe hair weaving.
A. SEBACEOUS B. HAIR INTEGRATION C. MICRO GRAFT D. DEPILATION

27. **B** — A substance used to relieve pain.
A. SEBACEOUS B. ANALGESIC C. DIODE D. NERVE ENDINGS

28. **D** — Contact dermatitis, it's a mild inflammation of the skin.
A. DEPILATION B. MICRO GRAFT C. SERUM D. ECZEMA

29. **B** — allows you to only pay attention to a particular area or panel of hair.
A. REMI B. SECTIONING C. BARBA D. INDENTATION

30. **D** — Relating to the skin.
A. ACCENT COLOR B. FOLLICULITIS C. DEPILATORIES D. CUTANEOUS

31. **D** — A water gel-like substance that is known for its ability to soothe irritated skin, especially sunburned skin.
A. MEDULLA B. SPRITZ C. STEAMING D. ALOE VERA

32. **A** — This is the end of the active growth period, and is marked by changes occurring in the follicle.
A. CATAGEN B. ELECTRIC TWEEZER C. FREEZING SPRAY D. DIAZOXIDE

33. **D** — A process of removing the top dead skin layers to reveal healthier, newer skin underneath.
A. SPLIT ENDS B. BLANCHING C. DEVELOPER D. EXFOLIATING

34. __B__ A natural water-soluble source of acid derived from liquid silk.
   A. FLUENCE   B. SILK PROTEIN   C. COAGULATION   D. DIMETHICONE

35. __C__ A drug sometimes linked to excess hair growth.
   A. PORE   B. PIGMENT   C. DANAZOL   D. CAPILLARIES

36. __B__ Pertaining to carbon - based compounds produced by living plants, animals or by synthetic processes.
   A. BETAINE   B. ORGANIC   C. HYDROLYZED KERATIN   D. ALOE VERA

37. __D__ Discolored skin that should be examined and approved by a physician before hair removal.
   A. ALOPECIA ADNATA   B. AZELAIC ACID   C. LENTIGO   D. BIRTHMARKS

38. __C__ A semi-conductive material which mainly lets energy travel one direction and not the other.
   A. FOLLICLES   B. BLEMISH   C. DIODE   D. T ZONE

39. __D__ a crystal silicate mineral compounded with elements such as aluminum, iron, magnesium, sodium, lithium, or potassium.
   A. SPLIT ENDS   B. ANAGEN CYCLE   C. APPLE CIDER VINEGAR   D. TOURMALINE

40. __D__ The structural protein of hair.
   A. SEMI PERMANENT   B. ALOPECIA ADNATA   C. DHT   D. HYDROLYZED KERATIN

41. __D__ Site where hair roots are taken from during transplant surgery.
   A. ELECTROLOGY   B. BLEMISH   C. LAYERING   D. DONOR SITE

42. __C__ Allergen is a substance that causes an allergic reaction.
   A. DEPTH   B. ALOE VERA   C. ALLERGEN   D. ADRENAL

43. __C__ A color which lasts from 6 - 8 shampoos.
   A. FLY-AWAY HAIR   B. ACID   C. SEMI PERMANENT   D. PERMANENT HAIR REDUCTION

44. __A__ The medical term for armpit, a common place for gonadal hair after puberty.
   A. AXILLA   B. LIPID LAYER   C. HYDROGEN PEROXIDE   D. INDENTATION

45. __B__ A mixture of wax, thickeners, and a group of chemicals used to coat the hair shaft and detangle after shampooing.
   A. CATAGEN   B. CREAM RINSE   C. EDEMA   D. CLIMBAZOLE

46. __D__ A disease of the skin and connective tissue that can cause hair loss over the affected areas.
   A. KELOIDS   B. PALMITATE   C. ALKALINE   D. SCLERODERMA

47. __C__ Detangling aid which conditions, protects against humidity, and adds shine.
   A. CLARIFIER   B. SCRUNCH DRY   C. DIMETHICONE   D. ALOPECIA UNIVERSALIS

48. __C__ Clinic based method of reducing the appearance of cellulite.
   A. BETAINE   B. CLARIFIER   C. CELLULITE REDUCTION   D. ACTIVATOR

49. __C__ Commonly used in the treatment of acne and other skin conditions.
   A. ANODE   B. DIMETHICONE   C. AZELAIC ACID   D. SEBORRHOEIC DERMATITIS

50. __D__ Usually a sharp, intense color used as a contrast or pickup for color scheme. It is used to add excitement to an overall effect
   A. FRAGRANCE FREE   B. HAIR INTEGRATION   C. RELAX   D. ACCENT COLOR

51. __A__ Medical term for beard.
   A. BARBA   B. ALCOHOL   C. NATURAL   D. CLARIFIER

52. B — Coarse, pigmented or non-pigmented, exist on the scalp and gain length at a rate of 1-2cm per month during a cyclical life of up to 10 years.
    A. CREAM RINSE   B. TERMINAL HAIRS   C. WATER RESISTANT   D. ENDOCRINE SYSTEM

53. A — The volume or springiness of hair.
    A. BODY   B. COHERENT LIGHT   C. FRAGRANCE FREE   D. ACID MANTLE

54. D — Natural substance that gives color (pigment) to hair and skin.
    A. ANODE   B. CAPILLARIES   C. CONTACT COOLING   D. MELANIN

55. C — A product which oxidizes artificial color pigment.
    A. LUVIMER   B. RELAX   C. DEVELOPER   D. OXIDATION COLOUR

56. B — The process of scraping or wearing hair away. Causing partial or complete absence of hair from areas.
    A. JOJOBA OIL   B. ABRASION   C. COMEDONES   D. CATIONIC POLYMER

57. A — A female hormone sometimes linked to increased hair growth.
    A. ESTROGEN   B. HYDRATE   C. ECZEMA   D. SCLERODERMA

58. D — a male hormone that is suggested to be the main cause for the miniaturization of the hair follicle and for hair loss.
    A. TONE   B. BETAINE   C. CHAMOMILE   D. DHT

59. D — A device that removes hair by grasping hairs above the skin's surface with an electrified tweezers.
    A. SCRUNCH DRY   B. AMPERE   C. BLEACH   D. ELECTRIC TWEEZER

60. B — To add moisture to the skin.
    A. EDEMA   B. HYDRATE   C. BARBA   D. WIG

61. B — Groupings of hair that grow together and share the same blood supply.
    A. SEMI PERMANENT   B. FOLLICULAR UNIT   C. IONIC   D. NORWOOD SCALE

62. D — Hormone that causes masculine characteristics and affects hair growth.
    A. BLANCHING   B. COUTURE CUT   C. BARBICIDE   D. ANDROGEN

63. B — Term for loose commercial hair. This hair is used for creating wefts or for services like fusion.
    A. MELASMA   B. BULK HAIR   C. JOJOBA OIL   D. FOLLICULITIS

64. A — Used in many products for blonde hair to enhance color.
    A. CHAMOMILE   B. ACNE   C. FASHION SHADE   D. ARNICA

65. A — Makes smooth or slippery by using oil to overcome friction.
    A. LUBRICATES   B. LEUCOTRICHIA   C. KELOIDS   D. HAIR WEAVING

66. C — A classification for stronger, thicker types of hair.
    A. KERATIN   B. CONGENITAL   C. COARSE   D. STEAMING

67. A — A whitening of the skin sometimes caused by some types of hair removal.
    A. BLANCHING   B. WEFTS   C. CATHODE   D. TERMINAL HAIRS

68. D — A clinical testing method in which neither patient nor doctor know what medication or procedure is being used.
    A. CARBOMER   B. EPIDERMIS   C. PH   D. DOUBLE BLIND

69. D — used in between Shampoo and Conditioner to put protein back into the hair.
    A. HYDROLYZED KERATIN   B. SEBACEOUS   C. SPLIT ENDS   D. TREATMENT

70. **D** — The main structure of the hair shaft. The cortex determines the color and texture of the hair. The largest section of a single hair, containing the main bulk of the hair.
A. ELECTROLYSIS B. APPLE CIDER VINEGAR C. SILK PROTEIN D. CORTEX

71. **B** — A point midway up the hair follicle which researchers suspect must be damaged to induce permanent hair removal
A. HENNA B. BULGE C. PERMANENTLY D. NERVE ENDINGS

72. **D** — A technique for drying your hair which creates a style at the same time.
A. COUTURE CUT B. KELOIDS C. TOPICALLY D. SCRUNCH DRY

73. **A** — A negative electrode in a cell or circuit.
A. CATHODE B. HAIR WEAVING C. CHILLTIP D. DERMAL SHEATH

74. **B** — A group of glands which maintain the body's internal environment through the production of hormones.
A. SPRITZ B. ENDOCRINE SYSTEM C. COAGULATION D. ACTIVATOR

75. **D** — The temporary removal of hair.
A. INFUSION B. T ZONE C. DERMATITIS D. DEPILATION

76. **B** — Ingredients extracted directly from plants, earth minerals, or animal products as opposed to being produced synthetically.
A. BLEACH B. NATURAL C. T ZONE D. DOUBLE BLIND

77. **C** — In women, a major source of female hormones. Certain conditions involving the ovaries can lead to excess hair growth, especially polycystic ovary syndrome (PCOS).
A. SEBACEOUS GLAND B. DEVELOPER C. OVARIES D. SPLIT ENDS

78. **D** — Refers to a congenital absence of pigment in a lock of hairs which will show as grey or white.
A. AXILLA B. TOURMALINE C. APPLE CIDER VINEGAR D. LEUCOTRICHIA

79. **C** — The hair follicle is the tiny blub under your scalp from which the hair grows.
A. ANODE B. DERMABRASION C. FOLLICLES D. T ZONE

80. **C** — Oil producing gland in the dermis.
A. CATHODE B. ELECTRIC TWEEZER C. SEBACEOUS GLAND D. ALEXANDRITE

81. **A** — A method used to disguise (not remove) hair by lightening its color.
A. BLEACH B. COUTURE CUT C. EDEMA D. OVARIES

82. **C** — Flexible resin.
A. ALCOHOL B. HENNA C. LUVIMER D. COAGULATION

83. **C** — Increases wet and dry combability.
A. SELECTIVE PHOTOTHERMOLYSIS B. AMMONIUM THIOGLYCOLATE C. SILICONE D. BLEMISH

84. **D** — A geometric bob with a straight fringe, so called because of the resemblance to the capital A, with it's horizontal line, the fringe and its legs the hair passing your ears.
A. SOAP B. CONTACT COOLING C. ALOPECIA UNIVERSALIS D. A LINE BOB

85. **C** — Receptors which respond to touch, pain, pressure, heat and cold.
A. ALEXANDRITE B. CARBOMER C. NERVE ENDINGS D. PIGMENT

86. **B** — In hair removal, the practice of epilation with electrified needles.
A. TRACK B. ELECTROLYSIS C. TREATMENT D. LAYERING

87. __C__ Contains superior properties to keep skin and hair soft. It is beneficial to dry hair.
    A. AXILLA B. ACNE C. JOJOBA OIL D. BULK HAIR

88. __D__ To chemically straighten the hair to gently smooth out curl, reduce frizz, or create a straight style.
    A. CREAM RINSE B. HENNA C. BULK HAIR D. RELAX

89. __D__ A gland that affects certain types of hair growth.
    A. WATER RESISTANT B. MEDULLA C. SEBACEOUS GLAND D. ADRENAL

90. __B__ Small blood vessels which connect the arteries and veins that feed the hair.
    A. COHERENT LIGHT B. CAPILLARIES C. CATAPHORESIS D. DHT

91. __D__ Pertaining to a drug that is produced for profit.
    A. ESTROGEN B. SOAP C. ACCENT COLOR D. PROPRIETARY

92. __B__ Used to oxidize (expand) artificial color molecules. Can also lighten natural color pigment.
    A. PIGMENT B. HYDROGEN PEROXIDE C. BLEND D. BASIC SHADE

93. __D__ A type of raised darkened scar, more common with dark skin. Due to a defect in the healing process.
    A. COCAMIDE DEA B. HAIR WEAVING C. LUVIMER D. KELOIDS

94. __D__ The term used to describe any hairpiece with a full cap which covers the hair on the head, or the entire area where hair normally grows, as a substitute for hair.
    A. HYDROGEN PEROXIDE B. ALEXANDRITE C. ACID MANTLE D. WIG

95. __D__ A very small hair graft usually consisting of one or two hairs.
    A. TAN B. DIODE C. DIET D. MICRO GRAFT

96. __A__ Area at the top of the head.
    A. CROWN B. COHERENT LIGHT C. EXFOLIATING D. FRAGRANCE FREE

97. __D__ Selectively targeting dermal structures with light energy, without causing damage to surrounding tissue.
    A. JOJOBA OIL B. COARSE C. CRUSTING D. SELECTIVE PHOTOTHERMOLYSIS

98. __C__ A medical term for swelling.
    A. AMPERE B. DANAZOL C. EDEMA D. CHILLTIP

99. __B__ The medulla is a central zone of cells usually only present in large thick hairs.
    A. COUTURE CUT B. MEDULLA C. TRACK D. ALOPECIA UNIVERSALIS

100. __B__ Metabolising stubborn fat deposits, typically in the lower body, using methods such as Eporex mesotherapy.
    A. EPIDERMIS B. TARGETED FAT REDUCTION C. KERATIN D. ANDROGEN

From the words provided for each clue, provide the letter of the word which best matches the clue.

101. __D__ Process where water molecules are broken down by ions into smaller droplets. This then allows the hair to absorb the moisture more easily.
    A. TERMINAL HAIRS B. THREAD VEIN C. HYPOPIGMENTATION D. IONIC

102. __C__ To weave strands of hair together. On the scalp braiding is used to form a base or track to sew on a commercial weft.
    A. WEAVE B. CURRENT C. BRAID D. DIODE

103. __C__ A protein that holds all connective tissue together under the skin.
A. SILICONE B. CHIGNON C. COLLAGEN D. ABDOMEN

104. __B__ The removal of dead skin cells to reveal softer skin underneath.
A. BARBICIDE B. EXFOLIATION C. SILICONE D. PUNCH GRAFT

105. __C__ The pigmented area surrounding the nipple. A very common area for hair growth.
A. HAIR INTEGRATION B. COAGULATION C. AREOLA D. LUBRICANT

106. __B__ Pertains to the skin.
A. PIGMENTED LESION B. SUBCUTANEOUS C. Q SWITCH D. CHEMICAL DEPILATORIES

107. __D__ The substructure that is responsible for the spectral selective absorption of electromagnetic radiation.
A. CARBOMER B. ALOPECIA UNIVERSALIS C. FINISHING SPRAY D. CHROMOPHORE

108. __B__ The small area at the base of the hair root which provides nutrients needed for growth.
A. ANODE B. PAPILLA C. CLUB HAIR D. MICRO LINKING TECHNIQUE

109. __C__ This drug is normally used to reduce sex drive in men who have an excessive sex drive. It is also prescribed to treat hirsutism and androgenic alopecia in women.
A. DERMABRASION B. LUBRICANT C. CYPROTERONE ACETATE D. PROPECIA

110. __B__ Hair extensions are pieces of real or synthetic weaved close to the scalp in order to achieve greater length or fullness.
A. ANTI ANDROGEN B. EXTENSION C. PERM D. BETAINE

111. __A__ This is the complete loss of scalp hair often combined with the loss of eyebrows and eyelashes.
A. ALOPECIA TOTALIS B. OVARIES C. MICRO LINKING TECHNIQUE D. DIODE

112. __C__ Congenital baldness or baldness at birth.
A. TRICHOTILLOMANIA B. SPRIONOLACTONE C. ALOPECIA ADNATA D. SEBACEOUS

113. __B__ A flat, discolored area of skin similar to a freckle.
A. SEBACEOUS GLAND B. LENTIGO C. TARGETED FAT REDUCTION D. PAPILLA

114. __C__ The body's shock absorber.
A. BULBOUS NEEDLE B. TRICHOTILLOMANIA C. SUBCUTANEOUS TISSUE D. PH

115. __C__ Powder or cream preparations that dissolve hair above the surface of the skin. Some find these products very irritating to the skin.
A. SEBACEOUS B. GENERIC C. CHEMICAL DEPILATORIES D. ESCHAR

116. __B__ A discoloration of skin from blood, sometimes caused by electrolysis, plucking, or waxing. Also known as Purpura.
A. DISCOMFORT B. BRUISE C. SPRIONOLACTONE D. LUBRICATES

117. __B__ Hormone that causes masculine characteristics and affects hair growth.
A. A LINE BOB B. ANDROGEN C. ANTIANDROGEN D. DONOR SITE

118. __B__ In hair removal, the practice of epilation with electrified needles.
A. DERMATITIS B. ELECTROLYSIS C. BARBICIDE D. CHIGNON

119. __D__ Flexible resin.
A. ALOE VERA B. DOUBLE BLIND C. T ZONE D. LUVIMER

120. __B__ A chemical substance found in plants and animals. The building blocks of hair.
A. DERMATITIS   B. AMINO ACID   C. PUNCH GRAFT   D. BOB

121. __A__ A sun tanning product that contains DHA, which reacts with amino acids in the top layer of skin, causing it to temporarily darken (2-4 days).
A. SELF TANNER   B. TEXTURIZER   C. BASIC SHADE   D. SILK PROTEIN

122. __C__ A smoothing product to stop your hair from frizzing, keeping it smooth and straight. You'll be able to find a serum that is specifically designed to your own hair type.
A. EPILATION   B. ISOPROPYL LANOLATE   C. SERUM   D. IONIC

123. __D__ Laser at 755nm used for hair removal.
A. LUBRICANT   B. ECCRINE GLAND   C. TRICHOPTILOSIS   D. ALEXANDRITE

124. __B__ a light mist or spray, which when used as verb means to lightly spray your hair.
A. ANAGEN CYCLE   B. SPRITZ   C. BLACK SKIN   D. ARRECTOR PILI

125. __D__ A test performed on the skin 24 hours before its use to determine sensitivity.
A. CHEMICAL DEPILATORIES   B. CLONE   C. DISTORTED HAIR FOLLICLES   D. PATCH TEST

126. __C__ A method used to disguise (not remove) hair by lightening its color.
A. MONOFILAMENT   B. KELOIDS   C. BLEACH   D. ANDROGEN

127. __B__ A device that produces short intense bursts of energy from a laser.
A. CURRENT   B. Q SWITCH   C. CHEMICAL DEPILATORIES   D. CYPROTERONE ACETATE

128. __C__ Also called vitamin B5 (a B vitamin), is a water-soluble vitamin required to sustain life (essential nutrient).
A. ELECTROLYSIS   B. PERMANENT   C. PANTOTHENIC ACID   D. ALLERGEN

129. __A__ Fine, transparent nylon or silk mesh with hairs individually hand-knotted into the mesh. Allows the hair to fall naturally and gives more versatility in styling.
A. MONOFILAMENT   B. SKIN REJUVENATION   C. ANTIBIOTIC   D. LEUCOTRICHIA

130. __C__ A group of genetically identical cells or organisms derived from a single common cell.
A. DERMIS   B. SLOUGH   C. CLONE   D. BETAINE

131. __A__ The brand name for finestaride. The only drug approved by the FDA to treat hair loss.
A. PROPECIA   B. FOLLICLES   C. EMOLLIENTS   D. CETYL ALCOHOL

132. __B__ Contains superior properties to keep skin and hair soft. It is beneficial to dry hair.
A. ELECTROLOGY   B. JOJOBA OIL   C. FINASTERIDE   D. LIPID LAYER

133. __C__ A geometric bob with a straight fringe, so called because of the resemblance to the capital A, with it's horizontal line, the fringe and its legs the hair passing your ears.
A. ALLERGEN   B. MONOFILAMENT   C. A LINE BOB   D. SLOUGH

134. __A__ Completely changing the natural color of the hair.
A. PERMANENTLY   B. DERMATITIS   C. ENERGY DENSITY   D. CARBON DIOXIDE LASER

135. __B__ The body transformation of food into energy.
A. AMMONIUM THIOGLYCOLATE   B. METABOLISM   C. LIPID LAYER   D. ARRECTOR PILI

136. __D__ Creamy hair product meant to be used after shampoo. Moisturizes and detangles hair.
A. ENERGY DENSITY   B. TERMINAL HAIRS   C. ELECTROCOAGULATION   D. CONDITIONER

137. __B__ The practice of hair removal through the use of electrified needles, invented in the 1870's.
A. BIOPSY B. ELECTROLOGY C. IONIC D. FOLLICLES

138. __C__ Optimum hold without overload.
A. TOURMALINE B. ACNE C. MICRO DIFFUSE D. DISTORTED HAIR FOLLICLES

139. __C__ The invisible spectrum of solar radiation. It is divided into three regions with increasing danger to the skin.
A. TOURMALINE B. NORWOOD SCALE C. UV D. HYPOPIGMENTATION

140. __D__ a crystal silicate mineral compounded with elements such as aluminum, iron, magnesium, sodium, lithium, or potassium.
A. ENERGY DENSITY B. FLY-AWAY HAIR C. Q SWITCH D. TOURMALINE

141. __D__ Is sometimes linked to excess hair growth, especially in the extremely obese and extremely anorexic.
A. GENERIC B. ISOPROPYL LANOLATE C. ARNICA D. DIET

142. __B__ The active stage in a hair growth cycle.
A. CORTISONE B. ANAGEN CYCLE C. SPRIONOLACTONE D. CLUB HAIR

143. __D__ Combating the signs of ageing using the latest innovative, non-invasive treatments that give you visibly younger, healthy, radiant skin.
A. ELECTRIC TWEEZER B. TREATMENT C. BLACKHEADS D. SKIN REJUVENATION

144. __B__ A color which lasts from 6 - 8 shampoos.
A. PERMANENTLY B. SEMI PERMANENT C. ISOPROPYL LANOLATE D. ESCHAR

145. __B__ Tiny hair-like blood vessels, some of which carry nutrient to the hair growth matrix.
A. FINISHING SPRAY B. CAPILLARIES C. ALLERGEN D. DIODE

146. __B__ A medical term for swelling.
A. EFFICACY B. EDEMA C. REMI D. DERMATITIS

147. __D__ The hair follicle is the tiny blub under your scalp from which the hair grows.
A. SILICONE B. EPILATION C. SOLUBLE D. FOLLICLES

148. __B__ Ingredients extracted directly from plants, earth minerals, or animal products as opposed to being produced synthetically.
A. ACNE B. NATURAL C. BLISTER D. DISCOMFORT

149. __A__ A color which requires oxygen to make it work.
A. OXIDATION COLOUR B. ALOPECIA TOTALIS C. EXTRACT D. TELOGEN

150. __D__ Substances used to dissolve hair above the skin's surface.
A. CARBOMER B. ESCHAR C. AMINOPHENOLS D. DEPILATORIES

151. __C__ allows you to only pay attention to a particular area or panel of hair.
A. PERMANENTLY B. CREAM RINSE C. SECTIONING D. DERMABRASION

152. __C__ Procedures that do not involve tools that break the skin or physically enter the body.
A. AMINO ACID B. CONDITIONER C. NON INVASIVE D. BROKEN CAPILLARIES

153. __C__ Refers to a congenital absence of pigment in a lock of hairs which will show as grey or white.
A. ENERGY DENSITY B. ABDOMEN C. LEUCOTRICHIA D. ESCHAR

154. __A__ A bodily reaction to an irritant. Skin allergies can be exacerbated by solutions put on the skin.
A. ALLERGY B. Q SWITCH C. CHELATING D. ALCOHOL

155. B An inflammation of the skin, a result of over production of oil and bacteria.
A. AMINOPHENOLS   B. ACNE   C. FLY-AWAY HAIR   D. INTENSE PULSED LIGHT

156. C Produced from starch by means of enzymatic conversion and are used in a wide range of applications in food, pharmaceutical and chemical industries.
A. DERMATITIS   B. DEPILATE   C. CYCLODEXTRINS   D. FOLLICLE SHEATH

157. D part of the structure of the hair and also form a protective barrier. They are composed of EFA's amongst other complicated scientific things.
A. DERMABRASION   B. PH   C. TARGETED FAT REDUCTION   D. LIPID LAYER

158. D A type of raised darkened scar, more common with dark skin. Due to a defect in the healing process.
A. CORTISONE   B. Q SWITCH   C. DISCOMFORT   D. KELOIDS

159. D Used to measure acidity in cosmetic preparations.
A. ACNE   B. ESCHAR   C. ACTINIC KERATOSIS   D. PH

160. A Creates "Goose Bumps" when stimulated.
A. ARRECTOR PILI   B. PROTEIN TREATMENT   C. ALLERGEN   D. PSORIASIS

161. A A hair weave is usually a hairpiece with layered gaps made into it.
A. WEAVE   B. OUTER ROOT SHEATH   C. EXFOLIATION   D. BARBA

162. D Allergen is a substance that causes an allergic reaction.
A. ANAGEN CYCLE   B. LIPID LAYER   C. HYPERPIGMENTATION   D. ALLERGEN

163. D A natural water-soluble source of acid derived from liquid silk.
A. ALEXANDRITE   B. FOLLICLES   C. HAIR INTEGRATION   D. SILK PROTEIN

164. C The term for hair loss which occurs over the entire body.
A. THREAD VEIN   B. WEAVE   C. ALOPECIA UNIVERSALIS   D. EMOLLIENTS

165. C Variety of skin conditions mainly the result of excess melanin. Commonly known as Café au Lait stains, birthmarks, age spots and freckles.
A. EPILATION   B. ANTI ANDROGEN   C. PIGMENTED LESION   D. AMINOPHENOLS

166. B Allows some light to pass through.
A. BROKEN CAPILLARIES   B. TRANSLUCENT   C. SPRITZ   D. EPILATION

167. A The soft area between the rib cage and the pubic area. A common area for excess hair, often in a line from the belly button to the pubic hair.
A. ABDOMEN   B. ALLERGY   C. SPLIT ENDS   D. CUTTING IN

168. D An anti-inflammatory sometimes linked to hair growth when taken internally.
A. HAIR INTEGRATION   B. CYPROTERONE ACETATE   C. DOUBLE BLIND   D. CORTISONE

169. D The removal of hair below the skin's surface.
A. INDENTATION   B. SILK PROTEIN   C. ALCOHOL   D. EPILATION

170. D Products so labeled may still contain small amounts of fragrances to mask the fatty odor of soap or other unpleasant odors.
A. BOTANICAL   B. DERMABRASION   C. SPRITZ   D. FRAGRANCE FREE

171. C A clinical testing method in which neither patient nor doctor know what medication or procedure is being used.
A. NORWOOD SCALE   B. SELF TANNER   C. DOUBLE BLIND   D. BROKEN CAPILLARIES

172. __D__ This form of hair loss is caused by pulling out one's own hair, usually without realizing it.
A. MICRO DIFFUSE B. HYPERPIGMENTATION C. ESTROGEN D. TRICHOTILLOMANIA

173. __C__ Split ends.
A. HYPERPIGMENTATION B. TRANSLUCENT C. TRICHOPTILOSIS D. BULB

174. __D__ A machine used to sterilize medical utensils and some hair removal devices.
A. HYPOPIGMENTATION B. BLEACH C. CYCLODEXTRINS D. AUTOCLAVE

175. __C__ creates curls by restructuring your hair molecules with a chemical, or heat treatment and is generally a long-lasting or permanent change to your hair.
A. CARBON DIOXIDE LASER B. TRICHOTILLOMANIA C. PERM D. PUNCH GRAFT

176. __C__ The resting phase in the hair cycle.
A. FOLLICLES B. DIET C. TELOGEN D. DERMIS

177. __A__ The thin outer layer of skin, on top of the thicker and deeper dermis.
A. EPIDERMIS B. CURRENT C. TRICHOPTILOSIS D. SEMI PERMANENT

178. __C__ A definition set by the American FDA that most laser and intense light source manufacturers claim to meet for hair removal.
A. BIOPSY B. AZELAIC ACID C. PERMANENT D. SUBCUTANEOUS

179. __B__ Atopic Dermatitis is also known as Eczema. Contact Dermatitis is an inflammation of the skin caused by direct contact with an irritating substance.
A. SOLUBLE B. DERMATITIS C. MELASMA D. SCHIZOTRICHIA

180. __D__ The process by which most synthetic fiber is curled at the factory.
A. ACNE B. SURFACTANTS C. BRAID D. STEAMING

181. __D__ The use of heat generated by electricity to change tissue from a fluid to a semi-solid, similar to cooking an egg.
A. MICRO LINKING TECHNIQUE B. BLEACH C. BASIC SHADE D. ELECTROCOAGULATION

182. __C__ A common ingredient in chemical depilatories.
A. SCHIZOTRICHIA B. ALOPECIA TOTALIS C. AMMONIUM THIOGLYCOLATE D. ACUPRESSURE

183. __D__ used in between Shampoo and Conditioner to put protein back into the hair.
A. SCHIZOTRICHIA B. THREAD VEIN C. MICRODERMABRASION D. TREATMENT

184. __C__ Possessing a positive electrical charge. Cationic detergents are often used in shampoos because they reduce static electricity and leave the hair manageable.
A. DERMABRASION B. OUTER ROOT SHEATH C. CATIONIC D. CHROMOPHORE

185. __D__ A soft thin layer surrounding the lower two-thirds of a hair.
A. BASIC SHADE B. SUNSCREEN C. DERMATITIS D. OUTER ROOT SHEATH

186. __D__ Refers to a product containing plants or ingredients made from plants.
A. COLLAGEN B. FLY-AWAY HAIR C. AMMONIUM THIOGLYCOLATE D. BOTANICAL

187. __D__ A medical term for sweat gland. These tiny pores do not contain hair follicles.
A. ANTIBIOTIC B. DIODE C. BOTANICAL D. ECCRINE GLAND

188. __C__ A plant extract that has been used to treat swelling, soreness and bruising.
A. EPIDERMIS B. BARBA C. ARNICA D. HUMECTANT

189. C — Products with ingredients that absorb UVA and UVB rays.
   A. BOB B. TREATMENT C. SUNSCREEN D. ANODE

190. A — The volume or springiness of hair.
   A. BODY B. ANODE C. AREOLA D. IONIC

191. B — In hair removal, a conductor through which electricity enters or leaves the body. An electrolysis needle is an electrode.
   A. TEXTURIZER B. ELECTRODE C. BLACK SKIN D. SECTIONING

192. A — Caused by an absence of melanocytes, whitening of the skin. Vitiligo is a common medical complaint.
   A. HYPOPIGMENTATION B. HYPERPIGMENTATION C. ALPHA HYDROXY ACID D. PATCH TEST

193. C — Small clumps of coagulated melanin.
   A. CUTICLE B. PUNCH GRAFT C. FRECKLES D. ALPHA HYDROXY ACID

194. A — Phenol derivatives used in combination with other chemicals in permanent (two step) hair dyes.
   A. AMINOPHENOLS B. SEBACEOUS C. HYPOPIGMENTATION D. SKIN REJUVENATION

195. C — A Synthetic moisturizer.
   A. PERMANENTLY B. EFFICACY C. ISOPROPYL LANOLATE D. ALOPECIA UNIVERSALIS

196. D — A hairspray with medium hold used on a finished style to maintain its shape and hold.
   A. MICRO LINKING TECHNIQUE B. HYPERPIGMENTATION C. PUNCH GRAFT D. FINISHING SPRAY

197. B — A type of electrolysis needle.
   A. SILK PROTEIN B. BULBOUS NEEDLE C. NON INVASIVE D. FLY-AWAY HAIR

198. C — A technique used by hairdressers to change the thickness of the hair, creating either a thinning or thicker appearance.
   A. T ZONE B. THREAD VEIN C. LAYERING D. CATAGEN

199. D — The process by which blood clots, and can be induced by heat or chemicals.
   A. REMI B. LUVIMER C. CUTICLE D. COAGULATION

200. D — Causes blackheads
   A. CUTICLE B. UV C. ALPHA HYDROXY ACID D. COMEDOGENIC

From the words provided for each clue, provide the letter of the word which best matches the clue.

201. B — Hair that has lost its pigment.
   A. BOAR BRISTLE B. GREY HAIR C. BLEACH D. TREATMENT

202. D — An oil or oil rich crème or lotion designed to lubricate the skin and slow moisture loss.
   A. TRANSLUCENT B. ACUPUNCTURE C. CHITOSAN D. LUBRICANT

203. C — Commonly used in the treatment of acne and other skin conditions.
   A. SPIDER VEIN B. BULBOUS NEEDLE C. AZELAIC ACID D. HYPERPIGMENTATION

204. A — A term meaning how well or effectively a cosmetic device works.
   A. EFFICACY B. BULK HAIR C. AMORTIZATION D. SELECTIVE PHOTOTHERMOLYSIS

205. D — Increases wet and dry combability.
   A. BOAR BRISTLE B. INDENTATION C. ELECTRIC TWEEZER D. SILICONE

206. **C** — A small rough spot on skin chronically exposed to the sun, occurs most frequently in fair skinned people.
A. SEBUM   B. BETAINE   C. ACTINIC KERATOSIS   D. ALOPECIA AREATA

207. **B** — The oily secretion of the sebaceous glands of the scalp, composed of keratin, fat or cellular debris.
A. FUSION   B. SEBUM   C. CATIONIC   D. SOLUBLE

208. **B** — A drug or product that limited the effects of androgens (male hormones).
A. HYDRATE   B. ANTI ANDROGEN   C. ALOPECIA SENILIS   D. ACTIVE INGREDIENT

209. **D** — A medical term for blackheads.
A. CATIONIC   B. BETAINE   C. SELF TANNER   D. COMEDONES

210. **A** — Synthetic moisturizer.
A. PALMITATE   B. ALOPECIA ADNATA   C. ACTIVE INGREDIENT   D. NORWOOD SCALE

211. **C** — Used to remove the moisture from wet hair.
A. BASIC SHADE   B. CORNROW   C. ROUGH BLOW DRY   D. PALMITATE

212. **B** — a male hormone that is suggested to be the main cause for the miniaturization of the hair follicle and for hair loss.
A. ALOPECIA TOTALIS   B. DHT   C. BLACKHEADS   D. EMLA

213. **D** — Drugs that sometimes cause increased hair growth.
A. DEPILATORIES   B. APPLE CIDER VINEGAR   C. TELOGEN   D. BIRTH CONTROL

214. **C** — The thin outer layer of skin, on top of the thicker and deeper dermis.
A. ANTIANDROGEN   B. EMLA   C. EPIDERMIS   D. SELECTIVE PHOTOTHERMOLYSIS

215. **B** — Either made synthetically or derived from the kernel of the coconut, it gives lather and cleans skin and hair.
A. ALOPECIA TOTALIS   B. COCAMIDE DEA   C. SOOTHING   D. CYST

216. **C** — A bristle commonly used in natural bristle brushes.
A. GLYCERIN   B. CORTEX   C. BOAR BRISTLE   D. AMORTIZATION

217. **B** — Refers to a congenital absence of pigment in a lock of hairs which will show as grey or white.
A. ADRENAL   B. LEUCOTRICHIA   C. MYRISTATE   D. DEPILATION

218. **C** — Selectively targeting dermal structures with light energy, without causing damage to surrounding tissue.
A. ACUPUNCTURE   B. CELLULITE REDUCTION   C. SELECTIVE PHOTOTHERMOLYSIS   D. CHELATING

219. **D** — A relatively rare condition in which the follicle is not straight.
A. FASHION SHADE   B. ALOPECIA SENILIS   C. GLYCERIN   D. DISTORTED HAIR FOLLICLES

220. **D** — The process of converting one enzyme to another.
A. DERMABRASION   B. HYPERPIGMENTATION   C. FUSION   D. AMORTIZATION

221. **C** — Thin hair that is charged by static and is a particular problem with straight looks as the hair just won't lie properly and can spoil your look.
A. MEDULLA   B. FUSION   C. FLY-AWAY HAIR   D. CONTACT COOLING

222. **D** — A group of genetically identical cells or organisms derived from a single common cell.
A. ALOPECIA TOTALIS   B. HAIR GROWTH CYCLE   C. ANTIANDROGEN   D. CLONE

223. **A** — To cancel or reduce effect.
A. NEUTRALISE   B. ELASTICITY   C. HYDROLYZED KERATIN   D. PALMITATE

224. A — A basic color with added tone.
A. FASHION SHADE   B. METABOLISM   C. ARRECTOR PILI   D. DERMIS

225. A — A method in which hair is maintained or tightened using a tool.
A. INTERLOCKING   B. ALOPECIA   C. RUBY   D. AMPHOTERIC

226. A — Ability to absorb moisture.
A. POROSITY   B. PANTOTHENIC ACID   C. ACNE   D. ALOPECIA ANDROGENETIC

227. C — A technique used by hairdressers to change the thickness of the hair, creating either a thinning or thicker appearance.
A. POROSITY   B. DEXAMETHOSONE   C. LAYERING   D. ROUGH BLOW DRY

228. B — Receptors which respond to touch, pain, pressure, heat and cold.
A. BACTERIA   B. NERVE ENDINGS   C. TEMPORARY COLOR   D. CELLULITE REDUCTION

229. D — In women, a major source of female hormones. Certain conditions involving the ovaries can lead to excess hair growth, especially polycystic ovary syndrome (PCOS).
A. DISTORTED HAIR FOLLICLES   B. FRAGRANCE   C. ABDOMEN   D. OVARIES

230. D — Used to oxidize (expand) artificial color molecules. Can also lighten natural color pigment.
A. NORWOOD SCALE   B. BIRTH CONTROL   C. CILIA   D. HYDROGEN PEROXIDE

231. B — The hair's ability to stretch without breaking and then return to its original shape.
A. BLEACH   B. ELASTICITY   C. NORWOOD SCALE   D. LASER

232. D — A mild nonirritating surfactant often used in shampoos; leaves hair manageable and is gentle enough for chemically treated hair.
A. ACNE   B. NEUTRALISE   C. DERMABRASION   D. AMPHOTERIC

233. D — A drug sometimes linked to excess hair growth.
A. NERVE ENDINGS   B. ALOPECIA AREATA   C. APPLE CIDER VINEGAR   D. DILANTIN

234. B — Products that reflect all the sun's rays, such as zinc oxide and titanium dioxide. They permit minimal tanning, and are a good choice for those who are sensitive to chemicals.
A. HEATCLAMPS   B. SUNBLOCK   C. SOLUBLE   D. SCLERODERMA

235. D — The enzyme superoxide, catalyzes the dis-mutation of superoxide into oxygen and hydrogen peroxide.
A. CHELATING   B. CORTEX   C. EFFICACY   D. SUPEROXIDE DISMUTASE

236. B — Contains superior properties to keep skin and hair soft. It is beneficial to dry hair.
A. HYPERPIGMENTATION   B. JOJOBA OIL   C. LUVIMER   D. HYDROLYZED KERATIN

237. B — Small clumps of coagulated melanin.
A. INTERLOCKING   B. FRECKLES   C. CORTEX   D. ACCELERATOR

238. C — has been called a more extensive and severe form of dandruff.
A. BIRTH CONTROL   B. DIATHERMY   C. SEBORRHOEIC DERMATITIS   D. CORTEX

239. C — A condition that is hereditary. Excess hair often runs in the family.
A. LUBRICANT   B. HAIR GROWTH CYCLE   C. CONGENITAL   D. HUMIDITY

240. B — The body's shock absorber.
A. COCAMIDE DEA   B. SUBCUTANEOUS TISSUE   C. ROUGH BLOW DRY   D. ANAESTHETIC

241. __A__ Used to measure acidity in cosmetic preparations.
A. PH   B. COARSE   C. DEPILATION   D. DEXAMETHOSONE

242. __D__ Is sometimes linked to excess hair growth, especially in the extremely obese and extremely anorexic.
A. GLYCERIN   B. SILICONE   C. TRICLOSAN   D. DIET

243. __D__ Split ends.
A. HAIR EXTENSIONS   B. ARNICA   C. CASTRATION   D. TRICHOPTILOSIS

244. __C__ Refers to unflattering warm tones in hair color created by chemicals or damage.
A. HEATCLAMPS   B. AZELAIC ACID   C. BRASSY   D. ACTIVATOR

245. __B__ Blocks the effects of androgens, normally by blocking the receptor sites.
A. SERUM   B. ANTIANDROGEN   C. FASHION SHADE   D. MELANOMA

246. __B__ An alkaline ingredient used in some permanent hair color. An ingredient that results in a chemical action that decolorizes the hair.
A. UV   B. AMMONIA   C. DEXAMETHOSONE   D. OVARIES

247. __B__ To add moisture to the skin.
A. ADRENAL   B. HYDRATE   C. DEPILATORIES   D. TESTOSTERONE

248. __A__ Probably the most difficult type of skin from which to remove hair.
A. BLACK SKIN   B. TELOGEN   C. TRICHOPTILOSIS   D. FLY-AWAY HAIR

249. __D__ Small blood vessels which connect the arteries and veins that feed the hair.
A. SACRUM   B. SEBUM   C. CARBOMER   D. CAPILLARIES

250. __B__ Is effective against most bacteria occurring on the skin.
A. NERVE ENDINGS   B. TRICLOSAN   C. ALOPECIA AREATA   D. BLEACH

251. __A__ This is the complete loss of scalp hair often combined with the loss of eyebrows and eyelashes.
A. ALOPECIA TOTALIS   B. DRUG TREATMENT   C. ARRECTOR PILI   D. AZELAIC ACID

252. __D__ Commonly used laser for hair and tattoo removal.
A. MICRO DIFFUSE   B. HYDRATE   C. CARBOMER   D. RUBY

253. __B__ A device that removes hair by grasping hairs above the skin's surface with an electrified tweezers.
A. CICATRICIAL ALOPECIA   B. ELECTRIC TWEEZER   C. ALKALI   D. CAPILLARIES

254. __C__ A form of skin cancer.
A. DHT   B. DIABETES   C. MELANOMA   D. SUPEROXIDE DISMUTASE

255. __B__ A hair color formula that lasts only until you shampoo your hair.
A. TOPICALLY   B. TEMPORARY COLOR   C. ABDOMEN   D. TRICHOPTILOSIS

256. __A__ The active dissolving ingredient in many cream depilatories
A. CALCIUM THIOGLYCOLATE   B. ACCELERATOR   C. TEA TREE OIL   D. ALOPECIA ADNATA

257. __A__ Detangling aid which conditions, protects against humidity, and adds shine.
A. DIMETHICONE   B. PANTOTHENIC ACID   C. PH   D. BRAID

258. __A__ A small opening of the sweat glands of the skin.
A. PORE   B. SERUM   C. FUSION   D. ALOPECIA SENILIS

259. **D** — A type of electrolysis needle.
A. CAPILLARIES B. DERMIS C. CLEARING D. BULBOUS NEEDLE

260. **B** — Loss of hair, especially from the head, which either happens naturally or is caused by disease
A. MELANOMA B. ALOPECIA C. OVARIES D. DIMETHICONE

261. **A** — Being able to dissolve into, or being compatible with, another substance.
A. SOLUBLE B. SPIDER VEIN C. ACTIVATOR D. DISTORTED HAIR FOLLICLES

262. **B** — Clinic based method of reducing the appearance of cellulite.
A. HYDRATE B. CELLULITE REDUCTION C. ALOPECIA D. NEUTRALISE

263. **B** — A type of clogged pore in the skin with a visible black plug.
A. SUNBLOCK B. BLACKHEADS C. SCLERODERMA D. MEDULLA

264. **D** — To attach wefted hair to the natural hair with a latex or surgical type adhesive.
A. DEPILATE B. FOLLICLE SHEATH C. ACTIVATOR D. BONDING

265. **D** — A method of hair removal in which all hair in an area is removed at once, as opposed to thinning.
A. JOJOBA OIL B. NEUTRALISE C. FUSION D. CLEARING

266. **D** — A trademark for a Japanese-made synthetic fiber which is used extensively in the manufacture of wigs and hairpieces
A. AMORTIZATION B. NORWOOD SCALE C. COMEDOGENIC D. KANEKALON

267. **C** — A chemically based permanent waving product that has a pH from 7.5 to 9.5. Stronger than acid perms, alkaline perms are designed to produce tight, firm, springy curls.
A. PATCH TEST B. ACTIVATOR C. ALKALINE PERM D. NERVE ENDINGS

268. **C** — Another name for thermolysis.
A. BLEACH B. BONDING C. DIATHERMY D. INFUSION

269. **C** — A method used to disguise (not remove) hair by lightening its color.
A. CONGENITAL B. SPLIT ENDS C. BLEACH D. DHT

270. **D** — Term for loose commercial hair. This hair is used for creating wefts or for services like fusion.
A. SELF TANNER B. DEPILATORIES C. RELAX D. BULK HAIR

271. **B** — The deepest layers of the skin, where blood vessels, lymph channels, nerve endings, sweat glands, sebaceous glands, fat cells, hair follicles and muscles are located.
A. CILIA B. DERMIS C. BIRTH CONTROL D. SUPEROXIDE DISMUTASE

272. **C** — Tiny hair-like blood vessels, some of which carry nutrient to the hair growth matrix.
A. ROUGH BLOW DRY B. SERUM C. CAPILLARIES D. HEATCLAMPS

273. **C** — A natural or neutral color.
A. CATAPHORESIS B. POROSITY C. BASIC SHADE D. GLYCERIN

274. **C** — A doctor specializing in skin and hair conditions.
A. DIABETES B. BLEACH C. DERMATOLOGIST D. PANTHENOL

275. **B** — Aids detangling. Provides volume, control and shine.
A. CATAGEN B. PANTHENOL C. CASTRATION D. EMLA

276. __B__ Products so labeled may still contain small amounts of fragrances to mask the fatty odor of soap or other unpleasant odors.
A. PANTHENOL B. FRAGRANCE FREE C. PATCH TEST D. DEPILATE

277. __B__ Reducing skin discomforts from irritation, blemishes, burning skin, etc.
A. FACE LIFT B. SOOTHING C. DIMETHICONE D. ROUGH BLOW DRY

278. __C__ When your skin is damaged by exposure to the UVA and UVB rays of the sun, its reaction is to produce more melanin as an attempt to protect itself against further damage.
A. CAPILLARIES B. FACE LIFT C. TAN D. ALOPECIA ADNATA

279. __C__ Also known as eczema.
A. CLARIFIER B. ANTISEPTIC C. ATOPIC DERMATITIS D. DILANTIN

280. __D__ In hair removal, a conductor through which electricity enters or leaves the body. An electrolysis needle is an electrode.
A. PORE B. CORTEX C. DISCOMFORT D. ELECTRODE

281. __C__ A small temporary scab that occurs sometimes after electrolysis, especially after overtreatment.
A. INFUSION B. PANTHENOL C. ESCHAR D. HYDRATE

282. __A__ The invisible spectrum of solar radiation. It is divided into three regions with increasing danger to the skin.
A. UV B. TRANSLUCENT C. CELLULITE REDUCTION D. DISCOMFORT

283. __C__ A chemical ingredients that is specifically added to hair bleach to speed up the action of the bleach without unnecessarily damaging the hair.
A. CHITOSAN B. BULBOUS NEEDLE C. ACTIVATOR D. FOLLICULITIS

284. __C__ A substance used to relieve all feeling.
A. JOJOBA OIL B. DIMETHICONE C. ANAESTHETIC D. DIATHERMY

285. __B__ Trichoptilosis
A. APPLE CIDER VINEGAR B. SPLIT ENDS C. EXTRACT D. HYPERPIGMENTATION

286. __A__ An herbal concentrate produced by separating the essential or active part of an herb into a solvent material.
A. EXTRACT B. FRAGRANCE FREE C. HAIR EXTENSIONS D. ADRENAL

287. __C__ A non- shiny surface that absorbs light; a dead or dull finish.
A. DEPILATORIES B. FRECKLES C. MATTE D. LUBRICANT

288. __C__ An organism responsible for infection.
A. BETAINE B. CALAMINE C. BACTERIA D. EMLA

289. __C__ A natural conditioning substance for example: from molasses or sugar beet.
A. ROUGH BLOW DRY B. WEFTS C. BETAINE D. FRECKLES

290. __A__ An over excitation of melanocytes, darkening of the skin. Can be seen as sun-induced freckles or melasma.
A. HYPERPIGMENTATION B. CORNROW C. CALCIUM THIOGLYCOLATE D. INTERLOCKING

291. __D__ This is the common name for male or female pattern baldness which depends on the genetic predisposition of the hair follicles and the levels of DHT in the body.
A. HYDROGEN PEROXIDE B. SACRUM C. ELASTICITY D. ALOPECIA ANDROGENETIC

292. __A__ A natural solvent in oils and creams. It acidifies products.
A. APPLE CIDER VINEGAR B. BIRTH CONTROL C. BARBICIDE D. LASER

293. __C__ Excessive development of the male breasts.
A. ALOPECIA AREATA B. ALOPECIA SENILIS C. GYNECOMASTIA D. CONGENITAL

294. __C__ The process of attaching small pieces of human hair with a special adhesive and a thermal gun.
A. ELASTICITY B. ARNICA C. FUSION D. ELECTRIC TWEEZER

295. __D__ Synthetic moisturizer.
A. DEPILATE B. BARBICIDE C. POROSITY D. MYRISTATE

296. __B__ A common disorder characterized by inflammation of the hair follicle.
A. GLABELLA B. FOLLICULITIS C. NERVE ENDINGS D. OVARIES

297. __C__ Medical term for eyelashes. Ingrown eyelashes should never be removed except under the supervision of a trained medical specialist
A. FACE LIFT B. CHELATING C. CILIA D. CORNROW

298. __A__ A liquid with a pH higher than 7.
A. ALKALI B. HAIR EXTENSIONS C. DEXAMETHOSONE D. CONGENITAL

299. __C__ Causes blackheads
A. BACTERIA B. BULBOUS NEEDLE C. COMEDOGENIC D. CORNROW

300. __B__ Proteins that catalyze (i.e. accelerate) and control the rates of chemical reactions.
A. ELECTRIC TWEEZER B. ENZYME C. CORNROW D. ACNE

From the words provided for each clue, provide the letter of the word which best matches the clue.

301. __A__ A hollow or pocket in the skin.
A. INDENTATION B. SPRITZ C. DISCOMFORT D. PALM ROLLING

302. __D__ The use of heat generated by electricity to change tissue from a fluid to a semi-solid, similar to cooking an egg.
A. BIOPSY B. TEA TREE OIL C. BULGE D. ELECTROCOAGULATION

303. __D__ Temporarily straightening the hair with a heated iron.
A. DOUBLE BLIND B. LASER C. COHERENT LIGHT D. THERMAL PROCESS

304. __B__ This is the complete loss of scalp hair often combined with the loss of eyebrows and eyelashes.
A. ELECTROCOAGULATION B. ALOPECIA TOTALIS C. ANAGEN D. ANTI ANDROGEN

305. __C__ The main structure of the hair shaft. The cortex determines the color and texture of the hair. The largest section of a single hair, containing the main bulk of the hair.
A. ACUPRESSURE B. BETAINE C. CORTEX D. ALLERGY

306. __A__ A basic color with added tone.
A. FASHION SHADE B. ROSACEA C. TOURMALINE D. DIAZOXIDE

307. __A__ A hair weave is usually a hairpiece with layered gaps made into it.
A. WEAVE B. DIAMETER C. EXFOLIATING D. DHT

308. __C__ A relatively rare condition in which the follicle is not straight.
A. SCLERODERMA B. FOLLICULITIS C. DISTORTED HAIR FOLLICLES D. PARFUM

309. __D__ Refers to unflattering warm tones in hair color created by chemicals or damage.
A. CLUB HAIR B. SUPEROXIDE DISMUTASE C. ACCENT COLOR D. BRASSY

310. __B__ Loss of hair, especially from the head, which either happens naturally or is caused by disease
A. ELECTRIC TWEEZER B. ALOPECIA C. STEAMING D. DIAZOXIDE

311. __A__ A whitening of the skin sometimes caused by some types of hair removal.
A. BLANCHING B. DILANTIN C. CONDITIONER D. BULGE

312. __B__ Caused by an absence of melanocytes, whitening of the skin. Vitiligo is a common medical complaint.
A. BIOPSY B. HYPOPIGMENTATION C. BETAINE D. BRUISE

313. __D__ Removal of hair on the surface of the skin. Examples include shaving or the use of depilatory creams.
A. TOPICALLY B. BIOPSY C. TRICHOPTILOSIS D. DEPILATE

314. __D__ A common ingredient in chemical depilatories.
A. TEA TREE OIL B. CHIGNON C. WEFTS D. AMMONIUM THIOGLYCOLATE

315. __D__ An over excitation of melanocytes, darkening of the skin. Can be seen as sun-induced freckles or melasma.
A. EFFICACY B. ALOPECIA NEUROTICA C. MEDULLA D. HYPERPIGMENTATION

316. __B__ The greying of hair. A pigment deficiency frequently seen in middle-aged people of either sex.
A. ANODE B. CANITIES C. INGROWN HAIR D. HUMECTANT

317. __A__ The combination of sweat and sebum that provides the skin's protective coating.
A. ACID MANTLE B. CHEMICAL DEPILATORIES C. LUVIMER D. WEFT

318. __D__ a light mist or spray, which when used as verb means to lightly spray your hair.
A. MEDULLA B. COHERENT LIGHT C. CICATRICIAL ALOPECIA D. SPRITZ

319. __B__ Products that reflect all the sun's rays, such as zinc oxide and titanium dioxide. They permit minimal tanning, and are a good choice for those who are sensitive to chemicals.
A. MEDULLA B. SUNBLOCK C. WHITE HAIR D. HUMIDITY

320. __C__ A device that removes hair by grasping hairs above the skin's surface with an electrified tweezers.
A. CATHODE B. GYNECOMASTIA C. ELECTRIC TWEEZER D. BARBA

321. __D__ Varies greatly by individual and body area. Electrolysis is generally considered most painful, followed by laser, plucking, waxing and finally pulse light sources.
A. TEMPORARY COLOR B. SUPEROXIDE DISMUTASE C. HYPERPIGMENTATION D. DISCOMFORT

322. __B__ An antiandrogen and is used in the treatment of androgen related disorders such as female pattern baldness and hirsutism.
A. PANTOTHENIC ACID B. SPRIONOLACTONE C. LASER D. ERYTHEMA

323. __D__ A disease of the skin and connective tissue that can cause hair loss over the affected areas.
A. CANITIES B. SELF TANNER C. EXFOLIATION D. SCLERODERMA

324. __C__ Baldness following a nervous disorder or injury to the nervous system.
A. Q SWITCH B. BLONDE HAIR C. ALOPECIA NEUROTICA D. WEAVE

325. __C__ A drug sometimes linked to excess hair growth.
A. EXFOLIATING B. ACETONE C. DIAZOXIDE D. CLARIFIER

326. __C__ The process of converting one enzyme to another.
A. COHERENT LIGHT B. HUMECTANT C. AMORTIZATION D. DEPILATORIES

327. **D** — The deepest layers of the skin, where blood vessels, lymph channels, nerve endings, sweat glands, sebaceous glands, fat cells, hair follicles and muscles are located.
A. ANTI ANDROGEN B. FASHION SHADE C. BRUISE D. DERMIS

328. **C** — A form of skin cancer.
A. NORWOOD SCALE B. PUNCH GRAFT C. MELANOMA D. A LINE BOB

329. **C** — Dark skin discoloration on sun-exposed areas of the face and neck. Young women with brownish skin tones are at greatest risk.
A. DISTORTED HAIR FOLLICLES B. EXFOLIATING C. MELASMA D. DIAZOXIDE

330. **C** — Protects the hair during its growth stage.
A. SPRITZ B. FASHION SHADE C. FOLLICLE SHEATH D. PARFUM

331. **C** — has been called a more extensive and severe form of dandruff.
A. CAPILLARIES B. ACUPUNCTURE C. SEBORRHOEIC DERMATITIS D. EXFOLIATING

332. **D** — Distribution of ashen and warm pigments, visual effect of gold or ash in the hair.
A. FOLLICULITIS B. ANTI ANDROGEN C. COHERENT LIGHT D. TONE

333. **B** — One of a group of hormonal steroid compounds that promote the development of female secondary sex characteristics.
A. BARBICIDE B. ESTROGEN C. EXFOLIATING D. FASHION SHADE

334. **B** — A common disorder characterized by inflammation of the hair follicle.
A. ALCOHOL B. FOLLICULITIS C. DEPILATE D. SERUM

335. **D** — The medical term for armpit, a common place for gonadal hair after puberty.
A. COHERENT LIGHT B. LANUGO HAIRS C. Q SWITCH D. AXILLA

336. **C** — A hair that does not break the surface of the skin, and grows back inward. Can be severe and cause inflammation, soreness and infection.
A. NORWOOD SCALE B. BRASSY C. INGROWN HAIR D. BRUISE

337. **B** — A clinical testing method in which neither patient nor doctor know what medication or procedure is being used.
A. ALOPECIA UNIVERSALIS B. DOUBLE BLIND C. WHITE HAIR D. INFUSION

338. **D** — Excessive development of the male breasts.
A. BLISTER B. ACID PERM C. EXFOLIATION D. GYNECOMASTIA

339. **B** — Usually a sharp, intense color used as a contrast or pickup for color scheme. It is used to add excitement to an overall effect
A. CATOGEN B. ACCENT COLOR C. OVERTREATMENT D. CATHODE

340. **D** — A drug sometimes linked to excess hair growth.
A. WEFTS B. FLY-AWAY HAIR C. SPRITZ D. DANAZOL

341. **D** — The space between the eyebrows.
A. HAIR GROWTH CYCLE B. ALLERGY C. SERUM D. GLABELLA

342. **B** — Hair loss which occurs in patches on the scalp.
A. NATURAL B. ALOPECIA AREATA C. ESTROGEN D. ALKALI

343. **C** — Excess hair can be increased or decreased by certain drugs. These drugs often affect hormonal levels.
A. EXFOLIATING B. ARRECTOR PILI C. DRUG TREATMENT D. CATHODE

344. __A__ A polymer on the basis of acrylic acid. Provides a thickening, gelling action and consistency regulator for cosmetic products.
A. CARBOMER B. CAPILLARIES C. INDENTATION D. WEFT

345. __B__ Tea made by steeping an herb's leaves or flowers in hot water.
A. ALOPECIA ANDROGENETIC B. INFUSION C. SUPEROXIDE DISMUTASE D. GLYCERIN

346. __C__ Laser at 755nm used for hair removal.
A. SELF TANNER B. JOULE C. ALEXANDRITE D. AMMONIUM THIOGLYCOLATE

347. __A__ Color.
A. PIGMENT B. AXILLA C. RELAXER D. AMPERE

348. __B__ Repels moisture or water; not readily removed with water.
A. ANDROGEN B. WATER RESISTANT C. CLUB HAIR D. CHILLTIP

349. __B__ The medulla is a central zone of cells usually only present in large thick hairs.
A. CARBOMER B. MEDULLA C. ANTISEPTIC D. FUSION

350. __A__ Thin hair that is charged by static and is a particular problem with straight looks as the hair just won't lie properly and can spoil your look.
A. FLY-AWAY HAIR B. SEMI PERMANENT C. PARFUM D. PERMANENT HAIR REDUCTION

351. __A__ Proteins that catalyze (i.e. accelerate) and control the rates of chemical reactions.
A. ENZYME B. PARFUM C. DISTORTED HAIR FOLLICLES D. BULGE

352. __D__ Having no pigment. Possible causes: Genetic. Vitamin B deficiency. Drugs for treatment of arthritis. Other health factors.
A. LUVIMER B. CLARIFIER C. ENERGY DENSITY D. WHITE HAIR

353. __C__ Natural substance that gives color (pigment) to hair and skin.
A. SEBACEOUS B. BULK HAIR C. MELANIN D. BRUISE

354. __D__ A unit of energy. Describes energy output for pulsed light based systems.
A. COLD SORE B. DHT C. TEA TREE OIL D. JOULE

355. __C__ Overly aggressive treatment to remove hair which leads to temporary or permanent skin damage.
A. ANODE B. TOPICALLY C. OVERTREATMENT D. EFFICACY

356. __B__ A drug sometimes linked to excess hair growth.
A. CHIGNON B. DILANTIN C. COLOGNE D. LASER

357. __C__ The resting stage of the hair cycle.
A. BULGE B. AXILLA C. CATOGEN D. CROWN

358. __A__ A point midway up the hair follicle which researchers suspect must be damaged to induce permanent hair removal
A. BULGE B. BLEND C. TELOGEN D. GLABELLA

359. __D__ To become shed or cast off.
A. ACUPUNCTURE B. RUBY C. ANTIBIOTIC D. SLOUGH

360. __D__ an extraction from the Melaleuca tree.
A. TERMINAL HAIRS B. FOLLICLES C. HIGHLIGHTS D. TEA TREE OIL

361. C — This is the growing phase of the hair cycle which lasts about seven years in a healthy person. The active stage in a hair growth cycle.
A. ACID PERM B. SCLERODERMA C. ANAGEN D. REMI

362. B — The subtle lifting of color in specific sections of hair.
A. HAIR INTEGRATION B. HIGHLIGHTS C. DIODE D. SCLERODERMA

363. D — A combination of water containing alcohol and fragrant oils. Not to be confused with a concentrated perfume.
A. HIRSUTISM B. DIAZOXIDE C. SPRIONOLACTONE D. COLOGNE

364. D — A clarifying shampoo is slightly stronger than everyday shampoos and is designed to remove products, hard water or chlorine residue that have built-up over time.
A. ANTI ANDROGEN B. BARBA C. CHIGNON D. CLARIFIER

365. C — Products so labeled may still contain small amounts of fragrances to mask the fatty odor of soap or other unpleasant odors.
A. CILIA B. DANAZOL C. FRAGRANCE FREE D. GREY HAIR

366. D — Commonly used laser for hair and tattoo removal.
A. EYELASHES B. AMPERE C. BLEND D. RUBY

367. C — A chemical process by which the hair is permanently straightened. New-growth areas have to be maintained via 'touch-ups' to continue the straightened pattern.
A. HAIR GROWTH CYCLE B. OVARIES C. RELAXER D. MELASMA

368. D — A recessive hereditary trait which presents as white hair due to defective melanin production thought to be caused by a mutation within genes.
A. FOLLICULITIS B. REMI C. ACCENT COLOR D. ALBINISM

369. D — A fibrous protein found in hair, nails, and skin.
A. GLABELLA B. MEDULLA C. SELF TANNER D. KERATIN

370. A — Flexible resin.
A. LUVIMER B. ANTIBIOTIC C. HUMECTANT D. OVERTREATMENT

371. C — Split ends.
A. CICATRICIAL ALOPECIA B. DEPILATORIES C. TRICHOPTILOSIS D. HAIR GROWTH CYCLE

372. D — Aids detangling. Provides volume, control and shine.
A. MELANOMA B. ACUPUNCTURE C. HAIR EXTENSIONS D. PANTHENOL

373. C — This drug is normally used to reduce sex drive in men who have an excessive sex drive. It is also prescribed to treat hirsutism and androgenic alopecia in women.
A. BETAINE B. LASER C. CYPROTERONE ACETATE D. ACCENT COLOR

374. C — Powder or cream preparations that dissolve hair above the surface of the skin. Some find these products very irritating to the skin.
A. SPRIONOLACTONE B. HAIR INTEGRATION C. CHEMICAL DEPILATORIES D. CARBOMER

375. D — Means to apply directly onto the scalp.
A. CICATRICIAL ALOPECIA B. NORWOOD SCALE C. OVERTREATMENT D. TOPICALLY

376. B — Produces permanent hair waves with curls that are actually softer than an alkaline perm. It also has a pH from 6.5 to 8.0.
A. AMPHOTERIC B. ACID PERM C. ANALGESIC D. ALOPECIA ANDROGENETIC

377. D Creates "Goose Bumps" when stimulated.
A. CLARIFIER B. PERMANENT HAIR REDUCTION C. HIGHLIGHTS D. ARRECTOR PILI

378. B Wefts are temporary hair extensions which are glued into your hair.
A. FACE LIFT B. WEFTS C. ANTISEPTIC D. AXILLA

379. B Increases wet and dry combability.
A. SLOUGH B. SILICONE C. DHT D. CALAMINE

380. D A semi-conductive material which mainly lets energy travel one direction and not the other.
A. ALOPECIA ADNATA B. ANDROGEN C. BULGE D. DIODE

381. B The process by which most synthetic fiber is curled at the factory.
A. CATOGEN B. STEAMING C. LASER D. SLOUGH

382. C A method of hair removal in which all hair in an area is removed at once, as opposed to thinning.
A. CHEMICAL DEPILATORIES B. CLUB HAIR C. CLEARING D. ACID MANTLE

383. C A disorder involving chronic inflammation of the cheeks, nose, chin, forehead or eyelids. It may cause redness, vascularity, swelling or hyperplasia.
A. CLUB HAIR B. ELECTROCOAGULATION C. ROSACEA D. TRACK

384. C Creamy hair product meant to be used after shampoo. Moisturizes and detangles hair.
A. ENERGY DENSITY B. TELOGEN C. CONDITIONER D. ACETONE

385. A A treatment consisting of short pulses of light sent out through an applicator that is gently pressed against the skin.
A. INTENSE PULSED LIGHT B. FOLLICLES C. EYELASHES D. ANDROGENS

386. A A pink ointment sometimes used to treat skin irritation
A. CALAMINE B. EFFICACY C. INDENTATION D. SPLIT ENDS

387. C Congenital baldness or baldness at birth.
A. PALM ROLLING B. ACID PERM C. ALOPECIA ADNATA D. ALOPECIA AREATA

388. D A mild nonirritating surfactant often used in shampoos; leaves hair manageable and is gentle enough for chemically treated hair.
A. CALAMINE B. BLONDE HAIR C. WEAVE D. AMPHOTERIC

389. B A modality of electrolysis which uses both thermolysis and galvanic methods.
A. TEXTURIZER B. BLEND C. ANALGESIC D. CARBOMER

390. C A chemical formed in the blood when the body uses fat instead of glucose (sugar) for energy.
A. AXILLA B. PIGMENT C. ACETONE D. BRUISE

391. C An amount of hair or fiber which is doubled over and MACHINE-SEWN along the top to create a long strand of hair.
A. ARRECTOR PILI B. EYELASHES C. WEFT D. AMPHOTERIC

392. C The most concentrated and most fragrant scent and therefore the most expensive.
A. CATHODE B. DRUG TREATMENT C. PARFUM D. BARBA

393. A Hair passes through a series of cycles known as Anagen (growing phase), Catagen (resting phase) and Telogen (dormant phase).
A. HAIR GROWTH CYCLE B. ANTIBIOTIC C. WATER RESISTANT D. CHILLTIP

394. __D__ Coarse, pigmented or non-pigmented, exist on the scalp and gain length at a rate of 1-2cm per month during a cyclical life of up to 10 years.
A. HENNA B. EFFICACY C. CATOGEN D. TERMINAL HAIRS

395. __D__ The temporary removal of hair.
A. CALAMINE B. CATHODE C. ALOPECIA ANDROGENETIC D. DEPILATION

396. __C__ A drug or preparation used to prevent and treat infection.
A. CLEARING B. ANDROGEN C. ANTIBIOTIC D. ACID MANTLE

397. __B__ Term used to measure the output energy for Lasers and Pulsed Light Sources.
A. SUNBLOCK B. ENERGY DENSITY C. CROWN D. INGROWN HAIR

398. __D__ A bodily reaction to an irritant. Skin allergies can be exacerbated by solutions put on the skin.
A. AUTOCLAVE B. TERMINAL HAIRS C. CHILLTIP D. ALLERGY

399. __B__ A positive electrode.
A. RUBY B. ANODE C. WEFT D. SILICONE

400. __D__ A negative electrode in a cell or circuit.
A. DISTORTED HAIR FOLLICLES B. BLANCHING C. LUVIMER D. CATHODE

Matching
Provide the word that best matches each clue.

1. _____ A protein that holds all connective tissue together under the skin.

2. _____ These solutions are used as exfoliants. They can help reduce ingrown hairs and improve the look of skin.

3. _____ Contact dermatitis, it's a mild inflammation of the skin.

4. _____ allows you to only pay attention to a particular area or panel of hair.

5. _____ The pigmented area surrounding the nipple. A very common area for hair growth.

6. _____ Also known as eczema.

7. _____ An organism responsible for infection.

8. _____ A collection of fat cells resulting from poor lymphatic drainage, fluid retention, poor circulation, not drinking enough water, a sedentary lifestyle and hormones.

9. _____ The classic look of the 50s and 60s; the style was short and straight but blow-dried and curled under.

10. _____ Protective hairs on the eyelid. Some people get ingrown hairs here, which should only be treated under a physician's care, preferably an ophthalmologist.

11. _____ Positively charges the hair to provide manageability and reduces static.

12. _____ To become shed or cast off.

13. _____ A method of relieving pain by pressing down on an area of the body.

14. _____ A group of glands which maintain the body's internal environment through the production of hormones.

15. _____ A rounded, thick, tightly curled hair style.

16. _____ An area of tissue erosion. They are always depressed and are due to irritation. They may become infected and inflamed as they grow.

17. _____ Used to add volume or length to your hair by bonding synthetic or real hair at your roots.

18. _____ A substance used to relieve pain.

19. _____ An inflammation of the skin, a result of over production of oil and bacteria.

20. _____ A term meaning how well or effectively a cosmetic device works.

21. _____ A sophisticated, elegant up style, where long hair is twisted (either in a roll or knot) and pinned from the nape of neck.

22. _____ A liquid, usually corrosive with a pH lower than 7, opposite of an alkali.

23. _____ A measurement across the width of the hair.

24. _____ Small blood vessels which connect the arteries and veins that feed the hair.

25. _____ A measurement of electrical current.

A. EFFICACY	B. ATOPIC DERMATITIS	C. HAIR EXTENSIONS
D. SLOUGH	E. BACTERIA	F. AMPERE
G. ACUPRESSURE	H. DIAMETER	I. CHIGNON
J. AREOLA	K. AFRO HAIRSTYLE	L. CATIONIC POLYMER
M. ACID	N. EYELASHES	O. COLLAGEN
P. CAPILLARIES	Q. ENDOCRINE SYSTEM	R. ANALGESIC
S. BOB	T. CELLULITE	U. ULCER
V. SECTIONING	W. ALPHA HYDROXY ACID	X. ECZEMA
Y. ACNE		

Provide the word that best matches each clue.

26. _____ A female hormone sometimes linked to increased hair growth.

27. _____ Brand name of sanitizer used to disinfect salon implements.

28. _____ Fine, transparent nylon or silk mesh with hairs individually hand-knotted into the mesh. Allows the hair to fall naturally and gives more versatility in styling.

29. _____ A technique under development which could make an unlimited crop of donor hair available for transplanting.

30. _____ A non- shiny surface that absorbs light; a dead or dull finish.

31. _____ A polymer on the basis of acrylic acid. Provides a thickening, gelling action and consistency regulator for cosmetic products.

32. _____ part of the structure of the hair and also form a protective barrier. They are composed of EFA's amongst other complicated scientific things.

33. _____ The process by which blood clots, and can be induced by heat or chemicals.

34. _____ An emollient cream used to hydrate the skin.

35. _____ The term used to describe any hairpiece with a full cap which covers the hair on the head, or the entire area where hair normally grows, as a substitute for hair.

36. _____ Light that stays focused, a property of lasers.

37. _____ Makes smooth or slippery by using oil to overcome friction.

38. _____ A chemical agent that prevent the growth of bacteria.

39. _____ A natural conditioning substance for example: from molasses or sugar beet.

40. _____ Area at the top of the head.

41. _____ Cells within the extracellular matrix that produce new collagen molecules when stimulated.

42. _____ A small opening of the sweat glands of the skin.

43. _____ Commonly used laser for hair and tattoo removal.

44. _____ A device that removes hair by grasping hairs above the skin's surface with an electrified tweezers.

45. _____ Tiny hair-like blood vessels, some of which carry nutrient to the hair growth matrix.

46. _____ A bristle commonly used in natural bristle brushes.

47. _____ A section of skin tissue removed for clinical observation.

48. _____ An antiandrogen and is used in the treatment of androgen related disorders such as female pattern baldness and hirsutism.

49. _____ A vegetable dye made from its leaves and stems into a powder. Traditionally, it imparts a reddish cast to the hair by coating it.

50. _____ The medical term for armpit, a common place for gonadal hair after puberty.

A. PORE
B. BARBICIDE
C. FIBROBLASTS
D. ESTROGEN
E. HENNA
F. MATTE
G. RUBY
H. CAPILLARIES
I. CROWN
J. AXILLA
K. COHERENT LIGHT
L. WIG
M. MOISTURIZER
N. BOAR BRISTLE
O. ANTISEPTIC
P. SPRIONOLACTONE
Q. LIPID LAYER
R. BETAINE
S. ELECTRIC TWEEZER
T. LUBRICATES
U. MONOFILAMENT
V. COAGULATION
W. BIOPSY
X. HAIR CLONING

Y. CARBOMER

Provide the word that best matches each clue.

51. _____ The type of electricity that comes from a wall outlet (AC), as opposed to direct current (DC).

52. _____ The oily secretion of the sebaceous glands of the scalp, composed of keratin, fat or cellular debris.

53. _____ A geometric bob with a straight fringe, so called because of the resemblance to the capital A, with it's horizontal line, the fringe and its legs the hair passing your ears.

54. _____ Protective hairs on the eyelid. Some people get ingrown hairs here, which should only be treated under a physician's care, preferably an ophthalmologist.

55. _____ The amount of moisture available in the air.

56. _____ Commonly used laser for hair and tattoo removal.

57. _____ A smoothing product to stop your hair from frizzing, keeping it smooth and straight. You'll be able to find a serum that is specifically designed to your own hair type.

58. _____ Clinic based method of reducing the appearance of cellulite.

59. _____ A deep cleansing process which strips the hair lightly before a chemical service. Also known as clarifying.

60. _____ The active stage in a hair growth cycle.

61. _____ The use of heat generated by electricity to change tissue from a fluid to a semi-solid, similar to cooking an egg.

62. _____ The substructure that is responsible for the spectral selective absorption of electromagnetic radiation.

63. _____ A disorder involving chronic inflammation of the cheeks, nose, chin, forehead or eyelids. It may cause redness, vascularity, swelling or hyperplasia.

64. _____ An organism responsible for infection.

65. _____ The darkness or lightness of a color.

66. _____ Also known as eczema.

67. _____ A natural conditioning substance for example: from molasses or sugar beet.

68. _____ Esters found in sunscreen and cosmetic products that can make skin sensitive.

69. _____ This drug is normally used to reduce sex drive in men who have an excessive sex drive. It is also prescribed to treat hirsutism and androgenic alopecia in women.

70. _____ A method of relieving pain by inserting needles into the skin.

71. _____ A hairspray with the firmest hold used to maintain style of hard to hold hair.

72. _____ Overly aggressive treatment to remove hair which leads to temporary or permanent skin damage.

73. _____ Term used to measure the output energy, for Lasers and Pulsed Light Sources that is delivered to tissue.

74. _____ a crystal silicate mineral compounded with elements such as aluminum, iron, magnesium, sodium, lithium, or potassium.

75. _____ A measurement of electrical current.

A. CHELATING	B. FREEZING SPRAY	C. OVERTREATMENT
D. EYELASHES	E. SERUM	F. FLUENCE
G. RUBY	H. ANAGEN CYCLE	I. CHROMOPHORE
J. A LINE BOB	K. TOURMALINE	L. AMPERE
M. ELECTROCOAGULATION	N. ALTERNATING CURRENT	O. CELLULITE REDUCTION
P. HUMIDITY	Q. ATOPIC DERMATITIS	R. BACTERIA
S. ROSACEA	T. BETAINE	U. CYPROTERONE ACETATE
V. DEPTH	W. PABA	X. SEBUM
Y. ACUPUNCTURE		

Provide the word that best matches each clue.

76. _____ A product which oxidizes artificial color pigment.

77. _____ A patented contact cooling device used in laser hair removal.

78. _____ A cosmetic procedure used to smooth skin and reduce scars.

79. _____ The type of electricity that comes from a wall outlet (AC), as opposed to direct current (DC).

80. _____ Protects the hair during its growth stage.

81. _____ A method of hair removal in which all hair in an area is removed at once, as opposed to thinning.

82. _____ A chemical process by which the hair is permanently straightened. New-growth areas have to be maintained via 'touch-ups' to continue the straightened pattern.

83. _____ Refers to a congenital absence of pigment in a lock of hairs which will show as grey or white.

84. _____ Relating to the skin.

85. _____ A natural herb that has been shown to be an effective anti-androgen.

86. _____ The pigmented area surrounding the nipple. A very common area for hair growth.

87. _____ A unit of energy. Describes energy output for pulsed light based systems.

88. _____ A non-living hair in the last stages of the hair growth cycle, it is detached from the follicle but has not yet shed.

89. _____ Hair shafts are produced by follicles within the skin in all but few locations

90. _____ The small area at the base of the hair root which provides nutrients needed for growth.

91. _____ The hair's ability to stretch without breaking and then return to its original shape.

92. _____ The process of converting one enzyme to another.

93. _____ The deepest layers of the skin, where blood vessels, lymph channels, nerve endings, sweat glands, sebaceous glands, fat cells, hair follicles and muscles are located.

94. _____ Chronic skin inflammation characterized by frequent episodes of redness, itching and thick, dry scales.

95. _____ A drug sometimes linked to excess hair growth.

96. _____ An area of tissue erosion. They are always depressed and are due to irritation. They may become infected and inflamed as they grow.

97. _____ Distribution of ashen and warm pigments, visual effect of gold or ash in the hair.

98. _____ Treatments, especially IPL, where the follicle is disabled by the light energy making it unable to support any more hair growth.

99. _____ A device that removes hair by grasping hairs above the skin's surface with an electrified tweezers.

100. _____ A group of glands which maintain the body's internal environment through the production of hormones.

A. CHILLTIP
B. PERMANENT HAIR REDUCTION
C. CLEARING
D. ELECTRIC TWEEZER
E. DEVELOPER
F. AREOLA
G. PAPILLA
H. TELOGEN EFFLUVIUM
I. FOLLICLE SHEATH
J. DILANTIN
K. JOULE
L. ALTERNATING CURRENT
M. RELAXER
N. SAW PALMETTO
O. AMORTIZATION
P. DERMIS
Q. ENDOCRINE SYSTEM
R. PSORIASIS
S. TONE
T. LEUCOTRICHIA
U. DERMABRASION
V. CLUB HAIR
W. ELASTICITY
X. CUTANEOUS
Y. ULCER

Provide the word that best matches each clue.

101. _____ Pertaining to a drug that is produced for profit.

102. _____ Overly aggressive treatment to remove hair which leads to temporary or permanent skin damage.

103. _____ A small fluid-filled bubble on the skin caused by heat from over treatment with certain types of hair removal.

104. _____ allows you to only pay attention to a particular area or panel of hair.

105. _____ The soft area between the rib cage and the pubic area. A common area for excess hair, often in a line from the belly button to the pubic hair.

106. _____ A hollow or pocket in the skin.

107. _____ Esters found in sunscreen and cosmetic products that can make skin sensitive.

108. _____ The practice of hair removal through the use of electrified needles, invented in the 1870's.

109. _____ The root of a hair, so named because it's wider at the base.

110. _____ A geometric bob with a straight fringe, so called because of the resemblance to the capital A, with it's horizontal line, the fringe and its legs the hair passing your ears.

111. _____ A relatively rare condition which makes certain hair removal methods more difficult and can lead to ingrown hairs.

112. _____ The classic look of the 50s and 60s; the style was short and straight but blow-dried and curled under.

113. _____ Phenol derivatives used in combination with other chemicals in permanent (two step) hair dyes.

114. _____ Commonly used laser for hair and tattoo removal.

115. _____ A type of raised darkened scar, more common with dark skin. Due to a defect in the healing process.

116. _____ Excess hair can be increased or decreased by certain drugs. These drugs often affect hormonal levels.

117. _____ The removal of hair below the skin's surface.

118. _____ A drug or product that limited the effects of androgens (male hormones).

119. _____ Receptors which respond to touch, pain, pressure, heat and cold.

120. _____ A common ingredient in chemical depilatories.

121. _____ To weave strands of hair together. On the scalp braiding is used to form a base or track to sew on a commercial weft.

122. _____ Powder or cream preparations that dissolve hair above the surface of the skin. Some find these products very irritating to the skin.

123. _____ A deep cleansing process which strips the hair lightly before a chemical service. Also known as clarifying.

124. _____ Dried fluid that seeps from skin in some clients following hair removal such as laser, electrolysis, and depilatories.

125. _____ A bodily reaction to an irritant. Skin allergies can be exacerbated by solutions put on the skin.

A. SECTIONING
C. ABDOMEN
E. BLISTER
G. DRUG TREATMENT
I. PABA
K. A LINE BOB
M. ELECTROLOGY
O. INDENTATION
Q. EPILATION
S. NERVE ENDINGS
U. CHEMICAL DEPILATORIES
W. BRAID
Y. CURVED FOLLICLES

B. ALLERGY
D. BULB
F. RUBY
H. BOB
J. AMINOPHENOLS
L. PROPRIETARY
N. AMMONIUM THIOGLYCOLATE
P. CRUSTING
R. KELOIDS
T. OVERTREATMENT
V. CHELATING
X. ANTI ANDROGEN

Provide the word that best matches each clue.

126. _____ The subtle lifting of color in specific sections of hair.

127. _____ A collection of fat cells resulting from poor lymphatic drainage, fluid retention, poor circulation, not drinking enough water, a sedentary lifestyle and hormones.

128. _____ A small rough spot on skin chronically exposed to the sun, occurs most frequently in fair skinned people.

129. _____ A substance with a pH greater than 7; non acidic.

130. _____ The process of scraping or wearing hair away. Causing partial or complete absence of hair from areas.

131. _____ Term used to measure the output energy for Lasers and Pulsed Light Sources.

132. _____ Is sometimes linked to excess hair growth, especially in the extremely obese and extremely anorexic.

133. _____ A machine used to sterilize medical utensils and some hair removal devices.

134. _____ A small hair graft usually consisting of between three to ten hair roots.

135. _____ Varies greatly by individual and body area. Electrolysis is generally considered most painful, followed by laser, plucking, waxing and finally pulse light sources.

136. _____ Alopecia senilis is baldness due to old age.

137. _____ Jelly like material formed by the coagulation of a liquid. Semi-solid emulsion that liquefies when applied to the skin.

138. _____ A viral infection that appears around the mouth. Hair removal, especially electrolysis and lasers, should not be performed around visible cold sores.

139. _____ A chemical process by which the hair is permanently straightened. New-growth areas have to be maintained via 'touch-ups' to continue the straightened pattern.

140. _____ The forcing of substances into the skin from a positive to a negative pole. It is sometimes used after electrolysis to firm skin and reduce redness.

141. _____ A vegetable dye made from its leaves and stems into a powder. Traditionally, it imparts a reddish cast to the hair by coating it.

142. _____ Overly aggressive treatment to remove hair which leads to temporary or permanent skin damage.

143. _____ A small temporary scab that occurs sometimes after electrolysis, especially after overtreatment.

144. _____ Metabolising stubborn fat deposits, typically in the lower body, using methods such as Eporex mesotherapy.

145. _____ Are usually shed during the 7th month of fetal life following primary folliculo-genesis.

146. _____ Fatty or greasy, usually referring to the oil-secreting glans of the scalp.

147. _____ Form a protective layer which covers the shaft of hair. If your hair is colored or bleached they can spread out, split or become bloated due to over processing.

148. _____ Is not as visible, but it's also harder to treat. Lasers have limited effects on it because of its lack of pigment, and it is difficult to see against the skin.

149. _____ a light mist or spray, which when used as verb means to lightly spray your hair.

150. _____ A modern term used to describe hair weaving.

A. AUTOCLAVE   B. CATAPHORESIS

C. SEBACEOUS
E. SPRITZ
G. ABRASION
I. HAIR INTEGRATION
K. CELLULITE
M. ALOPECIA SENILIS
O. CUTICLES
Q. MINI GRAFT
S. BLONDE HAIR
U. DIET
W. HIGHLIGHTS
Y. TARGETED FAT REDUCTION

D. RELAXER
F. ESCHAR
H. HENNA
J. LANUGO HAIRS
L. ALKALINE
N. ENERGY DENSITY
P. DISCOMFORT
R. OVERTREATMENT
T. GEL
V. ACTINIC KERATOSIS
X. COLD SORE

Provide the word that best matches each clue.

151. _____ Hair loss due to inflammation of hair follicles.

152. _____ A natural herb that has been shown to be an effective anti-androgen.

153. _____ Substances used to dissolve hair above the skin's surface.

154. _____ The process by which most synthetic fiber is curled at the factory.

155. _____ A discoloration of skin from blood, sometimes caused by electrolysis, plucking, or waxing. Also known as Purpura.

156. _____ A technique under development which could make an unlimited crop of donor hair available for transplanting.

157. _____ The generic name of the brand name drug Rogaine. The first drug to be approved by the FDA for the treatment of androgenetic alopecia.

158. _____ Cells within the extracellular matrix that produce new collagen molecules when stimulated.

159. _____ The process of attaching hair wefts without braids. The links are sewn on to the wefted hair. The user's natural hair is pulled through and locked secure.

160. _____ In hair removal, a conductor through which electricity enters or leaves the body. An electrolysis needle is an electrode.

161. _____ A liquid with a pH higher than 7.

162. _____ Completely changing the natural color of the hair.

163. _____ The enzyme superoxide, catalyzes the dis-mutation of superoxide into oxygen and hydrogen peroxide.

164. _____ A device that removes hair by grasping hairs above the skin's surface with an electrified tweezers.

165. _____ allows you to only pay attention to a particular area or panel of hair.

166. _____ The removal of dead skin cells to reveal softer skin underneath.

167. _____ The practice of hair removal through the use of electrified needles, invented in the 1870's.

168. _____ A process by which a hair piece is attached to existing hair on the head through braiding or a weaving process.

169. _____ Small clumps of coagulated melanin.

170. _____ A medical term for blackheads.

171. _____ The body transformation of food into energy.

172. _____ A liquid, usually corrosive with a pH lower than 7, opposite of an alkali.

173. _____ An amount of hair or fiber which is doubled over and MACHINE-SEWN along the top to create a long strand of hair.

174. _____ Products that reflect all the sun's rays, such as zinc oxide and titanium dioxide. They permit minimal tanning, and are a good choice for those who are sensitive to chemicals.

175. _____ A gentle humectant, lather booster, and emulsifier. In hair products, it is used to smooth and soften the hair cuticle.

A. COMEDONES
B. ALKALI
C. BRUISE
D. MICRO LINKING TECHNIQUE
E. FRECKLES
F. MINOXIDIL
G. SAW PALMETTO
H. FIBROBLASTS
I. PERMANENTLY
J. WEFT
K. DEPILATORIES
L. EXFOLIATION
M. SUPEROXIDE DISMUTASE
N. SECTIONING
O. HAIR CLONING
P. ELECTRODE
Q. SUNBLOCK
R. STEAMING
S. ACID
T. ALOPECIA FOLLICULARIS
U. METABOLISM
V. CETYL ALCOHOL
W. ELECTROLOGY
X. ELECTRIC TWEEZER

Y. HAIR WEAVING

Provide the word that best matches each clue.

176. _____ Causes blackheads

177. _____ The small area at the base of the hair root which provides nutrients needed for growth.

178. _____ The surgical removal of one or both testicles or ovaries.

179. _____ A classification for stronger, thicker types of hair.

180. _____ A method in which hair is maintained or tightened using a tool.

181. _____ Products that reflect all the sun's rays, such as zinc oxide and titanium dioxide. They permit minimal tanning, and are a good choice for those who are sensitive to chemicals.

182. _____ A protein that holds all connective tissue together under the skin.

183. _____ Is sometimes linked to excess hair growth, especially in the extremely obese and extremely anorexic.

184. _____ A clinical testing method in which neither patient nor doctor know what medication or procedure is being used.

185. _____ Variety of skin conditions mainly the result of excess melanin. Commonly known as Café au Lait stains, birthmarks, age spots and freckles.

186. _____ Refers to human hair (usually Indian in origin) which has been harvested from root to end, with all of the cuticle going in the same direction.

187. _____ A type of raised darkened scar, more common with dark skin. Due to a defect in the healing process.

188. _____ a crystal silicate mineral compounded with elements such as aluminum, iron, magnesium, sodium, lithium, or potassium.

189. _____ The hard outer protective layer of the hair. Impart sheen to the hair.

190. _____ Clinic based method of reducing the appearance of cellulite.

191. _____ A natural solvent in oils and creams. It acidifies products.

192. _____ Used to measure acidity in cosmetic preparations.

193. _____ When your skin is damaged by exposure to the UVA and UVB rays of the sun, its reaction is to produce more melanin as an attempt to protect itself against further damage.

194. _____ A cosmetic procedure used to smooth skin and reduce scars.

195. _____ Also known as eczema.

196. _____ The temporary removal of hair.

197. _____ A medical term for the redness that sometimes follows hair removal and skin rejuvenation.

198. _____ A device that produces short intense bursts of energy from a laser.

199. _____ An anti-inflammatory sometimes linked to hair growth when taken internally.

200. _____ Pertaining to a drug that is produced for profit.

A. CORTISONE
B. ATOPIC DERMATITIS
C. CELLULITE REDUCTION
D. Q SWITCH
E. CUTICLE
F. CASTRATION
G. ERYTHEMA
H. DIET
I. COMEDOGENIC
J. TAN
K. DERMABRASION
L. KELOIDS
M. PH
N. PAPILLA
O. PROPRIETARY
P. SUNBLOCK
Q. COARSE
R. DOUBLE BLIND
S. TOURMALINE
T. REMI
U. DEPILATION
V. COLLAGEN
W. APPLE CIDER VINEGAR
X. INTERLOCKING
Y. PIGMENTED LESION

Provide the word that best matches each clue.

201. _____ Hair that has lost its pigment.

202. _____ A natural herb that has been shown to be an effective anti-androgen.

203. _____ In hair removal, a conductor through which electricity enters or leaves the body. An electrolysis needle is an electrode.

204. _____ Distribution of ashen and warm pigments, visual effect of gold or ash in the hair.

205. _____ Used in many products for blonde hair to enhance color.

206. _____ A whitening of the skin sometimes caused by some types of hair removal.

207. _____ Allows some light to pass through.

208. _____ Increases wet and dry combability.

209. _____ A Synthetic moisturizer.

210. _____ A disease where the body improperly produces insulin, sometimes linked to excess hair growth.

211. _____ A substance, such as a vitamin, which provides elements for the ongoing functioning of the body's metabolic processes.

212. _____ A unit of energy. Describes energy output for pulsed light based systems.

213. _____ A combination of water containing alcohol and fragrant oils. Not to be confused with a concentrated perfume.

214. _____ Flexible resin.

215. _____ The surgical removal of one or both testicles or ovaries.

216. _____ Discolored skin that should be examined and approved by a physician before hair removal.

217. _____ Also called vitamin B5 (a B vitamin), is a water-soluble vitamin required to sustain life (essential nutrient).

218. _____ The combination of sweat and sebum that provides the skin's protective coating.

219. _____ A fibrous protein found in hair, nails, and skin.

220. _____ The darkness or lightness of a color.

221. _____ A predominantly male hormone which promotes the development of male characteristics.

222. _____ The forehead, nose and chin areas, which tend to be oilier than the cheeks.

223. _____ A hollow or pocket in the skin.

224. _____ This is the common name for male or female pattern baldness which depends on the genetic predisposition of the hair follicles and the levels of DHT in the body.

225. _____ A method of relieving pain by inserting needles into the skin.

A. T ZONE   B. NUTRIENT   C. ALOPECIA ANDROGENETIC

D. PANTOTHENIC ACID
E. INDENTATION
F. GREY HAIR
G. ISOPROPYL LANOLATE
H. COLOGNE
I. LUVIMER
J. ACUPUNCTURE
K. TRANSLUCENT
L. BLANCHING
M. TONE
N. SAW PALMETTO
O. KERATIN
P. BIRTHMARKS
Q. ACID MANTLE
R. ELECTRODE
S. JOULE
T. DIABETES
U. DEPTH
V. CASTRATION
W. CHAMOMILE
X. TESTOSTERONE
Y. SILICONE

Provide the word that best matches each clue.

226. _____ A liquid with a pH higher than 7.

227. _____ Drugs that sometimes cause increased hair growth.

228. _____ Area at the top of the head.

229. _____ An inflammation of the skin, a result of over production of oil and bacteria.

230. _____ an extraction from the Melaleuca tree.

231. _____ The most concentrated and most fragrant scent and therefore the most expensive.

232. _____ A pink ointment sometimes used to treat skin irritation

233. _____ In women, a major source of female hormones. Certain conditions involving the ovaries can lead to excess hair growth, especially polycystic ovary syndrome (PCOS).

234. _____ Combating the signs of ageing using the latest innovative, non-invasive treatments that give you visibly younger, healthy, radiant skin.

235. _____ Clinic based method of reducing the appearance of cellulite.

236. _____ Makes smooth or slippery by using oil to overcome friction.

237. _____ Cleansing agent that is a sodium or potassium salt of animal or vegetable fat.

238. _____ Is not as visible, but it's also harder to treat. Lasers have limited effects on it because of its lack of pigment, and it is difficult to see against the skin.

239. _____ In hair removal, the practice of epilation with electrified needles.

240. _D. FIBROBLASTS_ — Cells within the extracellular matrix that produce new collagen molecules when stimulated.

241. _M. NEUTRALISE_ — To cancel or reduce effect.

242. _B. MICRO LINKING TECHNIQUE_ — The process of attaching hair wefts without braids. The links are sewn on to the wefted hair. The user's natural hair is pulled through and locked secure.

243. _H. CATOGEN_ — The resting stage of the hair cycle.

244. _T. ANDROGEN_ — Hormone that causes masculine characteristics and affects hair growth.

245. _L. HEATCLAMPS_ — A heat gun that is used to seal synthetic hair. Used for creating warlocks and other styles.

246. _S. MINOXIDIL_ — The generic name of the brand name drug Rogaine. The first drug to be approved by the FDA for the treatment of androgenetic alopecia.

247. _X. CLONE_ — A group of genetically identical cells or organisms derived from a single common cell.

248. _F. HYDRATE_ — To add moisture to the skin.

249. _U. ANTI ANDROGEN_ — A drug or product that limited the effects of androgens (male hormones).

250. _N. EXFOLIATING_ — A process of removing the top dead skin layers to reveal healthier, newer skin underneath.

A. LUBRICATES	B. MICRO LINKING TECHNIQUE
C. BLONDE HAIR	D. FIBROBLASTS
E. ALKALI	F. HYDRATE
G. CROWN	H. CATOGEN
I. TEA TREE OIL	J. ELECTROLYSIS
K. OVARIES	L. HEATCLAMPS
M. NEUTRALISE	N. EXFOLIATING
O. SOAP	P. SKIN REJUVENATION
Q. ACNE	R. CALAMINE
S. MINOXIDIL	T. ANDROGEN
U. ANTI ANDROGEN	V. CELLULITE REDUCTION
W. BIRTH CONTROL	X. CLONE
Y. PARFUM	

Provide the word that best matches each clue.

251. _____ To weave strands of hair together. On the scalp braiding is used to form a base or track to sew on a commercial weft.

252. _____ Probably the most difficult type of skin from which to remove hair.

253. _____ Pertaining to a substance, product or drug that is not protected by trademark. It is identical in chemical composition but not necessarily equivalent in therapeutic effect.

254. _____ Used to add volume or length to your hair by bonding synthetic or real hair at your roots.

255. _____ Flaking scalp due to excessive cell production.

256. _____ The process of converting one enzyme to another.

257. _____ Protective hairs on the eyelid. Some people get ingrown hairs here, which should only be treated under a physician's care, preferably an ophthalmologist.

258. _____ The process of attaching small pieces of human hair with a special adhesive and a thermal gun.

259. _____ Often referred to as male hormones.

260. _____ Used to remove the moisture from wet hair.

261. _____ Selectively targeting dermal structures with light energy, without causing damage to surrounding tissue.

262. _____ The medulla is a central zone of cells usually only present in large thick hairs.

263. _____ A disease caused by a tumor on the adrenal gland, which can cause excess hair growth.

264. _____ A small hair graft usually consisting of between three to ten hair roots.

265. _____ A thickening agent or binding agent added to products to change their physical composition (joins two or more ingredients together).

266. _____ Color.

267. _____ A measurement across the width of the hair.

268. _____ A small fluid-filled bubble on the skin caused by heat from over treatment with certain types of hair removal.

269. _____ The pigmented area surrounding the nipple. A very common area for hair growth.

270. _____ This form of hair loss is caused by pulling out one's own hair, usually without realizing it.

271. _____ The small area at the base of the hair root which provides nutrients needed for growth.

272. _____ A liquid with a pH higher than 7.

273. _____ Aids detangling. Provides volume, control and shine.

274. _____ Thin hair that is charged by static and is a particular problem with straight looks as the hair just won't lie properly and can spoil your look.

275. _____ Parting or a cornrow that establishes the placement pattern of wefts or strand additions.

A. EYELASHES
B. PIGMENT
C. ROUGH BLOW DRY
D. FLY-AWAY HAIR
E. PAPILLA
F. ANDROGENS
G. AREOLA
H. MINI GRAFT
I. TRACK
J. EMULSIFIER
K. CUSHING SYNDROME
L. BLACK SKIN
M. FUSION
N. SELECTIVE PHOTOTHERMOLYSIS
O. DIAMETER
P. DANDRUFF
Q. BLISTER
R. MEDULLA
S. HAIR EXTENSIONS
T. AMORTIZATION
U. ALKALI
V. BRAID
W. GENERIC
X. PANTHENOL
Y. TRICHOTILLOMANIA

Provide the word that best matches each clue.

276. _____ Pertains to the skin.

277. _____ A trademark for a Japanese-made synthetic fiber which is used extensively in the manufacture of wigs and hairpieces

278. _____ The practice of hair removal through the use of electrified needles, invented in the 1870's.

279. _____ A unit of energy. Describes energy output for pulsed light based systems.

280. _____ has been called a more extensive and severe form of dandruff.

281. _____ Detangling aid which conditions, protects against humidity, and adds shine.

282. _____ A hollow or pocket in the skin.

283. _____ One of a group of hormonal steroid compounds that promote the development of female secondary sex characteristics.

284. _____ The resting stage of the hair cycle.

285. _____ A plant extract that has been used to treat swelling, soreness and bruising.

286. _____ The hair follicle is the tiny blub under your scalp from which the hair grows.

287. _____ Also known as eczema.

288. _____ The old fashioned way of removing grafts for hair transplants, usually carried out using an instrument called a trephine.

289. _____ A method used to disguise (not remove) hair by lightening its color.

290. _____ A hairspray with medium hold used on a finished style to maintain its shape and hold.

291. _____ A measurement of electrical current.

292. _____ Protects the hair during its growth stage.

293. _____ The process of attaching small pieces of human hair with a special adhesive and a thermal gun.

294. _____ In hair removal, a conductor through which electricity enters or leaves the body. An electrolysis needle is an electrode.

295. _____ A substance with a pH greater than 7; non acidic.

296. _____ The process of converting one enzyme to another.

297. _____ A color which lasts from 6 - 8 shampoos.

298. _____ This is the complete loss of scalp hair often combined with the loss of eyebrows and eyelashes.

299. _____ The subtle lifting of color in specific sections of hair.

300. _____ The root of a hair, so named because it's wider at the base.

A. ALKALINE	B. BLEACH	C. SEMI PERMANENT
D. SEBORRHOEIC DERMATITIS	E. KANEKALON	F. INDENTATION
G. ARNICA	H. FOLLICLE SHEATH	I. HIGHLIGHTS
J. AMPERE	K. ALOPECIA TOTALIS	L. ELECTROLOGY
M. JOULE	N. FOLLICLES	O. FINISHING SPRAY
P. DIMETHICONE	Q. ESTROGEN	R. ELECTRODE
S. PUNCH GRAFT	T. ATOPIC DERMATITIS	U. FUSION
V. SUBCUTANEOUS	W. AMORTIZATION	X. CATOGEN
Y. BULB		

Provide the word that best matches each clue.

301. _____ The resting phase in the hair cycle.

302. _____ A group of glands which maintain the body's internal environment through the production of hormones.

303. _____ The term used to describe getting a 'hair cut' and having your new hairpiece styled for the first time when you first receive it.

304. _____ A natural conditioning substance for example: from molasses or sugar beet.

305. _____ A clarifying shampoo is slightly stronger than everyday shampoos and is designed to remove products, hard water or chlorine residue that have built-up over time.

306. _____ A type of clogged pore in the skin with a visible black plug.

307. _____ The process of converting one enzyme to another.

308. _____ A thickening agent or binding agent added to products to change their physical composition (joins two or more ingredients together).

309. _____ The bald or thinning area where hair grafts or plugs a transplanted.

310. _____ To become shed or cast off.

311. _____ Used to remove the moisture from wet hair.

312. _____ A viral infection that appears around the mouth. Hair removal, especially electrolysis and lasers, should not be performed around visible cold sores.

313. _____ Creates "Goose Bumps" when stimulated.

314. _____ Ability to absorb moisture.

315. _____ A chemical process by which the hair is permanently straightened. New-growth areas have to be maintained via 'touch-ups' to continue the straightened pattern.

316. _____ The root of a hair, so named because it's wider at the base.

317. _____ a male hormone that is suggested to be the main cause for the miniaturization of the hair follicle and for hair loss.

318. _____ The medical term for armpit, a common place for gonadal hair after puberty.

319. _____ A vegetable dye made from its leaves and stems into a powder. Traditionally, it imparts a reddish cast to the hair by coating it.

320. _____ This is the growing phase of the hair cycle which lasts about seven years in a healthy person. The active stage in a hair growth cycle.

321. _____ A small temporary scab that occurs sometimes after electrolysis, especially after overtreatment.

322. _____ Refers to a congenital absence of pigment in a lock of hairs which will show as grey or white.

323. _____ Also known as eczema.

324. _____ Having no pigment. Possible causes: Genetic. Vitamin B deficiency. Drugs for treatment of arthritis. Other health factors.

325. _____ An antiandrogen and is used in the treatment of androgen related disorders such as female pattern baldness and hirsutism.

A. ROUGH BLOW DRY
B. TELOGEN
C. DHT
D. COLD SORE
E. ATOPIC DERMATITIS
F. EMULSIFIER
G. AXILLA
H. POROSITY
I. ESCHAR
J. ENDOCRINE SYSTEM
K. SLOUGH
L. SPRIONOLACTONE
M. AMORTIZATION
N. ARRECTOR PILI
O. BULB
P. CLARIFIER
Q. WHITE HAIR
R. CUTTING IN
S. LEUCOTRICHIA
T. BLACKHEADS
U. RECIPIENT SITE
V. HENNA
W. BETAINE
X. RELAXER
Y. ANAGEN

Provide the word that best matches each clue.

326. _____ A liquid with a pH higher than 7.

327. _____ The pigmented area surrounding the nipple. A very common area for hair growth.

328. _____ A hair color formula that lasts only until you shampoo your hair.

329. _____ Hair passes through a series of cycles known as Anagen (growing phase), Catagen (resting phase) and Telogen (dormant phase).

330. _____ This is baldness due to scarring. The follicles are absent in scar tissue.

331. _____ The most concentrated and most fragrant scent and therefore the most expensive.

332. _____ In hair removal, a conductor through which electricity enters or leaves the body. An electrolysis needle is an electrode.

333. _____ Being able to dissolve into, or being compatible with, another substance.

334. _____ Wefts are temporary hair extensions which are glued into your hair.

335. _____ A bodily reaction to an irritant. Skin allergies can be exacerbated by solutions put on the skin.

336. _____ A small opening of the sweat glands of the skin.

337. _____ Positively charges the hair to provide manageability and reduces static.

338. _____ In hair removal, the practice of epilation with electrified needles.

339. _____ A non-living hair in the last stages of the hair growth cycle, it is detached from the follicle but has not yet shed.

340. _____ Allergen is a substance that causes an allergic reaction.

341. _____ Dark skin discoloration on sun-exposed areas of the face and neck. Young women with brownish skin tones are at greatest risk.

342. _____ Excessive development of the male breasts.

343. _____ The removal of dead skin cells to reveal softer skin underneath.

344. _____ Baldness following a nervous disorder or injury to the nervous system.

345. _____ Combating the signs of ageing using the latest innovative, non-invasive treatments that give you visibly younger, healthy, radiant skin.

346. _____ A relatively rare condition which makes certain hair removal methods more difficult and can lead to ingrown hairs.

347. _____ A hairspray with medium hold used on a finished style to maintain its shape and hold.

348. _____ The hair's ability to stretch without breaking and then return to its original shape.

349. _____ Are usually shed during the 7th month of fetal life following primary folliculo-genesis.

350. _____ has been called a more extensive and severe form of dandruff.

A. SEBORRHOEIC DERMATITIS	B. CURVED FOLLICLES	C. LANUGO HAIRS
D. ELECTRODE	E. ALLERGEN	F. PARFUM
G. CICATRICIAL ALOPECIA	H. GYNECOMASTIA	I. MELASMA
J. PORE	K. ELECTROLYSIS	L. EXFOLIATION
M. TEMPORARY COLOR	N. ALOPECIA NEUROTICA	O. HAIR GROWTH CYCLE
P. WEFTS	Q. ALKALI	R. SOLUBLE
S. ALLERGY	T. ELASTICITY	U. FINISHING SPRAY
V. AREOLA	W. CLUB HAIR	X. SKIN REJUVENATION
Y. CATIONIC POLYMER		

Provide the word that best matches each clue.

351. _____ A common disorder characterized by inflammation of the hair follicle.

352. _____ A drug or preparation used to prevent and treat infection.

353. _____ A chemical formed in the blood when the body uses fat instead of glucose (sugar) for energy.

354. _____ A disease of the skin and connective tissue that can cause hair loss over the affected areas.

355. _____ A technique under development which could make an unlimited crop of donor hair available for transplanting.

356. _____ This is baldness due to scarring. The follicles are absent in scar tissue.

357. _____ A smoothing product to stop your hair from frizzing, keeping it smooth and straight. You'll be able to find a serum that is specifically designed to your own hair type.

358. _____ Term used to describe an on the scalp braid. These braids can be used to form a track for the cornrow weaving method.

359. _____ A small temporary scab that occurs sometimes after electrolysis, especially after overtreatment.

360. _____ A group of genetically identical cells or organisms derived from a single common cell.

361. _____ An over excitation of melanocytes, darkening of the skin. Can be seen as sun-induced freckles or melasma.

362. _____ A chemical process by which the hair is permanently straightened. New-growth areas have to be maintained via 'touch-ups' to continue the straightened pattern.

363. _____ Fatty or greasy, usually referring to the oil-secreting glans of the scalp.

364. _____ The generic name of the brand name drug Rogaine. The first drug to be approved by the FDA for the treatment of androgenetic alopecia.

365. _____ A substance, such as a vitamin, which provides elements for the ongoing functioning of the body's metabolic processes.

366. _____ A hairspray with medium hold used on a finished style to maintain its shape and hold.

367. _____ An acronym for Light Amplification by the Stimulated Emission of Radiation. A commonly used tool for cosmetic and surgical procedures.

368. _____ A hairspray with the firmest hold used to maintain style of hard to hold hair.

369. _____ A closed sac or capsule usually filled with fluid or semisolid material.

370. _____ A sun tanning product that contains DHA, which reacts with amino acids in the top layer of skin, causing it to temporarily darken (2-4 days).

371. _____ Increases wet and dry combability.

372. _____ Used to add volume or length to your hair by bonding synthetic or real hair at your roots.

373. _____ Creamy hair product meant to be used after shampoo. Moisturizes and detangles hair.

374. _____ A modality of electrolysis which uses both thermolysis and galvanic methods.

375. _____ creates curls by restructuring your hair molecules with a chemical, or heat treatment and is generally a long-lasting or permanent change to your hair.

A. HAIR EXTENSIONS   B. SEBACEOUS   C. ANTIBIOTIC
D. LASER   E. SERUM   F. NUTRIENT
G. HAIR CLONING   H. BLEND   I. ACETONE
J. CORNROW   K. RELAXER   L. FREEZING SPRAY
M. SELF TANNER   N. FINISHING SPRAY   O. CONDITIONER
P. HYPERPIGMENTATION   Q. CYST   R. SCLERODERMA
S. PERM   T. SILICONE   U. MINOXIDIL
V. ESCHAR   W. CICATRICIAL ALOPECIA X. CLONE
Y. FOLLICULITIS

Provide the word that best matches each clue.

376. _____ Metabolising stubborn fat deposits, typically in the lower body, using methods such as Eporex mesotherapy.

377. _____ A chemical process by which the hair is permanently straightened. New-growth areas have to be maintained via 'touch-ups' to continue the straightened pattern.

378. _____ Loss of hair, especially from the head, which either happens naturally or is caused by disease

379. _____ A cosmetic procedure used to smooth skin and reduce scars.

380. _____ A device that removes hair by grasping hairs above the skin's surface with an electrified tweezers.

381. _____ When your skin is damaged by exposure to the UVA and UVB rays of the sun, its reaction is to produce more melanin as an attempt to protect itself against further damage.

382. _____ A small temporary scab that occurs sometimes after electrolysis, especially after overtreatment.

383. _____ A bodily reaction to an irritant. Skin allergies can be exacerbated by solutions put on the skin.

384. _____ A medical term for blackheads.

385. _____ A technique under development which could make an unlimited crop of donor hair available for transplanting.

386. L. INGROWN HAIR — A hair that does not break the surface of the skin, and grows back inward. Can be severe and cause inflammation, soreness and infection.

387. P. WEFTS — Wefts are temporary hair extensions which are glued into your hair.

388. O. OXIDATION COLOUR — A color which requires oxygen to make it work.

389. M. ROUGH BLOW DRY — Used to remove the moisture from wet hair.

390. N. STEAMING — The process by which most synthetic fiber is curled at the factory.

391. E. FOLLICULAR UNIT — Groupings of hair that grow together and share the same blood supply.

392. H. ANDROGEN — Hormone that causes masculine characteristics and affects hair growth.

393. B. TAN — A bristle commonly used in natural bristle brushes.

394. J. SEBACEOUS — Fatty or greasy, usually referring to the oil-secreting glans of the scalp.

395. K. ALLERGY — Allergen is a substance that causes an allergic reaction.

396. (highlighting) — The subtle lifting of color in specific sections of hair.

397. C. COCAMIDE DEA — Either made synthetically or derived from the kernel of the coconut, it gives lather and cleans skin and hair.

398. D. JOJOBA OIL — Contains superior properties to keep skin and hair soft. It is beneficial to dry hair.

399. A. BOTANICAL — Refers to a product containing plants or ingredients made from plants.

400. S. MOISTURIZER — An emollient cream used to hydrate the skin.

A. BOTANICAL
B. TAN
C. COCAMIDE DEA
D. JOJOBA OIL
E. FOLLICULAR UNIT
F. ELECTRIC TWEEZER
G. ESCHAR
H. ANDROGEN
I. DERMABRASION
J. SEBACEOUS
K. ALLERGY
L. INGROWN HAIR
M. ROUGH BLOW DRY
N. STEAMING
O. OXIDATION COLOUR
P. WEFTS
Q. HAIR CLONING
R. TARGETED FAT REDUCTION
S. MOISTURIZER
T. ALOPECIA

U. ALLERGEN
W. HIGHLIGHTS
Y. COMEDONES

V. RELAXER
X. BOAR BRISTLE

Provide the word that best matches each clue.

1. COLLAGEN — A protein that holds all connective tissue together under the skin.

2. ALPHA HYDROXY ACID — These solutions are used as exfoliants. They can help reduce ingrown hairs and improve the look of skin.

3. ECZEMA — Contact dermatitis, it's a mild inflammation of the skin.

4. SECTIONING — allows you to only pay attention to a particular area or panel of hair.

5. AREOLA — The pigmented area surrounding the nipple. A very common area for hair growth.

6. ATOPIC DERMATITIS — Also known as eczema.

7. BACTERIA — An organism responsible for infection.

8. CELLULITE — A collection of fat cells resulting from poor lymphatic drainage, fluid retention, poor circulation, not drinking enough water, a sedentary lifestyle and hormones.

9. BOB — The classic look of the 50s and 60s; the style was short and straight but blow-dried and curled under.

10. EYELASHES — Protective hairs on the eyelid. Some people get ingrown hairs here, which should only be treated under a physician's care, preferably an ophthalmologist.

11. CATIONIC POLYMER — Positively charges the hair to provide manageability and reduces static.

12. SLOUGH — To become shed or cast off.

13. ACUPRESSURE — A method of relieving pain by pressing down on an area of the body.

14. ENDOCRINE SYSTEM — A group of glands which maintain the body's internal environment through the production of hormones.

15. AFRO HAIRSTYLE — A rounded, thick, tightly curled hair style.

16. ULCER — An area of tissue erosion. They are always depressed and are due to irritation. They may become infected and inflamed as they grow.

17. HAIR EXTENSIONS — Used to add volume or length to your hair by bonding synthetic or real hair at your roots.

18. ANALGESIC — A substance used to relieve pain.

19. ACNE — An inflammation of the skin, a result of over production of oil and bacteria.

20. EFFICACY — A term meaning how well or effectively a cosmetic device works.

21. CHIGNON — A sophisticated, elegant up style, where long hair is twisted (either in a roll or knot) and pinned from the nape of neck.

22. ACID — A liquid, usually corrosive with a pH lower than 7, opposite of an alkali.

23. DIAMETER — A measurement across the width of the hair.

24. CAPILLARIES — Small blood vessels which connect the arteries and veins that feed the hair.

25. AMPERE — A measurement of electrical current.

A. EFFICACY
B. ATOPIC DERMATITIS
C. HAIR EXTENSIONS
D. SLOUGH
E. BACTERIA
F. AMPERE
G. ACUPRESSURE
H. DIAMETER
I. CHIGNON
J. AREOLA
K. AFRO HAIRSTYLE
L. CATIONIC POLYMER
M. ACID
N. EYELASHES
O. COLLAGEN
P. CAPILLARIES
Q. ENDOCRINE SYSTEM
R. ANALGESIC
S. BOB
T. CELLULITE
U. ULCER
V. SECTIONING
W. ALPHA HYDROXY ACID
X. ECZEMA
Y. ACNE

Provide the word that best matches each clue.

26. ESTROGEN — A female hormone sometimes linked to increased hair growth.

27. BARBICIDE — Brand name of sanitizer used to disinfect salon implements.

28. MONOFILAMENT — Fine, transparent nylon or silk mesh with hairs individually hand-knotted into the mesh. Allows the hair to fall naturally and gives more versatility in styling.

29. HAIR CLONING — A technique under development which could make an unlimited crop of donor hair available for transplanting.

30. MATTE — A non- shiny surface that absorbs light; a dead or dull finish.

31. CARBOMER — A polymer on the basis of acrylic acid. Provides a thickening, gelling action and consistency regulator for cosmetic products.

32. LIPID LAYER — part of the structure of the hair and also form a protective barrier. They are composed of EFA's amongst other complicated scientific things.

33. COAGULATION — The process by which blood clots, and can be induced by heat or chemicals.

#	Term	Definition
34.	MOISTURIZER	An emollient cream used to hydrate the skin.
35.	WIG	The term used to describe any hairpiece with a full cap which covers the hair on the head, or the entire area where hair normally grows, as a substitute for hair.
36.	COHERENT LIGHT	Light that stays focused, a property of lasers.
37.	LUBRICATES	Makes smooth or slippery by using oil to overcome friction.
38.	ANTISEPTIC	A chemical agent that prevent the growth of bacteria.
39.	BETAINE	A natural conditioning substance for example: from molasses or sugar beet.
40.	CROWN	Area at the top of the head.
41.	FIBROBLASTS	Cells within the extracellular matrix that produce new collagen molecules when stimulated.
42.	PORE	A small opening of the sweat glands of the skin.
43.	RUBY	Commonly used laser for hair and tattoo removal.
44.	ELECTRIC TWEEZER	A device that removes hair by grasping hairs above the skin's surface with an electrified tweezers.
45.	CAPILLARIES	Tiny hair-like blood vessels, some of which carry nutrient to the hair growth matrix.
46.	BOAR BRISTLE	A bristle commonly used in natural bristle brushes.
47.	BIOPSY	A section of skin tissue removed for clinical observation.
48.	SPRIONOLACTONE	An antiandrogen and is used in the treatment of androgen related disorders such as female pattern baldness and hirsutism.
49.	HENNA	A vegetable dye made from its leaves and stems into a powder. Traditionally, it imparts a reddish cast to the hair by coating it.
50.	AXILLA	The medical term for armpit, a common place for gonadal hair after puberty.

A. PORE	B. BARBICIDE	C. FIBROBLASTS
D. ESTROGEN	E. HENNA	F. MATTE
G. RUBY	H. CAPILLARIES	I. CROWN
J. AXILLA	K. COHERENT LIGHT	L. WIG
M. MOISTURIZER	N. BOAR BRISTLE	O. ANTISEPTIC
P. SPRIONOLACTONE	Q. LIPID LAYER	R. BETAINE
S. ELECTRIC TWEEZER	T. LUBRICATES	U. MONOFILAMENT
V. COAGULATION	W. BIOPSY	X. HAIR CLONING

Y. CARBOMER

Provide the word that best matches each clue.

51. **ALTERNATING CURRENT** — The type of electricity that comes from a wall outlet (AC), as opposed to direct current (DC).

52. **SEBUM** — The oily secretion of the sebaceous glands of the scalp, composed of keratin, fat or cellular debris.

53. **A LINE BOB** — A geometric bob with a straight fringe, so called because of the resemblance to the capital A, with it's horizontal line, the fringe and its legs the hair passing your ears.

54. **EYELASHES** — Protective hairs on the eyelid. Some people get ingrown hairs here, which should only be treated under a physician's care, preferably an ophthalmologist.

55. **HUMIDITY** — The amount of moisture available in the air.

56. **RUBY** — Commonly used laser for hair and tattoo removal.

57. **SERUM** — A smoothing product to stop your hair from frizzing, keeping it smooth and straight. You'll be able to find a serum that is specifically designed to your own hair type.

58. **CELLULITE REDUCTION** — Clinic based method of reducing the appearance of cellulite.

59. **CHELATING** — A deep cleansing process which strips the hair lightly before a chemical service. Also known as clarifying.

60. **ANAGEN CYCLE** — The active stage in a hair growth cycle.

61. **ELECTROCOAGULATION** — The use of heat generated by electricity to change tissue from a fluid to a semi-solid, similar to cooking an egg.

62. **CHROMOPHORE** — The substructure that is responsible for the spectral selective absorption of electromagnetic radiation.

63. **ROSACEA** — A disorder involving chronic inflammation of the cheeks, nose, chin, forehead or eyelids. It may cause redness, vascularity, swelling or hyperplasia.

64. **BACTERIA** — An organism responsible for infection.

65. **DEPTH** — The darkness or lightness of a color.

66. **ATOPIC DERMATITIS** — Also known as eczema.

67. BETAINE — A natural conditioning substance for example: from molasses or sugar beet.

68. PABA — Esters found in sunscreen and cosmetic products that can make skin sensitive.

69. CYPROTERONE ACETATE — This drug is normally used to reduce sex drive in men who have an excessive sex drive. It is also prescribed to treat hirsutism and androgenic alopecia in women.

70. ACUPUNCTURE — A method of relieving pain by inserting needles into the skin.

71. FREEZING SPRAY — A hairspray with the firmest hold used to maintain style of hard to hold hair.

72. OVERTREATMENT — Overly aggressive treatment to remove hair which leads to temporary or permanent skin damage.

73. FLUENCE — Term used to measure the output energy, for Lasers and Pulsed Light Sources that is delivered to tissue.

74. TOURMALINE — a crystal silicate mineral compounded with elements such as aluminum, iron, magnesium, sodium, lithium, or potassium.

75. AMPERE — A measurement of electrical current.

A. CHELATING
B. FREEZING SPRAY
C. OVERTREATMENT
D. EYELASHES
E. SERUM
F. FLUENCE
G. RUBY
H. ANAGEN CYCLE
I. CHROMOPHORE
J. A LINE BOB
K. TOURMALINE
L. AMPERE
M. ELECTROCOAGULATION
N. ALTERNATING CURRENT
O. CELLULITE REDUCTION
P. HUMIDITY
Q. ATOPIC DERMATITIS
R. BACTERIA
S. ROSACEA
T. BETAINE
U. CYPROTERONE ACETATE
V. DEPTH
W. PABA
X. SEBUM
Y. ACUPUNCTURE

Provide the word that best matches each clue.

76. DEVELOPER — A product which oxidizes artificial color pigment.

77. CHILLTIP — A patented contact cooling device used in laser hair removal.

78. DERMABRASION — A cosmetic procedure used to smooth skin and reduce scars.

79. ALTERNATING CURRENT — The type of electricity that comes from a wall outlet (AC), as opposed to direct current (DC).

80. FOLLICLE SHEATH — Protects the hair during its growth stage.

81.	CLEARING	A method of hair removal in which all hair in an area is removed at once, as opposed to thinning.
82.	RELAXER	A chemical process by which the hair is permanently straightened. New-growth areas have to be maintained via 'touch-ups' to continue the straightened pattern.
83.	LEUCOTRICHIA	Refers to a congenital absence of pigment in a lock of hairs which will show as grey or white.
84.	CUTANEOUS	Relating to the skin.
85.	SAW PALMETTO	A natural herb that has been shown to be an effective anti-androgen.
86.	AREOLA	The pigmented area surrounding the nipple. A very common area for hair growth.
87.	JOULE	A unit of energy. Describes energy output for pulsed light based systems.
88.	CLUB HAIR	A non-living hair in the last stages of the hair growth cycle, it is detached from the follicle but has not yet shed.
89.	TELOGEN EFFLUVIUM	Hair shafts are produced by follicles within the skin in all but few locations
90.	PAPILLA	The small area at the base of the hair root which provides nutrients needed for growth.
91.	ELASTICITY	The hair's ability to stretch without breaking and then return to its original shape.
92.	AMORTIZATION	The process of converting one enzyme to another.
93.	DERMIS	The deepest layers of the skin, where blood vessels, lymph channels, nerve endings, sweat glands, sebaceous glands, fat cells, hair follicles and muscles are located.
94.	PSORIASIS	Chronic skin inflammation characterized by frequent episodes of redness, itching and thick, dry scales.
95.	DILANTIN	A drug sometimes linked to excess hair growth.
96.	ULCER	An area of tissue erosion. They are always depressed and are due to irritation. They may become infected and inflamed as they grow.

97. TONE — Distribution of ashen and warm pigments, visual effect of gold or ash in the hair.

98. PERMANENT HAIR REDUCTION — Treatments, especially IPL, where the follicle is disabled by the light energy making it unable to support any more hair growth.

99. ELECTRIC TWEEZER — A device that removes hair by grasping hairs above the skin's surface with an electrified tweezers.

100. ENDOCRINE SYSTEM — A group of glands which maintain the body's internal environment through the production of hormones.

A. CHILLTIP
B. PERMANENT HAIR REDUCTION
C. CLEARING
D. ELECTRIC TWEEZER
E. DEVELOPER
F. AREOLA
G. PAPILLA
H. TELOGEN EFFLUVIUM
I. FOLLICLE SHEATH
J. DILANTIN
K. JOULE
L. ALTERNATING CURRENT
M. RELAXER
N. SAW PALMETTO
O. AMORTIZATION
P. DERMIS
Q. ENDOCRINE SYSTEM
R. PSORIASIS
S. TONE
T. LEUCOTRICHIA
U. DERMABRASION
V. CLUB HAIR
W. ELASTICITY
X. CUTANEOUS
Y. ULCER

Provide the word that best matches each clue.

101. PROPRIETARY — Pertaining to a drug that is produced for profit.

102. OVERTREATMENT — Overly aggressive treatment to remove hair which leads to temporary or permanent skin damage.

103. BLISTER — A small fluid-filled bubble on the skin caused by heat from over treatment with certain types of hair removal.

104. SECTIONING — allows you to only pay attention to a particular area or panel of hair.

105. ABDOMEN — The soft area between the rib cage and the pubic area. A common area for excess hair, often in a line from the belly button to the pubic hair.

106. INDENTATION — A hollow or pocket in the skin.

107. PABA — Esters found in sunscreen and cosmetic products that can make skin sensitive.

108.	ELECTROLOGY	The practice of hair removal through the use of electrified needles, invented in the 1870's.
109.	BULB	The root of a hair, so named because it's wider at the base.
110.	A LINE BOB	A geometric bob with a straight fringe, so called because of the resemblance to the capital A, with it's horizontal line, the fringe and its legs the hair passing your ears.
111.	CURVED FOLLICLES	A relatively rare condition which makes certain hair removal methods more difficult and can lead to ingrown hairs.
112.	BOB	The classic look of the 50s and 60s; the style was short and straight but blow-dried and curled under.
113.	AMINOPHENOLS	Phenol derivatives used in combination with other chemicals in permanent (two step) hair dyes.
114.	RUBY	Commonly used laser for hair and tattoo removal.
115.	KELOIDS	A type of raised darkened scar, more common with dark skin. Due to a defect in the healing process.
116.	DRUG TREATMENT	Excess hair can be increased or decreased by certain drugs. These drugs often affect hormonal levels.
117.	EPILATION	The removal of hair below the skin's surface.
118.	ANTI ANDROGEN	A drug or product that limited the effects of androgens (male hormones).
119.	NERVE ENDINGS	Receptors which respond to touch, pain, pressure, heat and cold.
120.	AMMONIUM THIOGLYCOLATE	A common ingredient in chemical depilatories.
121.	BRAID	To weave strands of hair together. On the scalp braiding is used to form a base or track to sew on a commercial weft.
122.	CHEMICAL DEPILATORIES	Powder or cream preparations that dissolve hair above the surface of the skin. Some find these products very irritating to the skin.
123.	CHELATING	A deep cleansing process which strips the hair lightly before a chemical service. Also known as clarifying.
124.	CRUSTING	Dried fluid that seeps from skin in some clients following hair removal such as laser, electrolysis, and depilatories.

125. ALLERGY — A bodily reaction to an irritant. Skin allergies can be exacerbated by solutions put on the skin.

A. SECTIONING	B. ALLERGY
C. ABDOMEN	D. BULB
E. BLISTER	F. RUBY
G. DRUG TREATMENT	H. BOB
I. PABA	J. AMINOPHENOLS
K. A LINE BOB	L. PROPRIETARY
M. ELECTROLOGY	N. AMMONIUM THIOGLYCOLATE
O. INDENTATION	P. CRUSTING
Q. EPILATION	R. KELOIDS
S. NERVE ENDINGS	T. OVERTREATMENT
U. CHEMICAL DEPILATORIES	V. CHELATING
W. BRAID	X. ANTI ANDROGEN
Y. CURVED FOLLICLES	

Provide the word that best matches each clue.

126. HIGHLIGHTS — The subtle lifting of color in specific sections of hair.

127. CELLULITE — A collection of fat cells resulting from poor lymphatic drainage, fluid retention, poor circulation, not drinking enough water, a sedentary lifestyle and hormones.

128. ACTINIC KERATOSIS — A small rough spot on skin chronically exposed to the sun, occurs most frequently in fair skinned people.

129. ALKALINE — A substance with a pH greater than 7; non acidic.

130. ABRASION — The process of scraping or wearing hair away. Causing partial or complete absence of hair from areas.

131. ENERGY DENSITY — Term used to measure the output energy for Lasers and Pulsed Light Sources.

132. DIET — Is sometimes linked to excess hair growth, especially in the extremely obese and extremely anorexic.

133. AUTOCLAVE — A machine used to sterilize medical utensils and some hair removal devices.

134. MINI GRAFT — A small hair graft usually consisting of between three to ten hair roots.

135. DISCOMFORT — Varies greatly by individual and body area. Electrolysis is generally considered most painful, followed by laser, plucking, waxing and finally pulse light sources.

136. ALOPECIA SENILIS	Alopecia senilis is baldness due to old age.
137. GEL	Jelly like material formed by the coagulation of a liquid. Semi-solid emulsion that liquefies when applied to the skin.
138. COLD SORE	A viral infection that appears around the mouth. Hair removal, especially electrolysis and lasers, should not be performed around visible cold sores.
139. RELAXER	A chemical process by which the hair is permanently straightened. New-growth areas have to be maintained via 'touch-ups' to continue the straightened pattern.
140. CATAPHORESIS	The forcing of substances into the skin from a positive to a negative pole. It is sometimes used after electrolysis to firm skin and reduce redness.
141. HENNA	A vegetable dye made from its leaves and stems into a powder. Traditionally, it imparts a reddish cast to the hair by coating it.
142. OVERTREATMENT	Overly aggressive treatment to remove hair which leads to temporary or permanent skin damage.
143. ESCHAR	A small temporary scab that occurs sometimes after electrolysis, especially after overtreatment.
144. TARGETED FAT REDUCTION	Metabolising stubborn fat deposits, typically in the lower body, using methods such as Eporex mesotherapy.
145. LANUGO HAIRS	Are usually shed during the 7th month of fetal life following primary folliculo-genesis.
146. SEBACEOUS	Fatty or greasy, usually referring to the oil-secreting glans of the scalp.
147. CUTICLES	Form a protective layer which covers the shaft of hair. If your hair is colored or bleached they can spread out, split or become bloated due to over processing.
148. BLONDE HAIR	Is not as visible, but it's also harder to treat. Lasers have limited effects on it because of its lack of pigment, and it is difficult to see against the skin.
149. SPRITZ	a light mist or spray, which when used as verb means to lightly spray your hair.
150. HAIR INTEGRATION	A modern term used to describe hair weaving.

A. AUTOCLAVE   B. CATAPHORESIS

C. SEBACEOUS
E. SPRITZ
G. ABRASION
I. HAIR INTEGRATION
K. CELLULITE
M. ALOPECIA SENILIS
O. CUTICLES
Q. MINI GRAFT
S. BLONDE HAIR
U. DIET
W. HIGHLIGHTS
Y. TARGETED FAT REDUCTION

D. RELAXER
F. ESCHAR
H. HENNA
J. LANUGO HAIRS
L. ALKALINE
N. ENERGY DENSITY
P. DISCOMFORT
R. OVERTREATMENT
T. GEL
V. ACTINIC KERATOSIS
X. COLD SORE

Provide the word that best matches each clue.

151. ALOPECIA FOLLICULARIS — Hair loss due to inflammation of hair follicles.

152. SAW PALMETTO — A natural herb that has been shown to be an effective anti-androgen.

153. DEPILATORIES — Substances used to dissolve hair above the skin's surface.

154. STEAMING — The process by which most synthetic fiber is curled at the factory.

155. BRUISE — A discoloration of skin from blood, sometimes caused by electrolysis, plucking, or waxing. Also known as Purpura.

156. HAIR CLONING — A technique under development which could make an unlimited crop of donor hair available for transplanting.

157. MINOXIDIL — The generic name of the brand name drug Rogaine. The first drug to be approved by the FDA for the treatment of androgenetic alopecia.

158. FIBROBLASTS — Cells within the extracellular matrix that produce new collagen molecules when stimulated.

159. MICRO LINKING TECHNIQUE — The process of attaching hair wefts without braids. The links are sewn on to the wefted hair. The user's natural hair is pulled through and locked secure.

160. ELECTRODE — In hair removal, a conductor through which electricity enters or leaves the body. An electrolysis needle is an electrode.

161. ALKALI — A liquid with a pH higher than 7.

162. PERMANENTLY — Completely changing the natural color of the hair.

163. SUPEROXIDE DISMUTASE — The enzyme superoxide, catalyzes the dis-mutation of superoxide into oxygen and hydrogen peroxide.

164. ELECTRIC TWEEZER — A device that removes hair by grasping hairs above the skin's surface with an electrified tweezers.

165. SECTIONING — allows you to only pay attention to a particular area or panel of hair.

166. EXFOLIATION — The removal of dead skin cells to reveal softer skin underneath.

167. ELECTROLOGY — The practice of hair removal through the use of electrified needles, invented in the 1870's.

168. HAIR WEAVING — A process by which a hair piece is attached to existing hair on the head through braiding or a weaving process.

169. FRECKLES — Small clumps of coagulated melanin.

170. COMEDONES — A medical term for blackheads.

171. METABOLISM — The body transformation of food into energy.

172. ACID — A liquid, usually corrosive with a pH lower than 7, opposite of an alkali.

173. WEFT — An amount of hair or fiber which is doubled over and MACHINE-SEWN along the top to create a long strand of hair.

174. SUNBLOCK — Products that reflect all the sun's rays, such as zinc oxide and titanium dioxide. They permit minimal tanning, and are a good choice for those who are sensitive to chemicals.

175. CETYL ALCOHOL — A gentle humectant, lather booster, and emulsifier. In hair products, it is used to smooth and soften the hair cuticle.

A. COMEDONES
B. ALKALI
C. BRUISE
D. MICRO LINKING TECHNIQUE
E. FRECKLES
F. MINOXIDIL
G. SAW PALMETTO
H. FIBROBLASTS
I. PERMANENTLY
J. WEFT
K. DEPILATORIES
L. EXFOLIATION
M. SUPEROXIDE DISMUTASE
N. SECTIONING
O. HAIR CLONING
P. ELECTRODE
Q. SUNBLOCK
R. STEAMING
S. ACID
T. ALOPECIA FOLLICULARIS
U. METABOLISM
V. CETYL ALCOHOL
W. ELECTROLOGY
X. ELECTRIC TWEEZER

Y. HAIR WEAVING

Provide the word that best matches each clue.

#	Word	Clue
176.	COMEDOGENIC	Causes blackheads
177.	PAPILLA	The small area at the base of the hair root which provides nutrients needed for growth.
178.	CASTRATION	The surgical removal of one or both testicles or ovaries.
179.	COARSE	A classification for stronger, thicker types of hair.
180.	INTERLOCKING	A method in which hair is maintained or tightened using a tool.
181.	SUNBLOCK	Products that reflect all the sun's rays, such as zinc oxide and titanium dioxide. They permit minimal tanning, and are a good choice for those who are sensitive to chemicals.
182.	COLLAGEN	A protein that holds all connective tissue together under the skin.
183.	DIET	Is sometimes linked to excess hair growth, especially in the extremely obese and extremely anorexic.
184.	DOUBLE BLIND	A clinical testing method in which neither patient nor doctor know what medication or procedure is being used.
185.	PIGMENTED LESION	Variety of skin conditions mainly the result of excess melanin. Commonly known as Café au Lait stains, birthmarks, age spots and freckles.
186.	REMI	Refers to human hair (usually Indian in origin) which has been harvested from root to end, with all of the cuticle going in the same direction.
187.	KELOIDS	A type of raised darkened scar, more common with dark skin. Due to a defect in the healing process.
188.	TOURMALINE	a crystal silicate mineral compounded with elements such as aluminum, iron, magnesium, sodium, lithium, or potassium.
189.	CUTICLE	The hard outer protective layer of the hair. Impart sheen to the hair.
190.	CELLULITE REDUCTION	Clinic based method of reducing the appearance of cellulite.
191.	APPLE CIDER VINEGAR	A natural solvent in oils and creams. It acidifies products.
192.	PH	Used to measure acidity in cosmetic preparations.

193. TAN		When your skin is damaged by exposure to the UVA and UVB rays of the sun, its reaction is to produce more melanin as an attempt to protect itself against further damage.
194. DERMABRASION		A cosmetic procedure used to smooth skin and reduce scars.
195. ATOPIC DERMATITIS		Also known as eczema.
196. DEPILATION		The temporary removal of hair.
197. ERYTHEMA		A medical term for the redness that sometimes follows hair removal and skin rejuvenation.
198. Q SWITCH		A device that produces short intense bursts of energy from a laser.
199. CORTISONE		An anti-inflammatory sometimes linked to hair growth when taken internally.
200. PROPRIETARY		Pertaining to a drug that is produced for profit.

A. CORTISONE	B. ATOPIC DERMATITIS	C. CELLULITE REDUCTION
D. Q SWITCH	E. CUTICLE	F. CASTRATION
G. ERYTHEMA	H. DIET	I. COMEDOGENIC
J. TAN	K. DERMABRASION	L. KELOIDS
M. PH	N. PAPILLA	O. PROPRIETARY
P. SUNBLOCK	Q. COARSE	R. DOUBLE BLIND
S. TOURMALINE	T. REMI	U. DEPILATION
V. COLLAGEN	W. APPLE CIDER VINEGAR	X. INTERLOCKING
Y. PIGMENTED LESION		

Provide the word that best matches each clue.

201. GREY HAIR		Hair that has lost its pigment.
202. SAW PALMETTO		A natural herb that has been shown to be an effective anti-androgen.
203. ELECTRODE		In hair removal, a conductor through which electricity enters or leaves the body. An electrolysis needle is an electrode.
204. TONE		Distribution of ashen and warm pigments, visual effect of gold or ash in the hair.
205. CHAMOMILE		Used in many products for blonde hair to enhance color.
206. BLANCHING		A whitening of the skin sometimes caused by some types of hair removal.
207. TRANSLUCENT		Allows some light to pass through.

208. SILICONE — Increases wet and dry combability.

209. ISOPROPYL LANOLATE — A Synthetic moisturizer.

210. DIABETES — A disease where the body improperly produces insulin, sometimes linked to excess hair growth.

211. NUTRIENT — A substance, such as a vitamin, which provides elements for the ongoing functioning of the body's metabolic processes.

212. JOULE — A unit of energy. Describes energy output for pulsed light based systems.

213. COLOGNE — A combination of water containing alcohol and fragrant oils. Not to be confused with a concentrated perfume.

214. LUVIMER — Flexible resin.

215. CASTRATION — The surgical removal of one or both testicles or ovaries.

216. BIRTHMARKS — Discolored skin that should be examined and approved by a physician before hair removal.

217. PANTOTHENIC ACID — Also called vitamin B5 (a B vitamin), is a water-soluble vitamin required to sustain life (essential nutrient).

218. ACID MANTLE — The combination of sweat and sebum that provides the skin's protective coating.

219. KERATIN — A fibrous protein found in hair, nails, and skin.

220. DEPTH — The darkness or lightness of a color.

221. TESTOSTERONE — A predominantly male hormone which promotes the development of male characteristics.

222. T ZONE — The forehead, nose and chin areas, which tend to be oilier than the cheeks.

223. INDENTATION — A hollow or pocket in the skin.

224. ALOPECIA ANDROGENETIC — This is the common name for male or female pattern baldness which depends on the genetic predisposition of the hair follicles and the levels of DHT in the body.

225. ACUPUNCTURE — A method of relieving pain by inserting needles into the skin.

A. T ZONE   B. NUTRIENT   C. ALOPECIA ANDROGENETIC

D. PANTOTHENIC ACID
E. INDENTATION
F. GREY HAIR
G. ISOPROPYL LANOLATE
H. COLOGNE
I. LUVIMER
J. ACUPUNCTURE
K. TRANSLUCENT
L. BLANCHING
M. TONE
N. SAW PALMETTO
O. KERATIN
P. BIRTHMARKS
Q. ACID MANTLE
R. ELECTRODE
S. JOULE
T. DIABETES
U. DEPTH
V. CASTRATION
W. CHAMOMILE
X. TESTOSTERONE
Y. SILICONE

Provide the word that best matches each clue.

#	Term	Clue
226.	ALKALI	A liquid with a pH higher than 7.
227.	BIRTH CONTROL	Drugs that sometimes cause increased hair growth.
228.	CROWN	Area at the top of the head.
229.	ACNE	An inflammation of the skin, a result of over production of oil and bacteria.
230.	TEA TREE OIL	an extraction from the Melaleuca tree.
231.	PARFUM	The most concentrated and most fragrant scent and therefore the most expensive.
232.	CALAMINE	A pink ointment sometimes used to treat skin irritation
233.	OVARIES	In women, a major source of female hormones. Certain conditions involving the ovaries can lead to excess hair growth, especially polycystic ovary syndrome (PCOS).
234.	SKIN REJUVENATION	Combating the signs of ageing using the latest innovative, non-invasive treatments that give you visibly younger, healthy, radiant skin.
235.	CELLULITE REDUCTION	Clinic based method of reducing the appearance of cellulite.
236.	LUBRICATES	Makes smooth or slippery by using oil to overcome friction.
237.	SOAP	Cleansing agent that is a sodium or potassium salt of animal or vegetable fat.
238.	BLONDE HAIR	Is not as visible, but it's also harder to treat. Lasers have limited effects on it because of its lack of pigment, and it is difficult to see against the skin.
239.	ELECTROLYSIS	In hair removal, the practice of epilation with electrified needles.

240.	FIBROBLASTS	Cells within the extracellular matrix that produce new collagen molecules when stimulated.
241.	NEUTRALISE	To cancel or reduce effect.
242.	MICRO LINKING TECHNIQUE	The process of attaching hair wefts without braids. The links are sewn on to the wefted hair. The user's natural hair is pulled through and locked secure.
243.	CATOGEN	The resting stage of the hair cycle.
244.	ANDROGEN	Hormone that causes masculine characteristics and affects hair growth.
245.	HEATCLAMPS	A heat gun that is used to seal synthetic hair. Used for creating warlocks and other styles.
246.	MINOXIDIL	The generic name of the brand name drug Rogaine. The first drug to be approved by the FDA for the treatment of androgenetic alopecia.
247.	CLONE	A group of genetically identical cells or organisms derived from a single common cell.
248.	HYDRATE	To add moisture to the skin.
249.	ANTI ANDROGEN	A drug or product that limited the effects of androgens (male hormones).
250.	EXFOLIATING	A process of removing the top dead skin layers to reveal healthier, newer skin underneath.

A. LUBRICATES
B. MICRO LINKING TECHNIQUE
C. BLONDE HAIR
D. FIBROBLASTS
E. ALKALI
F. HYDRATE
G. CROWN
H. CATOGEN
I. TEA TREE OIL
J. ELECTROLYSIS
K. OVARIES
L. HEATCLAMPS
M. NEUTRALISE
N. EXFOLIATING
O. SOAP
P. SKIN REJUVENATION
Q. ACNE
R. CALAMINE
S. MINOXIDIL
T. ANDROGEN
U. ANTI ANDROGEN
V. CELLULITE REDUCTION
W. BIRTH CONTROL
X. CLONE
Y. PARFUM

Provide the word that best matches each clue.

251.	BRAID	To weave strands of hair together. On the scalp braiding is used to form a base or track to sew on a commercial weft.
252.	BLACK SKIN	Probably the most difficult type of skin from which to remove hair.
253.	GENERIC	Pertaining to a substance, product or drug that is not protected by trademark. It is identical in chemical composition but not necessarily equivalent in therapeutic effect.
254.	HAIR EXTENSIONS	Used to add volume or length to your hair by bonding synthetic or real hair at your roots.
255.	DANDRUFF	Flaking scalp due to excessive cell production.
256.	AMORTIZATION	The process of converting one enzyme to another.
257.	EYELASHES	Protective hairs on the eyelid. Some people get ingrown hairs here, which should only be treated under a physician's care, preferably an ophthalmologist.
258.	FUSION	The process of attaching small pieces of human hair with a special adhesive and a thermal gun.
259.	ANDROGENS	Often referred to as male hormones.
260.	ROUGH BLOW DRY	Used to remove the moisture from wet hair.
261.	SELECTIVE PHOTOTHERMOLYSIS	Selectively targeting dermal structures with light energy, without causing damage to surrounding tissue.
262.	MEDULLA	The medulla is a central zone of cells usually only present in large thick hairs.
263.	CUSHING SYNDROME	A disease caused by a tumor on the adrenal gland, which can cause excess hair growth.
264.	MINI GRAFT	A small hair graft usually consisting of between three to ten hair roots.
265.	EMULSIFIER	A thickening agent or binding agent added to products to change their physical composition (joins two or more ingredients together).
266.	PIGMENT	Color.
267.	DIAMETER	A measurement across the width of the hair.

268. BLISTER — A small fluid-filled bubble on the skin caused by heat from over treatment with certain types of hair removal.

269. AREOLA — The pigmented area surrounding the nipple. A very common area for hair growth.

270. TRICHOTILLOMANIA — This form of hair loss is caused by pulling out one's own hair, usually without realizing it.

271. PAPILLA — The small area at the base of the hair root which provides nutrients needed for growth.

272. ALKALI — A liquid with a pH higher than 7.

273. PANTHENOL — Aids detangling. Provides volume, control and shine.

274. FLY-AWAY HAIR — Thin hair that is charged by static and is a particular problem with straight looks as the hair just won't lie properly and can spoil your look.

275. TRACK — Parting or a cornrow that establishes the placement pattern of wefts or strand additions.

- A. EYELASHES
- B. PIGMENT
- C. ROUGH BLOW DRY
- D. FLY-AWAY HAIR
- E. PAPILLA
- F. ANDROGENS
- G. AREOLA
- H. MINI GRAFT
- I. TRACK
- J. EMULSIFIER
- K. CUSHING SYNDROME
- L. BLACK SKIN
- M. FUSION
- N. SELECTIVE PHOTOTHERMOLYSIS
- O. DIAMETER
- P. DANDRUFF
- Q. BLISTER
- R. MEDULLA
- S. HAIR EXTENSIONS
- T. AMORTIZATION
- U. ALKALI
- V. BRAID
- W. GENERIC
- X. PANTHENOL
- Y. TRICHOTILLOMANIA

Provide the word that best matches each clue.

276. SUBCUTANEOUS — Pertains to the skin.

277. KANEKALON — A trademark for a Japanese-made synthetic fiber which is used extensively in the manufacture of wigs and hairpieces

278. ELECTROLOGY — The practice of hair removal through the use of electrified needles, invented in the 1870's.

279.	JOULE	A unit of energy. Describes energy output for pulsed light based systems.
280.	SEBORRHOEIC DERMATITIS	has been called a more extensive and severe form of dandruff.
281.	DIMETHICONE	Detangling aid which conditions, protects against humidity, and adds shine.
282.	INDENTATION	A hollow or pocket in the skin.
283.	ESTROGEN	One of a group of hormonal steroid compounds that promote the development of female secondary sex characteristics.
284.	CATOGEN	The resting stage of the hair cycle.
285.	ARNICA	A plant extract that has been used to treat swelling, soreness and bruising.
286.	FOLLICLES	The hair follicle is the tiny blub under your scalp from which the hair grows.
287.	ATOPIC DERMATITIS	Also known as eczema.
288.	PUNCH GRAFT	The old fashioned way of removing grafts for hair transplants, usually carried out using an instrument called a trephine.
289.	BLEACH	A method used to disguise (not remove) hair by lightening its color.
290.	FINISHING SPRAY	A hairspray with medium hold used on a finished style to maintain its shape and hold.
291.	AMPERE	A measurement of electrical current.
292.	FOLLICLE SHEATH	Protects the hair during its growth stage.
293.	FUSION	The process of attaching small pieces of human hair with a special adhesive and a thermal gun.
294.	ELECTRODE	In hair removal, a conductor through which electricity enters or leaves the body. An electrolysis needle is an electrode.
295.	ALKALINE	A substance with a pH greater than 7; non acidic.
296.	AMORTIZATION	The process of converting one enzyme to another.
297.	SEMI PERMANENT	A color which lasts from 6 - 8 shampoos.

298. ALOPECIA TOTALIS — This is the complete loss of scalp hair often combined with the loss of eyebrows and eyelashes.

299. HIGHLIGHTS — The subtle lifting of color in specific sections of hair.

300. BULB — The root of a hair, so named because it's wider at the base.

A. ALKALINE	B. BLEACH	C. SEMI PERMANENT
D. SEBORRHOEIC DERMATITIS	E. KANEKALON	F. INDENTATION
G. ARNICA	H. FOLLICLE SHEATH	I. HIGHLIGHTS
J. AMPERE	K. ALOPECIA TOTALIS	L. ELECTROLOGY
M. JOULE	N. FOLLICLES	O. FINISHING SPRAY
P. DIMETHICONE	Q. ESTROGEN	R. ELECTRODE
S. PUNCH GRAFT	T. ATOPIC DERMATITIS	U. FUSION
V. SUBCUTANEOUS	W. AMORTIZATION	X. CATOGEN
Y. BULB		

Provide the word that best matches each clue.

301. TELOGEN — The resting phase in the hair cycle.

302. ENDOCRINE SYSTEM — A group of glands which maintain the body's internal environment through the production of hormones.

303. CUTTING IN — The term used to describe getting a 'hair cut' and having your new hairpiece styled for the first time when you first receive it.

304. BETAINE — A natural conditioning substance for example: from molasses or sugar beet.

305. CLARIFIER — A clarifying shampoo is slightly stronger than everyday shampoos and is designed to remove products, hard water or chlorine residue that have built-up over time.

306. BLACKHEADS — A type of clogged pore in the skin with a visible black plug.

307. AMORTIZATION — The process of converting one enzyme to another.

308. EMULSIFIER — A thickening agent or binding agent added to products to change their physical composition (joins two or more ingredients together).

309. RECIPIENT SITE — The bald or thinning area where hair grafts or plugs a transplanted.

310. SLOUGH — To become shed or cast off.

311. ROUGH BLOW DRY — Used to remove the moisture from wet hair.

312. COLD SORE — A viral infection that appears around the mouth. Hair removal, especially electrolysis and lasers, should not be performed around visible cold sores.

313. ARRECTOR PILI		Creates "Goose Bumps" when stimulated.
314. POROSITY		Ability to absorb moisture.
315. RELAXER		A chemical process by which the hair is permanently straightened. New-growth areas have to be maintained via 'touch-ups' to continue the straightened pattern.
316. BULB		The root of a hair, so named because it's wider at the base.
317. DHT		a male hormone that is suggested to be the main cause for the miniaturization of the hair follicle and for hair loss.
318. AXILLA		The medical term for armpit, a common place for gonadal hair after puberty.
319. HENNA		A vegetable dye made from its leaves and stems into a powder. Traditionally, it imparts a reddish cast to the hair by coating it.
320. ANAGEN		This is the growing phase of the hair cycle which lasts about seven years in a healthy person. The active stage in a hair growth cycle.
321. ESCHAR		A small temporary scab that occurs sometimes after electrolysis, especially after overtreatment.
322. LEUCOTRICHIA		Refers to a congenital absence of pigment in a lock of hairs which will show as grey or white.
323. ATOPIC DERMATITIS		Also known as eczema.
324. WHITE HAIR		Having no pigment. Possible causes: Genetic. Vitamin B deficiency. Drugs for treatment of arthritis. Other health factors.
325. SPRIONOLACTONE		An antiandrogen and is used in the treatment of androgen related disorders such as female pattern baldness and hirsutism.

A. ROUGH BLOW DRY	B. TELOGEN	C. DHT
D. COLD SORE	E. ATOPIC DERMATITIS	F. EMULSIFIER
G. AXILLA	H. POROSITY	I. ESCHAR
J. ENDOCRINE SYSTEM	K. SLOUGH	L. SPRIONOLACTONE
M. AMORTIZATION	N. ARRECTOR PILI	O. BULB
P. CLARIFIER	Q. WHITE HAIR	R. CUTTING IN
S. LEUCOTRICHIA	T. BLACKHEADS	U. RECIPIENT SITE
V. HENNA	W. BETAINE	X. RELAXER
Y. ANAGEN		

Provide the word that best matches each clue.

326. ALKALI A liquid with a pH higher than 7.

327. AREOLA — The pigmented area surrounding the nipple. A very common area for hair growth.

328. TEMPORARY COLOR — A hair color formula that lasts only until you shampoo your hair.

329. HAIR GROWTH CYCLE — Hair passes through a series of cycles known as Anagen (growing phase), Catagen (resting phase) and Telogen (dormant phase).

330. CICATRICIAL ALOPECIA — This is baldness due to scarring. The follicles are absent in scar tissue.

331. PARFUM — The most concentrated and most fragrant scent and therefore the most expensive.

332. ELECTRODE — In hair removal, a conductor through which electricity enters or leaves the body. An electrolysis needle is an electrode.

333. SOLUBLE — Being able to dissolve into, or being compatible with, another substance.

334. WEFTS — Wefts are temporary hair extensions which are glued into your hair.

335. ALLERGY — A bodily reaction to an irritant. Skin allergies can be exacerbated by solutions put on the skin.

336. PORE — A small opening of the sweat glands of the skin.

337. CATIONIC POLYMER — Positively charges the hair to provide manageability and reduces static.

338. ELECTROLYSIS — In hair removal, the practice of epilation with electrified needles.

339. CLUB HAIR — A non-living hair in the last stages of the hair growth cycle, it is detached from the follicle but has not yet shed.

340. ALLERGEN — Allergen is a substance that causes an allergic reaction.

341. MELASMA — Dark skin discoloration on sun-exposed areas of the face and neck. Young women with brownish skin tones are at greatest risk.

342. GYNECOMASTIA — Excessive development of the male breasts.

343. EXFOLIATION — The removal of dead skin cells to reveal softer skin underneath.

344. ALOPECIA NEUROTICA — Baldness following a nervous disorder or injury to the nervous system.

345.	SKIN REJUVENATION	Combating the signs of ageing using the latest innovative, non-invasive treatments that give you visibly younger, healthy, radiant skin.
346.	CURVED FOLLICLES	A relatively rare condition which makes certain hair removal methods more difficult and can lead to ingrown hairs.
347.	FINISHING SPRAY	A hairspray with medium hold used on a finished style to maintain its shape and hold.
348.	ELASTICITY	The hair's ability to stretch without breaking and then return to its original shape.
349.	LANUGO HAIRS	Are usually shed during the 7th month of fetal life following primary folliculo-genesis.
350.	SEBORRHOEIC DERMATITIS	has been called a more extensive and severe form of dandruff.

A. SEBORRHOEIC DERMATITIS	B. CURVED FOLLICLES	C. LANUGO HAIRS
D. ELECTRODE	E. ALLERGEN	F. PARFUM
G. CICATRICIAL ALOPECIA	H. GYNECOMASTIA	I. MELASMA
J. PORE	K. ELECTROLYSIS	L. EXFOLIATION
M. TEMPORARY COLOR	N. ALOPECIA NEUROTICA	O. HAIR GROWTH CYCLE
P. WEFTS	Q. ALKALI	R. SOLUBLE
S. ALLERGY	T. ELASTICITY	U. FINISHING SPRAY
V. AREOLA	W. CLUB HAIR	X. SKIN REJUVENATION
Y. CATIONIC POLYMER		

Provide the word that best matches each clue.

351.	FOLLICULITIS	A common disorder characterized by inflammation of the hair follicle.
352.	ANTIBIOTIC	A drug or preparation used to prevent and treat infection.
353.	ACETONE	A chemical formed in the blood when the body uses fat instead of glucose (sugar) for energy.
354.	SCLERODERMA	A disease of the skin and connective tissue that can cause hair loss over the affected areas.
355.	HAIR CLONING	A technique under development which could make an unlimited crop of donor hair available for transplanting.
356.	CICATRICIAL ALOPECIA	This is baldness due to scarring. The follicles are absent in scar tissue.
357.	SERUM	A smoothing product to stop your hair from frizzing, keeping it smooth and straight. You'll be able to find a serum that is specifically designed to your own hair type.

358.	CORNROW	Term used to describe an on the scalp braid. These braids can be used to form a track for the cornrow weaving method.
359.	ESCHAR	A small temporary scab that occurs sometimes after electrolysis, especially after overtreatment.
360.	CLONE	A group of genetically identical cells or organisms derived from a single common cell.
361.	HYPERPIGMENTATION	An over excitation of melanocytes, darkening of the skin. Can be seen as sun-induced freckles or melasma.
362.	RELAXER	A chemical process by which the hair is permanently straightened. New-growth areas have to be maintained via 'touch-ups' to continue the straightened pattern.
363.	SEBACEOUS	Fatty or greasy, usually referring to the oil-secreting glans of the scalp.
364.	MINOXIDIL	The generic name of the brand name drug Rogaine. The first drug to be approved by the FDA for the treatment of androgenetic alopecia.
365.	NUTRIENT	A substance, such as a vitamin, which provides elements for the ongoing functioning of the body's metabolic processes.
366.	FINISHING SPRAY	A hairspray with medium hold used on a finished style to maintain its shape and hold.
367.	LASER	An acronym for Light Amplification by the Stimulated Emission of Radiation. A commonly used tool for cosmetic and surgical procedures.
368.	FREEZING SPRAY	A hairspray with the firmest hold used to maintain style of hard to hold hair.
369.	CYST	A closed sac or capsule usually filled with fluid or semisolid material.
370.	SELF TANNER	A sun tanning product that contains DHA, which reacts with amino acids in the top layer of skin, causing it to temporarily darken (2-4 days).
371.	SILICONE	Increases wet and dry combability.
372.	HAIR EXTENSIONS	Used to add volume or length to your hair by bonding synthetic or real hair at your roots.
373.	CONDITIONER	Creamy hair product meant to be used after shampoo. Moisturizes and detangles hair.
374.	BLEND	A modality of electrolysis which uses both thermolysis and galvanic methods.

375. PERM _____ creates curls by restructuring your hair molecules with a chemical, or heat treatment and is generally a long-lasting or permanent change to your hair.

A. HAIR EXTENSIONS	B. SEBACEOUS	C. ANTIBIOTIC
D. LASER	E. SERUM	F. NUTRIENT
G. HAIR CLONING	H. BLEND	I. ACETONE
J. CORNROW	K. RELAXER	L. FREEZING SPRAY
M. SELF TANNER	N. FINISHING SPRAY	O. CONDITIONER
P. HYPERPIGMENTATION	Q. CYST	R. SCLERODERMA
S. PERM	T. SILICONE	U. MINOXIDIL
V. ESCHAR	W. CICATRICIAL ALOPECIA	X. CLONE
Y. FOLLICULITIS		

Provide the word that best matches each clue.

376. TARGETED FAT REDUCTION — Metabolising stubborn fat deposits, typically in the lower body, using methods such as Eporex mesotherapy.

377. RELAXER — A chemical process by which the hair is permanently straightened. New-growth areas have to be maintained via 'touch-ups' to continue the straightened pattern.

378. ALOPECIA — Loss of hair, especially from the head, which either happens naturally or is caused by disease

379. DERMABRASION — A cosmetic procedure used to smooth skin and reduce scars.

380. ELECTRIC TWEEZER — A device that removes hair by grasping hairs above the skin's surface with an electrified tweezers.

381. TAN — When your skin is damaged by exposure to the UVA and UVB rays of the sun, its reaction is to produce more melanin as an attempt to protect itself against further damage.

382. ESCHAR — A small temporary scab that occurs sometimes after electrolysis, especially after overtreatment.

383. ALLERGY — A bodily reaction to an irritant. Skin allergies can be exacerbated by solutions put on the skin.

384. COMEDONES — A medical term for blackheads.

385. HAIR CLONING — A technique under development which could make an unlimited crop of donor hair available for transplanting.

386. INGROWN HAIR — A hair that does not break the surface of the skin, and grows back inward. Can be severe and cause inflammation, soreness and infection.

387. WEFTS — Wefts are temporary hair extensions which are glued into your hair.

388. OXIDATION COLOUR — A color which requires oxygen to make it work.

389. ROUGH BLOW DRY — Used to remove the moisture from wet hair.

390. STEAMING — The process by which most synthetic fiber is curled at the factory.

391. FOLLICULAR UNIT — Groupings of hair that grow together and share the same blood supply.

392. ANDROGEN — Hormone that causes masculine characteristics and affects hair growth.

393. BOAR BRISTLE — A bristle commonly used in natural bristle brushes.

394. SEBACEOUS — Fatty or greasy, usually referring to the oil-secreting glans of the scalp.

395. ALLERGEN — Allergen is a substance that causes an allergic reaction.

396. HIGHLIGHTS — The subtle lifting of color in specific sections of hair.

397. COCAMIDE DEA — Either made synthetically or derived from the kernel of the coconut, it gives lather and cleans skin and hair.

398. JOJOBA OIL — Contains superior properties to keep skin and hair soft. It is beneficial to dry hair.

399. BOTANICAL — Refers to a product containing plants or ingredients made from plants.

400. MOISTURIZER — An emollient cream used to hydrate the skin.

A. BOTANICAL
B. TAN
C. COCAMIDE DEA
D. JOJOBA OIL
E. FOLLICULAR UNIT
F. ELECTRIC TWEEZER
G. ESCHAR
H. ANDROGEN
I. DERMABRASION
J. SEBACEOUS
K. ALLERGY
L. INGROWN HAIR
M. ROUGH BLOW DRY
N. STEAMING
O. OXIDATION COLOUR
P. WEFTS
Q. HAIR CLONING
R. TARGETED FAT REDUCTION
S. MOISTURIZER
T. ALOPECIA

U. ALLERGEN
W. HIGHLIGHTS
Y. COMEDONES

V. RELAXER
X. BOAR BRISTLE

Word Search

1. Find the hidden words. The words have been placed horizontally, vertically, or diagonally. When you locate a word, draw an ellipse around it.

A	L	O	P	E	C	I	A	F	O	L	L	I	C	U	L	A	R	I	S	R	O	F
K	A	O	Q	J	Z	U	O	F	W	J	B	O	A	R	B	R	I	S	T	L	E	A
S	C	S	S	S	X	Q	I	P	A	R	F	U	M	X	O	P	Y	R	J	D	H	C
J	U	T	V	U	U	X	P	A	N	T	O	T	H	E	N	I	C	A	C	I	D	E
Z	P	H	J	B	C	R	U	S	T	I	N	G	F	Q	F	E	M	B	I	W	Y	L
R	U	F	U	C	O	U	Q	X	Z	F	B	O	J	B	W	S	W	B	S	K	I	I
A	N	O	G	U	Z	U	H	W	C	J	R	M	B	S	L	W	V	G	E	S	A	F
Z	C	L	P	T	P	M	T	W	V	O	U	J	Q	F	N	M	T	D	C	U	D	T
B	T	L	C	A	E	S	S	E	N	T	I	A	L	O	I	L	X	D	T	K	X	M
L	U	I	D	N	A	V	H	T	S	N	S	M	V	D	S	X	L	V	I	W	H	J
D	R	C	F	E	N	Y	G	W	W	Z	E	A	I	O	R	T	U	D	O	V	W	P
R	E	L	D	O	O	B	P	B	N	U	Q	T	C	K	J	U	W	R	N	Z	H	U
S	T	E	X	U	D	L	Q	Q	P	D	N	T	T	C	Y	L	U	V	I	M	E	R
T	R	I	W	S	E	H	U	S	V	R	I	E	Q	L	H	E	L	M	N	F	L	W
S	M	I	S	O	P	R	O	P	Y	L	L	A	N	O	L	A	T	E	G	Z	L	B
Y	D	M	I	C	R	O	L	I	N	K	I	N	G	T	E	C	H	N	I	Q	U	E

1. A positive electrode.
2. Dried fluid that seeps from skin in some clients following hair removal such as laser, electrolysis, and depilatories.
3. Hair loss due to inflammation of hair follicles.
4. allows you to only pay attention to a particular area or panel of hair.
5. A bristle commonly used in natural bristle brushes.
6. The most concentrated and most fragrant scent and therefore the most expensive.
7. A method of relieving pain by inserting needles into the skin.
8. A discoloration of skin from blood, sometimes caused by electrolysis, plucking, or waxing. Also known as Purpura.
9. The essence of a plant, removed by compressing, steaming, dissolving or distilling.
10. A non- shiny surface that absorbs light; a dead or dull finish.
11. A Synthetic moisturizer.
12. Flexible resin.
13. Pertains to the skin.
14. The process of attaching hair wefts without braids. The links are sewn on to the wefted hair. The user's natural hair is pulled through and locked secure.
15. Surgical procedure that lifts and stretches the patient's skin to provide a firmer more youthful look.
16. The hair follicle houses the root of the hair. A pore in the skin from which a hair grows.
17. Also called vitamin B5 (a B vitamin), is a water-soluble vitamin required to sustain life (essential nutrient).

A. PARFUM
B. SUBCUTANEOUS
C. MATTE
D. LUVIMER
E. ALOPECIA FOLLICULARIS
F. ESSENTIAL OIL
G. BOAR BRISTLE
H. ACUPUNCTURE
I. BRUISE
J. SECTIONING
K. PANTOTHENIC ACID
L. FOLLICLE
M. ANODE
N. CRUSTING
O. ISOPROPYL LANOLATE
P. FACE LIFT
Q. MICRO LINKING TECHNIQUE

2. Find the hidden words. The words have been placed horizontally, vertically, or diagonally. When you locate a word, draw an ellipse around it.

A	M	L	S	U	P	E	R	O	X	I	D	E	D	I	S	M	U	T	A	S	E	C
L	O	T	S	S	I	P	T	B	X	O	X	H	M	D	J	D	M	E	M	E	C	H
B	X	B	X	J	M	I	C	U	G	G	X	E	T	F	J	F	U	W	S	P	V	R
L	S	L	C	H	W	D	H	A	M	O	R	T	I	Z	A	T	I	O	N	Y	L	O
A	A	W	H	B	Y	E	A	T	E	X	T	U	R	I	Z	E	R	M	Z	N	I	M
C	J	N	I	M	W	R	M	I	F	O	N	U	Z	K	E	B	C	X	P	G	T	O
K	O	R	T	M	R	M	O	Q	F	G	E	N	E	T	H	E	R	A	P	Y	Y	P
S	Y	M	O	X	E	I	M	F	E	A	T	H	E	R	I	N	G	I	L	E	F	H
K	W	Z	S	R	H	S	I	A	N	E	R	V	E	E	N	D	I	N	G	S	K	O
I	K	G	A	F	Q	I	L	M	U	P	J	X	Z	M	R	S	L	V	V	S	X	R
N	H	X	N	K	S	R	E	I	L	A	O	I	N	F	U	S	I	O	N	F	Y	E
E	D	F	H	S	E	M	I	P	E	R	M	A	N	E	N	T	G	J	E	C	L	H
A	H	S	E	O	P	Y	R	Q	S	F	A	C	U	P	U	N	C	T	U	R	E	T
J	A	H	U	A	C	Z	R	P	W	U	E	T	G	W	E	T	T	F	L	O	J	G
K	O	S	P	O	T	V	C	S	Q	M	V	V	M	O	D	W	L	G	D	W	J	M
W	K	V	O	M	F	A	S	H	I	O	N	S	H	A	D	E	I	K	V	N	F	M

1. Gene therapy is a treatment method which involves the manipulation of the genetic makeup.
2. The thin outer layer of skin, on top of the thicker and deeper dermis.
3. The most concentrated and most fragrant scent and therefore the most expensive.
4. Used in many products for blonde hair to enhance color.
5. The enzyme superoxide, catalyzes the dismutation of superoxide into oxygen and hydrogen peroxide.
6. Receptors which respond to touch, pain, pressure, heat and cold.
7. The substructure that is responsible for the spectral selective absorption of electromagnetic radiation.
8. Probably the most difficult type of skin from which to remove hair.
9. Area at the top of the head.
10. A method of relieving pain by inserting needles into the skin.
11. The process of converting one enzyme to another.
12. Tea made by steeping an herb's leaves or flowers in hot water.
13. A basic color with added tone.
14. A color which lasts from 6 - 8 shampoos.
15. Feathering is a cutting technique hairdressers use to take hard lines out of the hair. By cutting into the hair softer lines are created.
16. A natural polymer obtained from sea crustaceans protects the hair.
17. a mild relaxing treatment. Instead of causing the hair to be 'bone straight,' this chemical treatment is left on for a shorter period of time.

A. BLACK SKIN
B. CROWN
C. INFUSION
D. SEMI PERMANENT
E. FEATHERING
F. CHITOSAN
G. PARFUM
H. EPIDERMIS
I. FASHION SHADE
J. ACUPUNCTURE
K. TEXTURIZER
L. AMORTIZATION
M. GENE THERAPY
N. NERVE ENDINGS
O. CHAMOMILE
P. SUPEROXIDE DISMUTASE
Q. CHROMOPHORE

3. Find the hidden words. The words have been placed horizontally, vertically, or diagonally. When you locate a word, draw an ellipse around it.

E	J	M	Z	M	O	E	L	B	J	E	O	W	F	J	Y	U	I	H	M	A	X	I
W	Y	I	Z	U	N	E	X	U	B	C	K	L	H	N	E	Q	L	Y	I	Z	O	R
H	T	Z	O	N	E	H	G	L	V	T	F	X	A	E	L	Q	S	D	C	A	Z	J
I	X	W	O	V	J	S	M	G	H	R	D	J	Y	S	H	J	B	R	R	L	S	M
T	U	T	I	Q	B	D	P	E	U	W	N	Z	L	L	J	K	C	O	O	O	J	Q
E	P	E	M	U	L	S	I	F	I	E	R	F	U	S	I	O	N	G	D	P	U	C
H	G	C	K	P	D	L	U	N	W	Q	Q	D	S	E	X	G	A	E	I	E	H	U
A	L	G	P	W	Z	I	G	S	E	S	Z	N	P	Y	S	L	X	N	F	C	J	O
I	R	Y	A	Y	R	V	H	O	A	F	W	W	S	G	M	E	B	P	F	I	B	V
R	E	O	N	K	D	C	J	A	V	L	L	G	X	S	Y	R	V	E	U	A	U	J
P	B	G	W	T	K	H	Q	P	E	C	L	N	L	N	J	O	W	R	S	A	W	H
J	W	O	U	T	E	R	R	O	O	T	S	H	E	A	T	H	D	O	E	D	O	W
R	M	B	O	D	Y	D	I	A	T	H	E	R	M	Y	G	O	K	X	N	N	Y	F
X	D	R	U	G	T	R	E	A	T	M	E	N	T	M	D	P	Z	I	U	A	Z	K
D	C	E	T	Y	L	A	L	C	O	H	O	L	F	T	A	Q	W	D	A	T	X	W
J	E	L	E	C	T	R	O	L	Y	S	I	S	V	B	J	L	X	E	F	A	B	F

1. A thickening agent or binding agent added to products to change their physical composition (joins two or more ingredients together).
2. Another name for thermolysis.
3. A gentle humectant, lather booster, and emulsifier. In hair products, it is used to smooth and soften the hair cuticle.
4. Cleansing agent that is a sodium or potassium salt of animal or vegetable fat.
5. Congenital baldness or baldness at birth.
6. The volume or springiness of hair.
7. Used to oxidize (expand) artificial color molecules. Can also lighten natural color pigment.
8. Optimum hold without overload.
9. Excess hair can be increased or decreased by certain drugs. These drugs often affect hormonal levels.
10. A point midway up the hair follicle which researchers suspect must be damaged to induce permanent hair removal
11. The process of attaching small pieces of human hair with a special adhesive and a thermal gun.
12. In hair removal, the practice of epilation with electrified needles.
13. A soft thin layer surrounding the lower two-thirds of a hair.
14. The forehead, nose and chin areas, which tend to be oilier than the cheeks.
15. A hair weave is usually a hairpiece with layered gaps made into it.
16. Having no pigment. Possible causes: Genetic. Vitamin B deficiency. Drugs for treatment of arthritis. Other health factors.

A. WEAVE
B. EMULSIFIER
C. SOAP
D. MICRO DIFFUSE
E. DIATHERMY
F. ALOPECIA ADNATA
G. OUTER ROOT SHEATH
H. BODY
I. DRUG TREATMENT
J. CETYL ALCOHOL
K. WHITE HAIR
L. ELECTROLYSIS
M. BULGE
N. FUSION
O. T ZONE
P. HYDROGEN PEROXIDE

4. Find the hidden words. The words have been placed horizontally, vertically, or diagonally. When you locate a word, draw an ellipse around it.

H	L	L	D	F	S	K	I	N	R	E	J	U	V	E	N	A	T	I	O	N	B	O
J	Q	X	O	B	T	R	V	E	S	P	D	N	M	M	Z	A	T	C	A	Q	Q	I
S	Z	I	U	L	P	Z	I	D	Z	N	C	L	O	N	E	X	Q	A	G	K	Q	D
V	V	E	B	A	E	E	N	V	Z	Y	M	S	T	R	R	O	Y	T	H	B	N	K
U	P	S	L	C	R	V	F	K	E	P	I	L	A	T	I	O	N	A	I	X	P	R
H	H	B	E	K	M	J	U	M	E	T	A	B	O	L	I	S	M	G	T	X	I	R
D	W	P	B	H	A	E	S	R	R	W	L	A	B	L	O	N	D	E	H	A	I	R
F	Q	H	L	E	N	O	I	B	G	W	B	D	V	P	A	L	Z	N	L	W	G	F
H	R	F	I	A	E	Q	O	K	Y	U	I	L	A	N	U	G	O	H	A	I	R	S
F	H	D	N	D	N	E	N	X	F	C	N	X	V	V	E	R	P	B	Q	F	B	K
X	N	D	D	S	T	W	X	R	S	Z	I	I	Z	K	A	R	J	V	R	U	M	I
T	D	R	G	Q	L	N	D	P	E	G	S	E	Q	E	Q	Q	U	T	X	S	V	Y
I	Q	K	F	H	Y	P	O	P	I	G	M	E	N	T	A	T	I	O	N	I	O	G
A	P	P	L	E	C	I	D	E	R	V	I	N	E	G	A	R	R	W	D	O	L	J
A	C	S	W	X	S	R	X	P	S	I	M	M	V	S	V	T	K	X	Q	N	Y	V
O	A	D	C	I	C	A	T	R	I	C	I	A	L	A	L	O	P	E	C	I	A	S

1. A clinical testing method in which neither patient nor doctor know what medication or procedure is being used.
2. The removal of hair below the skin's surface.
3. The process of attaching small pieces of human hair with a special adhesive and a thermal gun.
4. A group of genetically identical cells or organisms derived from a single common cell.
5. Are usually shed during the 7th month of fetal life following primary folliculo-genesis.
6. Tea made by steeping an herb's leaves or flowers in hot water.
7. A recessive hereditary trait which presents as white hair due to defective melanin production thought to be caused by a mutation within genes.
8. Combating the signs of ageing using the latest innovative, non-invasive treatments that give you visibly younger, healthy, radiant skin.
9. Is not as visible, but it's also harder to treat. Lasers have limited effects on it because of its lack of pigment, and it is difficult to see against the skin.
10. This is baldness due to scarring. The follicles are absent in scar tissue.
11. A natural solvent in oils and creams. It acidifies products.
12. Caused by an absence of melanocytes, whitening of the skin. Vitiligo is a common medical complaint.
13. Completely changing the natural color of the hair.
14. The body transformation of food into energy.
15. This is the end of the active growth period, and is marked by changes occurring in the follicle.
16. A type of clogged pore in the skin with a visible black plug.

A. ALBINISM
B. CATAGEN
C. FUSION
D. BLONDE HAIR
E. INFUSION
F. CICATRICIAL ALOPECIA
G. BLACKHEADS
H. DOUBLE BLIND
I. SKIN REJUVENATION
J. HYPOPIGMENTATION
K. EPILATION
L. APPLE CIDER VINEGAR
M. PERMANENTLY
N. CLONE
O. METABOLISM
P. LANUGO HAIRS

5. Find the hidden words. The words have been placed horizontally, vertically, or diagonally. When you locate a word, draw an ellipse around it.

M	R	J	W	G	L	S	E	X	F	O	L	I	A	T	I	N	G	X	E	N	L	U
A	R	R	E	C	T	O	R	P	I	L	I	S	C	A	L	A	M	I	N	E	C	B
Z	G	F	A	D	I	R	E	C	T	C	U	R	R	E	N	T	D	Y	J	W	L	X
M	G	V	K	E	O	S	S	F	F	A	N	T	M	W	T	O	R	E	J	Z	S	U
O	Y	P	T	E	X	T	U	R	I	Z	E	R	I	A	A	U	C	V	Y	Y	U	B
A	F	X	M	Z	Z	T	B	N	W	B	M	N	T	D	J	J	S	S	B	X	T	O
B	L	G	M	O	F	S	S	K	C	E	O	U	R	R	W	B	R	E	Q	Y	E	A
D	Y	N	L	C	P	W	Q	K	K	C	W	A	A	T	Q	A	K	T	A	I	C	R
O	T	C	A	L	C	I	U	M	T	H	I	O	G	L	Y	C	O	L	A	T	E	B
M	W	X	S	B	M	T	M	H	A	C	U	P	U	N	C	T	U	R	E	B	N	R
E	L	Z	O	N	T	Z	A	M	Q	W	C	E	X	T	R	A	C	T	A	S	B	I
N	S	U	Q	X	G	O	B	G	L	P	P	C	E	Q	O	J	N	J	D	C	G	S
I	P	K	B	L	F	N	X	Z	Y	D	C	H	I	T	O	S	A	N	E	F	E	T
A	N	A	G	E	N	E	C	B	U	F	Y	K	O	G	G	U	B	W	J	M	L	L
C	L	I	M	B	A	Z	O	L	E	J	C	M	C	C	M	Z	X	J	M	H	S	E
F	S	J	C	I	R	O	U	G	H	B	L	O	W	D	R	Y	I	K	J	Z	C	W

1. The active dissolving ingredient in many cream depilatories
2. A natural polymer obtained from sea crustaceans protects the hair.
3. A method of relieving pain by inserting needles into the skin.
4. a mild relaxing treatment. Instead of causing the hair to be 'bone straight,' this chemical treatment is left on for a shorter period of time.
5. A bristle commonly used in natural bristle brushes.
6. This is the growing phase of the hair cycle which lasts about seven years in a healthy person. The active stage in a hair growth cycle.
7. Highly effective active anti-dandruff ingredient. Combats bacteria on the scalp.
8. A pink ointment sometimes used to treat skin irritation
9. The forehead, nose and chin areas, which tend to be oilier than the cheeks.
10. Used to remove the moisture from wet hair.
11. a type of electrical energy that travels in one direction.
12. A process of removing the top dead skin layers to reveal healthier, newer skin underneath.
13. Creates "Goose Bumps" when stimulated.
14. The soft area between the rib cage and the pubic area. A common area for excess hair, often in a line from the belly button to the pubic hair.
15. An herbal concentrate produced by separating the essential or active part of an herb into a solvent material.
16. Jelly like material formed by the coagulation of a liquid. Semi-solid emulsion that liquefies when applied to the skin.

A. CALCIUM THIOGLYCOLATE
B. ABDOMEN
C. GEL
D. DIRECT CURRENT
E. T ZONE
F. CLIMBAZOLE
G. BOAR BRISTLE
H. ROUGH BLOW DRY
I. TEXTURIZER
J. ARRECTOR PILI
K. CHITOSAN
L. EXTRACT
M. CALAMINE
N. ANAGEN
O. ACUPUNCTURE
P. EXFOLIATING

6. Find the hidden words. The words have been placed horizontally, vertically, or diagonally. When you locate a word, draw an ellipse around it.

I	L	C	U	W	W	N	N	O	R	Y	V	U	M	C	V	A	R	G	F	P	R	I
X	F	F	W	X	D	M	T	L	P	Z	N	H	G	R	D	R	A	S	C	A	B	W
Y	T	B	G	W	O	Q	M	I	R	T	D	U	S	O	L	N	L	F	W	N	X	Z
S	B	U	D	R	L	O	O	I	O	E	Z	Z	C	W	E	E	V	K	E	T	E	C
Z	A	I	N	A	L	S	W	S	P	V	S	S	R	N	L	D	M	U	C	H	I	O
E	X	T	E	N	S	I	O	N	E	V	D	P	U	J	U	H	I	A	A	E	H	N
I	I	T	F	Y	Q	Q	D	H	C	B	X	X	N	R	F	B	C	J	C	N	L	D
V	T	S	O	W	P	S	W	E	I	B	V	A	C	G	O	U	R	F	C	O	S	I
I	F	R	L	C	Y	X	B	F	A	O	L	J	H	G	X	L	O	C	E	L	U	T
U	E	U	L	O	A	P	D	R	P	M	O	W	D	U	Q	X	D	S	N	P	H	I
S	E	L	I	J	Z	J	G	N	X	R	N	H	R	E	J	P	I	H	T	A	Q	O
S	F	C	C	H	I	R	S	U	T	I	S	M	Y	L	K	F	F	E	C	B	D	N
E	N	E	L	C	B	L	E	M	I	S	H	Q	J	A	G	P	F	Q	O	A	T	E
B	O	R	E	S	C	A	T	A	P	H	O	R	E	S	I	S	U	C	L	D	K	R
N	Q	D	I	S	C	O	M	F	O	R	T	R	J	B	W	N	S	G	O	W	H	G
B	C	E	T	Y	L	A	L	C	O	H	O	L	K	L	H	C	E	N	R	B	E	M

1. Esters found in sunscreen and cosmetic products that can make skin sensitive.
2. The brand name for finestaride. The only drug approved by the FDA to treat hair loss.
3. Usually a sharp, intense color used as a contrast or pickup for color scheme. It is used to add excitement to an overall effect
4. Blood or pigment based visible mark.
5. The hair follicle houses the root of the hair. A pore in the skin from which a hair grows.
6. Hair extensions are pieces of real or synthetic weaved close to the scalp in order to achieve greater length or fullness.
7. A gentle humectant, lather booster, and emulsifier. In hair products, it is used to smooth and soften the hair cuticle.
8. Area at the top of the head.
9. A technique for drying your hair which creates a style at the same time.
10. Optimum hold without overload.
11. An area of tissue erosion. They are always depressed and are due to irritation. They may become infected and inflamed as they grow.
12. Creamy hair product meant to be used after shampoo. Moisturizes and detangles hair.
13. Excessive hair growth, accompanied by enlarged hair follicles and increased pigmentation.
14. The forcing of substances into the skin from a positive to a negative pole. It is sometimes used after electrolysis to firm skin and reduce redness.
15. Varies greatly by individual and body area. Electrolysis is generally considered most painful, followed by laser, plucking, waxing and finally pulse light sources.
16. Aids detangling. Provides volume, control and shine.

A. PABA
B. CROWN
C. CETYL ALCOHOL
D. CONDITIONER
E. FOLLICLE
F. EXTENSION
G. MICRO DIFFUSE
H. DISCOMFORT
I. ACCENT COLOR
J. HIRSUTISM
K. PANTHENOL
L. PROPECIA
M. BLEMISH
N. ULCER
O. CATAPHORESIS
P. SCRUNCH DRY

7. Find the hidden words. The words have been placed horizontally, vertically, or diagonally. When you locate a word, draw an ellipse around it.

H	Q	D	W	K	X	R	L	H	B	P	O	P	V	Y	H	T	O	V	B	I	A	W
U	B	U	E	S	F	F	L	Z	A	A	E	Q	X	Q	U	P	D	X	N	U	Y	E
E	C	Y	U	I	S	S	M	P	L	N	S	N	O	S	M	A	Z	W	L	L	W	C
C	C	O	L	L	A	G	E	N	K	F	T	S	M	Z	I	L	I	B	Y	Q	Y	W
R	C	A	T	I	O	N	I	C	A	A	R	G	T	X	D	M	I	O	N	I	C	E
X	D	X	X	C	Z	J	C	S	L	Q	O	R	Y	L	I	R	H	B	R	B	F	F
S	B	K	S	O	S	L	S	C	I	Q	G	T	U	B	T	O	N	L	X	N	G	T
U	V	C	T	N	O	N	W	S	N	Z	E	N	C	U	Y	L	A	A	W	U	G	S
P	T	Z	Y	E	V	A	E	L	E	K	N	V	H	G	P	L	B	N	F	S	E	R
Q	L	A	L	P	H	A	H	Y	D	R	O	X	Y	A	C	I	D	C	O	I	R	E
F	S	S	F	J	Y	B	T	Y	N	L	T	Y	O	K	U	N	Q	H	Q	I	S	G
E	N	E	R	G	Y	D	E	N	S	I	T	Y	Q	D	Y	G	H	I	J	P	J	F
I	S	H	C	U	T	D	B	A	S	I	C	S	H	A	D	E	H	N	Z	C	M	T
N	H	B	P	L	M	I	C	R	O	D	I	F	F	U	S	E	U	G	P	H	W	U
Y	Z	Y	Y	O	O	U	X	Z	I	S	N	Q	V	D	Q	E	V	H	M	R	N	W
Z	S	I	B	I	W	D	E	P	I	L	A	T	I	O	N	E	S	C	H	A	R	P

1. Optimum hold without overload.
2. A substance with a pH greater than 7; non acidic.
3. A technique used to smooth out the shaft of a lock by rolling it, with or without product, between the palms of the hands.
4. The temporary removal of hair.
5. Possessing a positive electrical charge. Cationic detergents are often used in shampoos because they reduce static electricity and leave the hair manageable.
6. The amount of moisture available in the air.
7. Term used to measure the output energy for Lasers and Pulsed Light Sources.
8. Process where water molecules are broken down by ions into smaller droplets. This then allows the hair to absorb the moisture more easily.
9. A whitening of the skin sometimes caused by some types of hair removal.
10. A small temporary scab that occurs sometimes after electrolysis, especially after overtreatment.
11. These solutions are used as exfoliants. They can help reduce ingrown hairs and improve the look of skin.
12. Increases wet and dry combability.
13. Wefts are temporary hair extensions which are glued into your hair.
14. A female hormone sometimes linked to increased hair growth.
15. A natural or neutral color.
16. A protein that holds all connective tissue together under the skin.

A. WEFTS
B. PALM ROLLING
C. DEPILATION
D. ENERGY DENSITY
E. COLLAGEN
F. HUMIDITY
G. SILICONE
H. BLANCHING
I. CATIONIC
J. BASIC SHADE
K. MICRO DIFFUSE
L. ALKALINE
M. ALPHA HYDROXY ACID
N. IONIC
O. ESCHAR
P. ESTROGEN

8. Find the hidden words. The words have been placed horizontally, vertically, or diagonally. When you locate a word, draw an ellipse around it.

Q	L	M	S	P	D	H	Q	X	Z	F	B	D	Q	M	P	Z	G	M	F	W	B	L
F	K	N	E	R	V	E	E	N	D	I	N	G	S	T	U	F	Z	X	O	Q	J	C
F	A	D	E	P	I	L	A	T	O	R	I	E	S	E	I	C	F	L	L	T	Y	M
H	Z	Z	H	C	X	P	S	H	K	Y	M	D	C	E	G	C	Y	U	L	X	L	I
S	G	P	D	V	C	M	D	U	N	U	V	T	Y	O	E	F	T	K	I	M	A	S
H	J	F	F	L	P	B	Y	M	A	C	A	G	Q	W	Q	F	E	U	C	A	Y	K
W	M	C	L	A	R	I	F	I	E	R	Z	L	M	F	Q	U	A	D	L	T	E	F
N	A	A	S	M	C	P	Y	D	N	A	E	N	T	E	L	S	T	A	E	M	R	N
E	W	I	E	X	F	O	L	I	A	T	I	N	G	U	D	I	R	V	S	N	I	Z
S	W	W	A	P	H	V	W	T	K	Z	C	H	U	N	G	O	E	R	H	G	N	Z
F	I	S	V	Z	L	S	D	Y	Y	W	W	T	X	F	E	N	E	M	E	K	G	T
C	A	M	M	O	N	I	U	M	T	H	I	O	G	L	Y	C	O	L	A	T	E	M
L	W	S	W	T	L	Y	F	S	R	P	R	N	D	P	F	H	I	X	T	W	K	I
L	T	E	L	O	G	E	N	E	F	F	L	U	V	I	U	M	L	I	H	Y	A	R
C	X	D	H	B	L	E	M	I	S	H	T	R	A	N	S	L	U	C	E	N	T	D
N	O	U	S	C	L	E	R	O	D	E	R	M	A	E	S	T	R	O	G	E	N	O

1. Blood or pigment based visible mark.
2. Protects the hair during its growth stage.
3. an extraction from the Melaleuca tree.
4. A female hormone sometimes linked to increased hair growth.
5. Hair shafts are produced by follicles within the skin in all but few locations
6. A process of removing the top dead skin layers to reveal healthier, newer skin underneath.
7. Substances used to dissolve hair above the skin's surface.
8. The amount of moisture available in the air.
9. A common ingredient in chemical depilatories.
10. The process of attaching small pieces of human hair with a special adhesive and a thermal gun.
11. A clarifying shampoo is slightly stronger than everyday shampoos and is designed to remove products, hard water or chlorine residue that have built-up over time.
12. Receptors which respond to touch, pain, pressure, heat and cold.
13. A disease of the skin and connective tissue that can cause hair loss over the affected areas.
14. A technique used by hairdressers to change the thickness of the hair, creating either a thinning or thicker appearance.
15. Allows some light to pass through.

A. BLEMISH
B. TRANSLUCENT
C. ESTROGEN
D. AMMONIUM THIOGLYCOLATE
E. TELOGEN EFFLUVIUM
F. SCLERODERMA
G. EXFOLIATING
H. TEA TREE OIL
I. CLARIFIER
J. HUMIDITY
K. FOLLICLE SHEATH
L. FUSION
M. DEPILATORIES
N. NERVE ENDINGS
O. LAYERING

9. Find the hidden words. The words have been placed horizontally, vertically, or diagonally. When you locate a word, draw an ellipse around it.

J	Q	H	V	B	O	M	M	K	H	G	E	F	U	P	Z	F	M	X	R	P	D	A
A	O	A	T	W	C	J	P	B	B	S	U	N	S	C	R	E	E	N	L	R	N	G
L	C	I	D	S	O	G	E	O	L	W	H	Y	V	B	B	S	W	L	I	O	H	L
O	D	R	B	Q	P	Q	R	A	X	Q	O	U	W	Z	Y	F	K	L	Z	T	T	Y
P	E	G	B	M	E	F	M	L	J	K	U	Q	P	T	I	Z	M	B	A	E	R	C
E	A	R	U	X	R	J	A	K	X	M	F	C	A	L	S	L	Y	C	N	I	K	E
C	B	O	H	N	M	U	N	A	B	U	L	K	H	A	I	R	Y	D	Y	N	T	R
I	H	W	Z	A	A	E	E	L	I	P	A	L	M	I	T	A	T	E	P	T	I	I
A	V	T	Z	G	N	E	N	I	Q	N	P	W	R	V	K	E	X	S	I	R	S	N
A	M	H	F	X	E	X	T	N	F	N	F	T	W	W	E	C	X	L	B	E	T	T
R	L	C	D	W	N	M	L	E	R	Y	X	X	L	L	V	Y	N	Z	A	A	B	O
E	Y	Y	H	O	T	Y	Y	K	R	D	H	T	N	H	U	I	N	Y	G	T	T	N
A	R	C	S	U	R	E	C	I	P	I	E	N	T	S	I	T	E	V	W	M	B	E
T	O	L	I	A	L	T	R	F	A	S	H	I	O	N	S	H	A	D	E	E	G	G
A	X	E	W	D	O	N	O	R	S	I	T	E	D	D	Q	X	D	I	T	N	A	O
S	A	L	T	E	R	N	A	T	I	N	G	C	U	R	R	E	N	T	E	T	Q	D

1. Hair loss which occurs in patches on the scalp.
2. Completely changing the natural color of the hair.
3. Products with ingredients that absorb UVA and UVB rays.
4. Distribution of ashen and warm pigments, visual effect of gold or ash in the hair.
5. A substance with a pH greater than 7; non acidic.
6. A humectant which absorbs moisture from the air to keep hair moist.
7. Site where hair roots are taken from during transplant surgery.
8. A definition set by the American FDA that most laser and intense light source manufacturers claim to meet for hair removal.
9. Hair passes through a series of cycles known as Anagen (growing phase), Catagen (resting phase) and Telogen (dormant phase).
10. Term for loose commercial hair. This hair is used for creating wefts or for services like fusion.
11. A treatment used on the hair. Designed to add strength and elasticity to the hair by adding protein to the cortex.
12. The type of electricity that comes from a wall outlet (AC), as opposed to direct current (DC).
13. Synthetic moisturizer.
14. A basic color with added tone.
15. The bald or thinning area where hair grafts or plugs a transplanted.

A. PERMANENTLY
B. PALMITATE
C. SUNSCREEN
D. PROTEIN TREATMENT
E. ALOPECIA AREATA
F. ALKALINE
G. BULK HAIR
H. FASHION SHADE
I. GLYCERIN
J. RECIPIENT SITE
K. PERMANENT
L. HAIR GROWTH CYCLE
M. DONOR SITE
N. TONE
O. ALTERNATING CURRENT

10. Find the hidden words. The words have been placed horizontally, vertically, or diagonally. When you locate a word, draw an ellipse around it.

O	Y	N	P	E	W	G	F	F	C	G	A	P	K	D	G	J	Q	M	G	K	E	X
R	O	U	G	H	B	L	O	W	D	R	Y	A	F	A	J	H	J	Q	I	Y	X	U
H	D	W	X	F	M	M	G	L	C	C	J	C	Q	N	Q	Y	B	K	W	O	F	Y
N	Q	Y	G	X	G	F	I	A	O	F	G	I	G	A	O	N	I	L	N	Y	O	Z
J	C	J	Y	T	D	N	K	S	W	T	H	D	L	Z	H	I	A	X	E	M	L	C
K	L	D	I	W	Z	R	A	E	D	X	A	M	Y	O	V	N	N	W	R	I	I	E
Z	C	S	B	U	E	A	U	R	N	K	V	A	C	L	A	N	A	X	V	B	A	G
I	U	A	M	D	X	I	P	C	K	L	I	N	E	V	V	C	E	S	E	X	T	A
K	D	C	H	B	I	R	T	H	C	O	N	T	R	O	L	G	S	V	E	R	I	X
J	Q	R	P	X	B	Y	D	D	B	R	S	L	I	B	A	S	T	L	N	L	O	V
K	Z	U	R	J	V	F	Y	L	P	O	R	E	N	S	Y	A	H	E	D	D	N	T
T	A	M	M	C	A	F	R	O	H	A	I	R	S	T	Y	L	E	N	I	O	T	G
T	R	A	L	H	B	L	I	S	T	E	R	F	T	E	J	Q	T	T	N	W	H	Y
I	X	G	E	I	C	E	S	D	F	C	Y	A	K	H	Q	G	I	I	G	Z	M	Z
M	I	C	R	O	D	I	F	F	U	S	E	F	B	S	Z	F	C	G	S	C	Q	L
U	C	C	C	S	F	K	W	U	H	T	M	O	N	Q	M	X	M	O	G	U	L	N

1. An acronym for Light Amplification by the Stimulated Emission of Radiation. A commonly used tool for cosmetic and surgical procedures.
2. The removal of dead skin cells to reveal softer skin underneath.
3. Optimum hold without overload.
4. Drugs that sometimes cause increased hair growth.
5. A flat, discolored area of skin similar to a freckle.
6. A substance used to relieve all feeling.
7. A drug sometimes linked to excess hair growth.
8. Bone in the lower back
9. A small fluid-filled bubble on the skin caused by heat from over treatment with certain types of hair removal.
10. A small opening of the sweat glands of the skin.
11. Receptors which respond to touch, pain, pressure, heat and cold.
12. Used to remove the moisture from wet hair.
13. A humectant which absorbs moisture from the air to keep hair moist.
14. The combination of sweat and sebum that provides the skin's protective coating.
15. A rounded, thick, tightly curled hair style.

A. ANAESTHETIC
B. LENTIGO
C. ACID MANTLE
D. SACRUM
E. BIRTH CONTROL
F. MICRO DIFFUSE
G. NERVE ENDINGS
H. EXFOLIATION
I. GLYCERIN
J. DANAZOL
K. ROUGH BLOW DRY
L. AFRO HAIRSTYLE
M. PORE
N. BLISTER
O. LASER

11. Find the hidden words. The words have been placed horizontally, vertically, or diagonally. When you locate a word, draw an ellipse around it.

N	E	O	T	R	I	C	H	O	P	T	I	L	O	S	I	S	L	S	G	D	H	K
S	U	R	F	A	C	T	A	N	T	S	L	Y	J	L	V	U	W	M	F	B	F	C
F	A	F	C	W	T	P	Y	D	F	O	L	L	I	C	U	L	I	T	I	S	A	P
U	P	C	G	X	R	O	K	G	L	A	B	E	L	L	A	N	O	A	D	V	M	F
L	R	A	B	K	E	C	N	R	Z	O	X	S	R	U	I	D	I	I	V	B	M	Q
E	D	R	V	R	A	T	H	R	E	A	D	V	E	I	N	J	C	O	H	L	O	J
J	Y	B	F	X	T	J	X	T	J	E	R	U	C	G	D	A	W	X	O	E	N	D
F	G	O	F	F	M	S	P	L	I	T	E	N	D	S	E	N	Q	B	P	A	I	A
S	H	M	O	G	E	H	Q	Q	S	U	I	X	O	U	E	Q	B	N	X	C	A	Z
U	U	E	L	O	N	C	A	S	T	R	A	T	I	O	N	K	B	C	D	H	S	A
K	T	R	V	D	T	J	M	K	G	W	Z	N	J	E	D	G	G	Q	M	B	O	C
Z	A	T	O	P	I	C	D	E	R	M	A	T	I	T	I	S	S	B	V	F	G	T
D	S	U	B	C	U	T	A	N	E	O	U	S	T	I	S	S	U	E	E	E	M	X
R	J	A	R	R	E	C	T	O	R	P	I	L	I	O	B	K	L	R	G	V	Q	Y
M	L	Q	I	H	E	K	Q	C	E	Y	K	A	T	I	D	F	R	C	R	U	A	L
M	T	R	E	G	B	J	I	H	J	U	Q	S	W	I	T	C	H	P	K	P	Y	L

1. An alkaline ingredient used in some permanent hair color. An ingredient that results in a chemical action that decolorizes the hair.
2. used in between Shampoo and Conditioner to put protein back into the hair.
3. broken capillaries.
4. A polymer on the basis of acrylic acid. Provides a thickening, gelling action and consistency regulator for cosmetic products.
5. A device that produces short intense bursts of energy from a laser.
6. Split ends.
7. The space between the eyebrows.
8. Trichoptilosis
9. Creates "Goose Bumps" when stimulated.
10. Active agent that allows oil to mix with water. Used in skincare products like cleansers, wetting agents, emulsifiers, solubizers, conditioning agents and foam stabilizers.
11. The surgical removal of one or both testicles or ovaries.
12. A common disorder characterized by inflammation of the hair follicle.
13. Also known as eczema.
14. A method used to disguise (not remove) hair by lightening its color.
15. The body's shock absorber.

A. GLABELLA
D. BLEACH
G. TREATMENT
J. FOLLICULITIS
M. SUBCUTANEOUS TISSUE
B. ARRECTOR PILI
E. Q SWITCH
H. TRICHOPTILOSIS
K. AMMONIA
N. CARBOMER
C. THREAD VEIN
F. SPLIT ENDS
I. CASTRATION
L. ATOPIC DERMATITIS
O. SURFACTANTS

12. Find the hidden words. The words have been placed horizontally, vertically, or diagonally. When you locate a word, draw an ellipse around it.

M	I	C	R	O	L	I	N	K	I	N	G	T	E	C	H	N	I	Q	U	E	Y	U
O	S	J	T	T	Z	O	I	C	H	A	M	P	E	R	E	M	P	S	Z	E	M	Z
D	C	A	P	Q	A	E	O	T	W	R	C	A	T	A	P	H	O	R	E	S	I	S
B	L	Z	G	E	Y	O	H	P	A	N	T	H	E	N	O	L	G	E	X	F	Q	E
S	E	E	S	T	C	O	N	T	A	C	T	C	O	O	L	I	N	G	D	V	E	C
U	R	L	W	S	O	J	Q	E	S	T	R	O	G	E	N	D	K	L	I	U	Y	C
P	O	A	Z	P	X	C	X	I	E	D	T	B	E	S	J	N	B	Y	V	G	K	R
V	D	I	M	E	A	U	W	D	C	R	Q	L	B	P	N	C	Y	L	G	H	F	I
A	E	C	V	Q	W	V	R	A	A	S	J	E	A	R	I	R	H	E	A	N	H	N
T	R	A	P	F	T	T	A	F	R	C	P	N	Q	I	F	X	H	T	S	U	L	E
U	M	C	Y	R	N	Z	T	E	T	B	J	D	Y	T	T	B	J	B	L	D	M	G
S	A	I	A	H	B	Q	Q	D	O	K	K	M	L	Z	T	R	P	Y	M	S	G	L
O	Q	D	G	P	L	O	A	Z	W	T	W	E	F	T	S	U	J	G	P	T	U	A
U	P	I	G	M	E	N	T	E	D	L	E	S	I	O	N	I	A	S	M	K	D	N
H	O	Y	P	J	R	H	H	U	Z	G	Q	V	X	M	G	S	D	O	T	B	R	D
U	J	F	D	V	O	U	T	E	R	R	O	O	T	S	H	E	A	T	H	S	R	Y

1. Commonly used in the treatment of acne and other skin conditions.
2. The forcing of substances into the skin from a positive to a negative pole. It is sometimes used after electrolysis to firm skin and reduce redness.
3. a light mist or spray, which when used as verb means to lightly spray your hair.
4. A method of cooling the epidermis immediately prior to laser irradiation in hopes of reducing or eliminating damage to the skin's surface.
5. A soft thin layer surrounding the lower two-thirds of a hair.
6. A medical term for sweat gland. These tiny pores do not contain hair follicles.
7. A female hormone sometimes linked to increased hair growth.
8. Aids detangling. Provides volume, control and shine.
9. A modality of electrolysis which uses both thermolysis and galvanic methods.
10. A discoloration of skin from blood, sometimes caused by electrolysis, plucking, or waxing. Also known as Purpura.
11. Variety of skin conditions mainly the result of excess melanin. Commonly known as Café au Lait stains, birthmarks, age spots and freckles.
12. A measurement of electrical current.
13. The process of attaching hair wefts without braids. The links are sewn on to the wefted hair. The user's natural hair is pulled through and locked secure.
14. Wefts are temporary hair extensions which are glued into your hair.
15. A disease of the skin and connective tissue that can cause hair loss over the affected areas.

A. PANTHENOL
B. BLEND
C. OUTER ROOT SHEATH
D. SCLERODERMA
E. BRUISE
F. WEFTS
G. SPRITZ
H. CONTACT COOLING
I. ESTROGEN
J. CATAPHORESIS
K. MICRO LINKING TECHNIQUE
L. ECCRINE GLAND
M. AZELAIC ACID
N. PIGMENTED LESION
O. AMPERE

13. Find the hidden words. The words have been placed horizontally, vertically, or diagonally. When you locate a word, draw an ellipse around it.

O	G	A	I	C	G	C	H	Z	B	W	S	R	C	T	C	P	T	W	I	N	X	D
A	L	T	E	R	N	A	T	I	N	G	C	U	R	R	E	N	T	T	J	M	N	E
T	L	O	Z	Q	I	C	F	T	G	D	I	S	R	K	Y	D	M	W	I	Z	S	Q
C	O	C	A	R	B	O	N	D	I	O	X	I	D	E	L	A	S	E	R	B	W	I
K	R	P	C	G	Z	H	P	S	Y	N	O	O	C	N	X	C	I	W	A	W	H	A
F	X	A	P	T	Q	E	W	A	M	O	V	N	R	Q	X	M	C	H	X	O	Q	A
I	C	N	Y	M	K	R	P	Z	Z	R	G	R	O	V	M	E	D	U	L	L	A	P
G	G	T	A	A	R	E	K	V	X	S	L	J	W	Y	D	X	E	S	C	H	A	R
K	Y	H	R	R	A	N	U	U	K	I	I	A	N	T	I	S	E	P	T	I	C	J
W	Y	E	E	X	G	T	L	E	E	T	R	X	U	V	Z	Y	K	Q	M	L	W	C
Q	E	N	O	Q	K	L	Z	A	D	E	R	M	A	L	P	A	P	I	L	L	A	B
M	Y	O	L	Y	E	I	E	P	I	D	E	R	M	I	S	L	G	N	F	K	H	C
K	Z	L	A	Q	T	G	U	M	D	H	Y	M	N	A	O	J	X	I	R	E	F	O
X	G	K	S	G	S	H	S	J	C	H	A	M	O	M	I	L	E	O	L	S	Z	J
D	I	S	T	O	R	T	E	D	H	A	I	R	F	O	L	L	I	C	L	E	S	J
A	X	B	R	O	K	E	N	C	A	P	I	L	L	A	R	I	E	S	L	X	K	E

1. Site where hair roots are taken from during transplant surgery.
2. Light that stays focused, a property of lasers.
3. The type of electricity that comes from a wall outlet (AC), as opposed to direct current (DC).
4. Area at the top of the head.
5. These tiny blood vessels at the surface of the skin appear as streaks or blotches.
6. The thin outer layer of skin, on top of the thicker and deeper dermis.
7. A relatively rare condition in which the follicle is not straight.
8. The pigmented area surrounding the nipple. A very common area for hair growth.
9. Aids detangling. Provides volume, control and shine.
10. A small temporary scab that occurs sometimes after electrolysis, especially after overtreatment.
11. Used in many products for blonde hair to enhance color.
12. Situated at the base of the hair follicle. Contains nerves and blood vessels which supply glucose for energy and amino acids to make keratin.
13. Also known as a CO2 laser, these are commonly used to perform skin resurfacing.
14. A chemical agent that prevent the growth of bacteria.
15. The medulla is a central zone of cells usually only present in large thick hairs.

A. CARBON DIOXIDE LASER
D. DISTORTED HAIR FOLLICLES
G. ANTISEPTIC
J. AREOLA
M. DONOR SITE
B. ALTERNATING CURRENT
E. PANTHENOL
H. CHAMOMILE
K. MEDULLA
N. COHERENT LIGHT
C. CROWN
F. BROKEN CAPILLARIES
I. ESCHAR
L. DERMAL PAPILLA
O. EPIDERMIS

14. Find the hidden words. The words have been placed horizontally, vertically, or diagonally. When you locate a word, draw an ellipse around it.

G	S	C	P	Y	Y	K	V	O	Y	W	B	E	T	E	O	V	A	R	I	E	S	E
P	X	N	B	D	E	V	E	L	O	P	E	R	T	U	T	M	T	O	Q	S	E	I
Z	W	C	O	M	E	D	O	N	E	S	U	U	B	H	F	D	U	U	H	U	H	X
U	P	C	O	A	R	S	E	P	R	V	Q	F	W	I	N	K	I	K	M	N	Z	P
V	K	H	G	M	H	O	B	B	G	D	L	Y	A	U	D	F	U	W	Z	S	D	X
C	T	A	Y	M	A	R	J	K	L	R	V	G	O	Y	K	A	B	K	G	C	O	N
K	R	E	G	V	I	N	K	E	O	O	M	V	S	T	R	G	H	A	W	R	S	H
C	I	C	A	T	R	I	C	I	A	L	A	L	O	P	E	C	I	A	R	E	V	I
L	Q	S	B	M	C	W	S	A	C	U	P	U	N	C	T	U	R	E	E	E	T	R
L	T	O	R	J	L	S	B	W	S	Q	D	Y	F	X	C	J	K	V	F	N	T	S
T	T	K	A	J	O	R	O	U	G	H	B	L	O	W	D	R	Y	B	O	D	Y	U
V	V	O	S	F	N	O	N	I	R	R	A	V	D	T	H	I	A	P	K	P	J	T
S	T	M	I	Y	I	J	G	H	Q	R	Z	K	Z	A	J	S	N	E	V	H	E	I
H	M	H	O	F	N	B	Z	Q	D	M	E	D	J	A	L	O	P	E	C	I	A	S
E	B	Q	N	C	G	J	Q	W	C	H	I	G	N	O	N	H	G	S	Z	S	P	M
V	C	J	O	V	W	S	U	N	B	L	O	C	K	U	C	K	B	G	M	H	W	J

1. Loss of hair, especially from the head, which either happens naturally or is caused by disease
2. Products that reflect all the sun's rays, such as zinc oxide and titanium dioxide. They permit minimal tanning, and are a good choice for those who are sensitive to chemicals.
3. A method of relieving pain by inserting needles into the skin.
4. A technique under development which could make an unlimited crop of donor hair available for transplanting.
5. In women, a major source of female hormones. Certain conditions involving the ovaries can lead to excess hair growth, especially polycystic ovary syndrome (PCOS).
6. A product which oxidizes artificial color pigment.
7. A sophisticated, elegant up style, where long hair is twisted (either in a roll or knot) and pinned from the nape of neck.
8. The volume or springiness of hair.
9. A medical term for blackheads.
10. Excessive hair growth, accompanied by enlarged hair follicles and increased pigmentation.
11. Products with ingredients that absorb UVA and UVB rays.
12. A classification for stronger, thicker types of hair.
13. This is baldness due to scarring. The follicles are absent in scar tissue.
14. Used to remove the moisture from wet hair.
15. The process of scraping or wearing hair away. Causing partial or complete absence of hair from areas.

A. HAIR CLONING
B. HIRSUTISM
C. SUNSCREEN
D. DEVELOPER
E. ALOPECIA
F. COARSE
G. CHIGNON
H. COMEDONES
I. OVARIES
J. ROUGH BLOW DRY
K. CICATRICIAL ALOPECIA
L. BODY
M. ACUPUNCTURE
N. SUNBLOCK
O. ABRASION

15. Find the hidden words. The words have been placed horizontally, vertically, or diagonally. When you locate a word, draw an ellipse around it.

Q	E	E	M	V	B	V	Z	A	L	O	P	E	C	I	A	T	O	T	A	L	I	S
S	Q	E	C	Y	P	R	O	T	E	R	O	N	E	A	C	E	T	A	T	E	N	N
Y	A	Y	P	M	B	R	O	K	E	N	C	A	P	I	L	L	A	R	I	E	S	A
A	C	T	I	V	E	I	N	G	R	E	D	I	E	N	T	O	P	O	G	W	G	T
P	R	I	J	H	T	Z	K	Q	B	U	M	Q	B	O	N	W	O	G	A	C	R	U
X	Q	I	W	C	M	L	T	X	R	P	N	K	P	M	D	M	U	A	B	A	H	R
A	M	E	T	A	B	O	L	I	S	M	D	T	L	J	W	B	Z	I	R	B	G	A
T	P	R	B	Z	M	E	C	Y	C	L	O	D	E	X	T	R	I	N	S	H	N	L
R	S	K	E	Z	G	M	H	B	K	K	T	Y	C	J	W	N	P	E	K	T	P	K
Q	S	W	I	T	C	H	E	U	F	P	J	T	V	X	A	L	E	Z	P	T	M	Q
I	T	O	L	C	J	A	L	O	H	H	H	R	G	U	B	N	J	B	C	L	S	D
X	M	U	U	G	L	P	A	Q	G	K	E	E	Q	S	D	K	E	R	A	T	I	N
O	U	B	Y	Q	G	J	T	F	Y	H	C	C	O	C	O	X	U	U	X	D	B	J
L	E	U	C	O	T	R	I	C	H	I	A	T	V	Y	M	U	F	I	R	U	K	I
W	D	C	A	N	F	T	N	I	D	V	L	T	R	N	E	M	S	S	E	W	M	S
L	N	A	C	G	Z	T	G	V	H	E	D	E	M	A	N	T	Z	E	L	Z	W	C

1. Produced from starch by means of enzymatic conversion and are used in a wide range of applications in food, pharmaceutical and chemical industries.
2. The body transformation of food into energy.
3. A deep cleansing process which strips the hair lightly before a chemical service. Also known as clarifying.
4. This drug is normally used to reduce sex drive in men who have an excessive sex drive. It is also prescribed to treat hirsutism and androgenic alopecia in women.
5. The soft area between the rib cage and the pubic area. A common area for excess hair, often in a line from the belly button to the pubic hair.
6. Refers to a congenital absence of pigment in a lock of hairs which will show as grey or white.
7. Ingredients extracted directly from plants, earth minerals, or animal products as opposed to being produced synthetically.
8. A fibrous protein found in hair, nails, and skin.
9. These tiny blood vessels at the surface of the skin appear as streaks or blotches.
10. The substance which, contained in a product, actually does the main part of the work that the product is used for.
11. A device that produces short intense bursts of energy from a laser.
12. A discoloration of skin from blood, sometimes caused by electrolysis, plucking, or waxing. Also known as Purpura.
13. The brand name for Minoxidil. A topical hair growth solution for hair loss.
14. This is the complete loss of scalp hair often combined with the loss of eyebrows and eyelashes.
15. A medical term for swelling.

A. BRUISE
B. EDEMA
C. Q SWITCH
D. METABOLISM
E. BROKEN CAPILLARIES
F. ROGAINE
G. ACTIVE INGREDIENT
H. NATURAL
I. CHELATING
J. CYPROTERONE ACETATE
K. KERATIN
L. ALOPECIA TOTALIS
M. CYCLODEXTRINS
N. ABDOMEN
O. LEUCOTRICHIA

16. Find the hidden words. The words have been placed horizontally, vertically, or diagonally. When you locate a word, draw an ellipse around it.

D	I	S	T	O	R	T	E	D	H	A	I	R	F	O	L	L	I	C	L	E	S	H
E	Z	B	B	W	H	A	I	R	C	L	O	N	I	N	G	D	L	T	I	P	P	A
C	H	E	M	I	C	A	L	D	E	P	I	L	A	T	O	R	I	E	S	B	C	I
H	M	C	A	U	H	C	H	E	L	A	T	I	N	G	R	X	I	C	A	T	L	R
O	M	Y	B	J	V	A	T	V	L	H	S	D	U	Q	O	Z	U	S	M	R	U	W
X	L	A	N	A	E	S	T	H	E	T	I	C	J	E	L	S	R	E	E	I	B	E
Z	T	C	R	U	S	T	I	N	G	B	Z	H	N	J	U	F	O	K	J	B	H	A
M	P	W	G	W	E	J	L	U	V	I	M	E	R	X	B	Z	G	R	D	O	A	V
X	O	C	L	I	M	B	A	Z	O	L	E	K	N	C	R	Q	A	B	O	B	I	I
W	R	R	V	L	W	R	G	T	V	H	G	I	P	K	I	F	I	W	U	R	R	N
P	E	V	V	F	N	F	B	F	Q	L	E	W	I	Q	C	O	N	S	V	U	K	G
K	E	X	Q	B	R	M	K	U	I	E	F	Q	I	Z	A	M	E	K	B	V	L	I
G	U	D	E	R	M	A	L	S	H	E	A	T	H	M	T	P	H	R	K	X	R	A
R	K	C	K	H	L	T	G	E	T	N	C	K	T	A	E	L	V	W	X	W	G	N
W	J	M	D	P	R	T	I	J	K	H	M	C	H	M	S	V	O	X	S	B	D	W
C	Y	F	V	B	L	E	E	M	V	M	B	L	N	V	A	Q	G	R	T	Y	V	I

1. Powder or cream preparations that dissolve hair above the surface of the skin. Some find these products very irritating to the skin.
2. Highly effective active anti-dandruff ingredient. Combats bacteria on the scalp.
3. Makes smooth or slippery by using oil to overcome friction.
4. A technique under development which could make an unlimited crop of donor hair available for transplanting.
5. A process by which a hair piece is attached to existing hair on the head through braiding or a weaving process.
6. The brand name for Minoxidil. A topical hair growth solution for hair loss.
7. Dried fluid that seeps from skin in some clients following hair removal such as laser, electrolysis, and depilatories.
8. A substance used to relieve all feeling.
9. A non-shiny surface that absorbs light; a dead or dull finish.
10. A non-living hair in the last stages of the hair growth cycle, it is detached from the follicle but has not yet shed.
11. The classic look of the 50s and 60s; the style was short and straight but blow-dried and curled under.
12. A relatively rare condition in which the follicle is not straight.
13. Flexible resin.
14. A deep cleansing process which strips the hair lightly before a chemical service. Also known as clarifying.
15. A lining around a hair.

A. CHEMICAL DEPILATORIES
B. ROGAINE
C. LUVIMER
D. HAIR CLONING
E. BOB
F. CLIMBAZOLE
G. HAIR WEAVING
H. DISTORTED HAIR FOLLICLES
I. CLUB HAIR
J. MATTE
K. CHELATING
L. CRUSTING
M. LUBRICATES
N. DERMAL SHEATH
O. ANAESTHETIC

17. Find the hidden words. The words have been placed horizontally, vertically, or diagonally. When you locate a word, draw an ellipse around it.

F	S	U	P	E	R	O	X	I	D	E	D	I	S	M	U	T	A	S	E	P	I	L
S	T	E	A	M	I	N	G	O	Q	G	C	H	R	O	M	O	P	H	O	R	E	Y
A	F	V	D	Q	U	L	G	I	O	F	D	X	P	U	L	R	U	R	U	X	R	A
M	H	F	E	A	T	B	R	O	K	E	N	C	A	P	I	L	L	A	R	I	E	S
P	S	R	P	N	Q	X	O	F	W	H	G	I	W	A	P	K	Y	C	N	E	V	Y
H	T	A	L	E	R	Q	X	V	S	E	C	T	I	O	N	I	N	G	J	A	G	E
O	N	G	Y	P	B	S	C	L	I	M	B	A	Z	O	L	E	Q	U	Y	R	I	P
T	S	R	S	M	F	I	X	Q	F	N	T	X	T	J	C	Z	H	L	W	S	Z	A
E	S	A	S	P	L	I	T	E	N	D	S	V	Q	C	S	J	G	Z	X	T	D	E
R	F	N	F	F	E	L	E	C	T	R	O	C	O	A	G	U	L	A	T	I	O	N
I	A	C	Y	Z	I	S	G	Q	V	N	G	T	O	M	B	L	F	X	Z	I	W	W
C	C	E	K	M	Z	R	R	H	D	E	V	E	L	O	P	E	R	U	P	T	O	D
X	Z	F	P	I	G	M	E	N	T	E	D	L	E	S	I	O	N	I	M	O	G	U
C	A	R	D	V	H	Y	D	R	O	L	Y	Z	E	D	K	E	R	A	T	I	N	Y
V	T	E	Y	L	O	G	D	O	U	B	L	E	B	L	I	N	D	F	X	J	J	Y
O	M	E	J	B	O	I	B	X	N	F	L	P	C	C	S	J	T	N	U	V	Z	O

1. Highly effective active anti-dandruff ingredient. Combats bacteria on the scalp.
2. Variety of skin conditions mainly the result of excess melanin. Commonly known as Café au Lait stains, birthmarks, age spots and freckles.
3. A clinical testing method in which neither patient nor doctor know what medication or procedure is being used.
4. The enzyme superoxide, catalyzes the dismutation of superoxide into oxygen and hydrogen peroxide.
5. Trichoptilosis
6. A common place for hair removal in older males.
7. The process by which most synthetic fiber is curled at the factory.
8. Products so labeled may still contain small amounts of fragrances to mask the fatty odor of soap or other unpleasant odors.
9. These tiny blood vessels at the surface of the skin appear as streaks or blotches.
10. allows you to only pay attention to a particular area or panel of hair.
11. A product which oxidizes artificial color pigment.
12. The use of heat generated by electricity to change tissue from a fluid to a semi-solid, similar to cooking an egg.
13. A mild nonirritating surfactant often used in shampoos; leaves hair manageable and is gentle enough for chemically treated hair.
14. The substructure that is responsible for the spectral selective absorption of electromagnetic radiation.
15. The structural protein of hair.

A. SUPEROXIDE DISMUTASE
B. BROKEN CAPILLARIES
C. HYDROLYZED KERATIN
D. CHROMOPHORE
E. EARS
F. FRAGRANCE FREE
G. DOUBLE BLIND
H. SECTIONING
I. PIGMENTED LESION
J. STEAMING
K. ELECTROCOAGULATION
L. AMPHOTERIC
M. SPLIT ENDS
N. CLIMBAZOLE
O. DEVELOPER

18. Find the hidden words. The words have been placed horizontally, vertically, or diagonally. When you locate a word, draw an ellipse around it.

O	E	X	T	W	F	M	J	O	R	U	N	A	U	Z	F	E	F	T	Z	F	I	T
J	D	V	J	V	W	I	M	J	D	E	R	M	A	B	R	A	S	I	O	N	P	N
Y	A	Y	F	E	A	C	V	M	B	E	T	A	I	N	E	V	N	Z	N	Q	C	B
I	T	D	O	I	N	R	A	M	O	R	T	I	Z	A	T	I	O	N	A	W	T	F
U	U	T	X	M	T	O	K	M	B	H	F	Z	C	C	T	B	A	A	K	H	E	R
I	F	T	B	U	I	D	A	C	S	X	B	O	R	N	E	U	E	E	L	K	X	Z
L	A	X	F	L	A	I	P	I	G	M	E	N	T	E	C	Y	O	X	S	D	O	Y
S	R	C	W	O	N	F	A	R	C	T	R	A	C	K	M	H	U	T	E	G	Q	I
X	Z	X	P	P	D	F	M	H	T	Q	L	A	I	Z	V	L	J	R	P	J	C	V
Z	C	Y	P	K	R	U	A	L	O	P	E	C	I	A	T	O	T	A	L	I	S	S
V	N	D	G	T	O	S	Y	U	T	B	P	V	O	Y	L	L	Y	C	L	L	O	S
R	H	T	A	R	G	E	T	E	D	F	A	T	R	E	D	U	C	T	I	O	N	A
X	E	U	E	U	E	A	L	O	P	E	C	I	A	N	E	U	R	O	T	I	C	A
I	V	B	H	E	N	X	R	U	P	K	R	B	N	G	U	V	O	B	K	R	K	A
R	M	B	R	A	N	N	F	C	Y	U	B	A	R	B	A	Z	K	G	O	N	J	B
E	L	E	C	T	R	O	D	E	R	O	S	A	C	E	A	U	Q	I	B	T	M	F

1. Parting or a cornrow that establishes the placement pattern of wefts or strand additions.
2. Baldness following a nervous disorder or injury to the nervous system.
3. This is the complete loss of scalp hair often combined with the loss of eyebrows and eyelashes.
4. The process of converting one enzyme to another.
5. An inflammation of the skin, a result of over production of oil and bacteria.
6. A disorder involving chronic inflammation of the cheeks, nose, chin, forehead or eyelids. It may cause redness, vascularity, swelling or hyperplasia.
7. A natural conditioning substance for example: from molasses or sugar beet.
8. Optimum hold without overload.
9. An herbal concentrate produced by separating the essential or active part of an herb into a solvent material.
10. A cosmetic procedure used to smooth skin and reduce scars.
11. Color.
12. Medical term for beard.
13. In hair removal, a conductor through which electricity enters or leaves the body. An electrolysis needle is an electrode.
14. Metabolising stubborn fat deposits, typically in the lower body, using methods such as Eporex mesotherapy.
15. A drug or product that limited the effects of androgens (male hormones).

A. ELECTRODE
B. TARGETED FAT REDUCTION
C. PIGMENT
D. MICRO DIFFUSE
E. ANTI ANDROGEN
F. TRACK
G. ACNE
H. ALOPECIA NEUROTICA
I. EXTRACT
J. BETAINE
K. DERMABRASION
L. AMORTIZATION
M. BARBA
N. ROSACEA
O. ALOPECIA TOTALIS

19. Find the hidden words. The words have been placed horizontally, vertically, or diagonally. When you locate a word, draw an ellipse around it.

H	L	E	M	E	J	D	K	M	K	T	R	A	N	S	L	U	C	E	N	T	I	D
Y	O	M	S	U	P	E	R	O	X	I	D	E	D	I	S	M	U	T	A	S	E	G
P	N	U	W	D	B	L	A	C	K	H	E	A	D	S	H	K	H	T	G	A	N	A
O	V	L	N	G	A	R	J	W	T	R	Q	T	O	M	O	B	I	V	Y	N	R	N
P	O	S	H	P	C	B	L	I	S	T	E	R	C	A	H	W	E	Q	J	A	E	A
I	Y	I	T	A	F	R	Q	Y	X	I	M	A	Q	Q	N	V	R	A	P	L	E
G	H	F	C	Y	O	J	E	Z	X	S	L	G	T	V	E	F	J	T	W	H	A	S
M	S	I	J	V	Y	C	F	R	E	E	Z	I	N	G	S	P	R	A	Y	O	X	T
E	K	E	N	M	N	R	Z	M	N	P	F	Q	V	X	O	L	J	J	V	R	E	H
N	G	R	T	X	N	R	P	Q	A	W	K	G	W	Q	C	I	F	I	Z	E	R	E
T	N	T	R	I	C	H	O	P	T	I	L	O	S	I	S	B	W	R	H	S	Y	T
A	C	R	O	P	G	W	B	C	U	A	H	Q	Y	J	M	X	C	B	B	I	O	I
T	L	T	X	W	R	H	S	P	R	Y	C	I	P	O	O	X	I	N	E	S	Y	C
I	O	V	R	R	P	M	Q	O	A	T	H	N	D	F	F	E	H	K	U	E	A	Z
O	N	A	F	Q	X	Y	U	K	L	S	C	B	B	Z	T	D	G	J	X	D	K	F
N	E	C	N	T	E	A	T	R	E	E	O	I	L	L	C	V	X	C	L	G	D	C

1. A type of clogged pore in the skin with a visible black plug.
2. The forcing of liquids into skin from the negative to the positive pole.
3. Caused by an absence of melanocytes, whitening of the skin. Vitiligo is a common medical complaint.
4. A small fluid-filled bubble on the skin caused by heat from over treatment with certain types of hair removal.
5. A substance used to relieve all feeling.
6. A group of genetically identical cells or organisms derived from a single common cell.
7. Split ends.
8. Ingredients extracted directly from plants, earth minerals, or animal products as opposed to being produced synthetically.
9. A hairspray with the firmest hold used to maintain style of hard to hold hair.
10. A thickening agent or binding agent added to products to change their physical composition (joins two or more ingredients together).
11. Allows some light to pass through.
12. An alternative to haircut, without any specific meaning to the style of the cut.
13. an extraction from the Melaleuca tree.
14. The enzyme superoxide, catalyzes the dismutation of superoxide into oxygen and hydrogen peroxide.
15. A chemical process by which the hair is permanently straightened. New-growth areas have to be maintained via 'touch-ups' to continue the straightened pattern.

A. TRANSLUCENT
B. RELAXER
C. FREEZING SPRAY
D. SUPEROXIDE DISMUTASE
E. HYPOPIGMENTATION
F. BLISTER
G. ANAESTHETIC
H. CROP
I. EMULSIFIER
J. TEA TREE OIL
K. BLACKHEADS
L. NATURAL
M. CLONE
N. TRICHOPTILOSIS
O. ANAPHORESIS

20. Find the hidden words. The words have been placed horizontally, vertically, or diagonally. When you locate a word, draw an ellipse around it.

F	D	M	T	Z	O	N	E	E	Y	P	A	U	R	S	P	R	I	T	Z	S	G	V
I	R	F	L	D	L	B	Y	Y	N	Q	T	V	W	M	T	O	C	A	R	Y	M	Y
N	Z	X	N	O	F	M	B	O	N	D	I	N	G	Q	J	D	M	S	Z	H	W	G
A	Q	R	P	H	L	I	B	N	I	Q	L	K	F	U	S	I	O	N	Q	I	M	V
S	S	M	R	C	I	C	A	T	R	I	C	I	A	L	A	L	O	P	E	C	I	A
T	E	Q	A	H	J	R	T	G	N	P	C	E	T	Y	L	A	L	C	O	H	O	L
E	C	X	W	I	P	O	K	E	B	V	F	O	L	L	I	C	U	L	I	T	I	S
R	T	P	P	D	N	G	X	K	P	Q	L	E	H	N	N	W	F	S	U	W	L	V
I	I	S	R	E	X	R	D	Z	C	B	O	F	F	T	G	H	I	U	S	W	I	O
D	O	H	B	P	J	A	P	R	O	T	E	I	N	T	R	E	A	T	M	E	N	T
E	N	W	F	T	L	F	S	A	S	R	D	N	S	Z	J	J	E	R	M	N	V	I
A	I	L	F	H	K	T	B	G	F	C	N	V	M	I	D	T	I	U	S	S	H	C
J	N	W	C	R	A	C	A	N	I	T	I	E	S	G	X	Z	Q	B	K	U	T	Y
A	G	Y	Q	U	J	M	V	Q	E	H	B	J	V	P	B	J	Z	U	G	S	Z	E
I	O	J	U	I	F	L	L	L	S	P	F	T	J	E	X	I	U	G	S	R	U	Q
R	L	I	Y	G	T	H	E	R	M	A	L	P	R	O	C	E	S	S	B	Q	N	A

1. a light mist or spray, which when used as verb means to lightly spray your hair.
2. The generic name of the brand name drug Proscar that is FDA approved for the treatment of benign prostate enlargement.
3. The forehead, nose and chin areas, which tend to be oilier than the cheeks.
4. A very small hair graft usually consisting of one or two hairs.
5. The greying of hair. A pigment deficiency frequently seen in middle-aged people of either sex.
6. To attach wefted hair to the natural hair with a latex or surgical type adhesive.
7. A common disorder characterized by inflammation of the hair follicle.
8. The process of attaching small pieces of human hair with a special adhesive and a thermal gun.
9. Used to measure acidity in cosmetic preparations.
10. allows you to only pay attention to a particular area or panel of hair.
11. A treatment used on the hair. Designed to add strength and elasticity to the hair by adding protein to the cortex.
12. This is baldness due to scarring. The follicles are absent in scar tissue.
13. A gentle humectant, lather booster, and emulsifier. In hair products, it is used to smooth and soften the hair cuticle.
14. The darkness or lightness of a color.
15. Temporarily straightening the hair with a heated iron.

A. FOLLICULITIS
B. FINASTERIDE
C. MICRO GRAFT
D. SECTIONING
E. CICATRICIAL ALOPECIA
F. PROTEIN TREATMENT
G. CETYL ALCOHOL
H. CANITIES
I. SPRITZ
J. THERMAL PROCESS
K. T ZONE
L. BONDING
M. FUSION
N. DEPTH
O. PH

1. Find the hidden words. The words have been placed horizontally, vertically, or diagonally. When you locate a word, draw an ellipse around it.

A	L	O	P	E	C	I	A	F	O	L	L	I	C	U	L	A	R	I	S	R	O	F
K	A	O	Q	J	Z	U	O	F	W	J	B	O	A	R	B	R	I	S	T	L	E	A
S	C	S	S	S	X	Q	I	P	A	R	F	U	M	X	O	P	Y	R	J	D	H	C
J	U	T	V	U	U	X	P	A	N	T	O	T	H	E	N	I	C	A	C	I	D	E
Z	P	H	J	B	C	R	U	S	T	I	N	G	F	Q	F	E	M	B	I	W	Y	L
R	U	F	U	C	O	U	Q	X	Z	F	B	O	J	B	W	S	W	B	S	K	I	I
A	N	O	G	U	Z	U	H	W	C	J	R	M	B	S	L	W	V	G	E	S	A	F
Z	C	L	P	T	P	M	T	W	V	O	U	J	Q	F	N	M	T	D	C	U	D	T
B	T	L	C	A	E	S	S	E	N	T	I	A	L	O	I	D	X	D	T	K	X	M
L	U	I	D	N	A	V	H	T	S	N	S	M	V	D	S	X	L	V	I	W	H	J
D	R	C	F	E	N	Y	G	W	W	Z	E	A	I	O	R	T	U	D	O	V	W	P
R	E	L	D	O	O	B	P	B	N	U	Q	T	C	K	J	U	W	R	N	Z	H	U
S	T	E	X	U	D	L	Q	Q	P	D	N	T	T	C	Y	L	U	V	I	M	E	R
T	R	I	W	S	E	H	U	S	V	R	I	E	Q	L	H	E	L	M	N	F	L	W
S	M	I	S	O	P	R	O	P	Y	L	L	A	N	O	L	A	T	E	G	Z	L	B
Y	D	M	I	C	R	O	L	I	N	K	I	N	G	T	E	C	H	N	I	Q	U	E

1. A positive electrode.
2. Dried fluid that seeps from skin in some clients following hair removal such as laser, electrolysis, and depilatories.
3. Hair loss due to inflammation of hair follicles.
4. allows you to only pay attention to a particular area or panel of hair.
5. A bristle commonly used in natural bristle brushes.
6. The most concentrated and most fragrant scent and therefore the most expensive.
7. A method of relieving pain by inserting needles into the skin.
8. A discoloration of skin from blood, sometimes caused by electrolysis, plucking, or waxing. Also known as Purpura.
9. The essence of a plant, removed by compressing, steaming, dissolving or distilling.
10. A non- shiny surface that absorbs light; a dead or dull finish.
11. A Synthetic moisturizer.
12. Flexible resin.
13. Pertains to the skin.
14. The process of attaching hair wefts without braids. The links are sewn on to the wefted hair. The user's natural hair is pulled through and locked secure.
15. Surgical procedure that lifts and stretches the patient's skin to provide a firmer more youthful look.
16. The hair follicle houses the root of the hair. A pore in the skin from which a hair grows.
17. Also called vitamin B5 (a B vitamin), is a water-soluble vitamin required to sustain life (essential nutrient).

A. PARFUM
D. LUVIMER
G. BOAR BRISTLE
J. SECTIONING
M. ANODE
P. FACE LIFT

B. SUBCUTANEOUS
E. ALOPECIA FOLLICULARIS
H. ACUPUNCTURE
K. PANTOTHENIC ACID
N. CRUSTING
Q. MICRO LINKING TECHNIQUE

C. MATTE
F. ESSENTIAL OIL
I. BRUISE
L. FOLLICLE
O. ISOPROPYL LANOLATE

2. Find the hidden words. The words have been placed horizontally, vertically, or diagonally. When you locate a word, draw an ellipse around it.

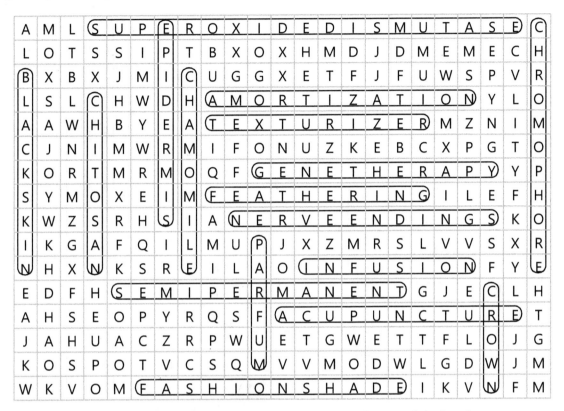

1. Gene therapy is a treatment method which involves the manipulation of the genetic makeup.
2. The thin outer layer of skin, on top of the thicker and deeper dermis.
3. The most concentrated and most fragrant scent and therefore the most expensive.
4. Used in many products for blonde hair to enhance color.
5. The enzyme superoxide, catalyzes the dismutation of superoxide into oxygen and hydrogen peroxide.
6. Receptors which respond to touch, pain, pressure, heat and cold.
7. The substructure that is responsible for the spectral selective absorption of electromagnetic radiation.
8. Probably the most difficult type of skin from which to remove hair.
9. Area at the top of the head.
10. A method of relieving pain by inserting needles into the skin.
11. The process of converting one enzyme to another.
12. Tea made by steeping an herb's leaves or flowers in hot water.
13. A basic color with added tone.
14. A color which lasts from 6 - 8 shampoos.
15. Feathering is a cutting technique hairdressers use to take hard lines out of the hair. By cutting into the hair softer lines are created.
16. A natural polymer obtained from sea crustaceans protects the hair.
17. a mild relaxing treatment. Instead of causing the hair to be 'bone straight,' this chemical treatment is left on for a shorter period of time.

A. BLACK SKIN
B. CROWN
C. INFUSION
D. SEMI PERMANENT
E. FEATHERING
F. CHITOSAN
G. PARFUM
H. EPIDERMIS
I. FASHION SHADE
J. ACUPUNCTURE
K. TEXTURIZER
L. AMORTIZATION
M. GENE THERAPY
N. NERVE ENDINGS
O. CHAMOMILE
P. SUPEROXIDE DISMUTASE
Q. CHROMOPHORE

3. Find the hidden words. The words have been placed horizontally, vertically, or diagonally. When you locate a word, draw an ellipse around it.

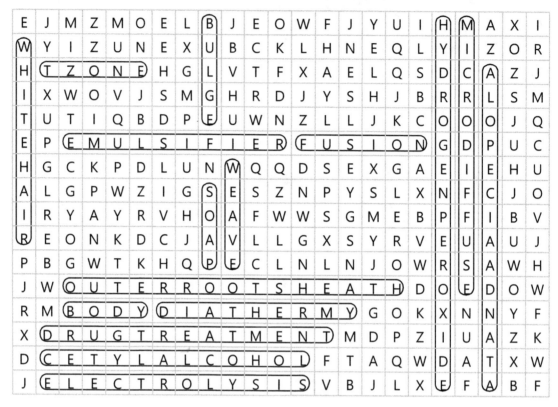

1. A thickening agent or binding agent added to products to change their physical composition (joins two or more ingredients together).
2. Another name for thermolysis.
3. A gentle humectant, lather booster, and emulsifier. In hair products, it is used to smooth and soften the hair cuticle.
4. Cleansing agent that is a sodium or potassium salt of animal or vegetable fat.
5. Congenital baldness or baldness at birth.
6. The volume or springiness of hair.
7. Used to oxidize (expand) artificial color molecules. Can also lighten natural color pigment.
8. Optimum hold without overload.
9. Excess hair can be increased or decreased by certain drugs. These drugs often affect hormonal levels.
10. A point midway up the hair follicle which researchers suspect must be damaged to induce permanent hair removal
11. The process of attaching small pieces of human hair with a special adhesive and a thermal gun.
12. In hair removal, the practice of epilation with electrified needles.
13. A soft thin layer surrounding the lower two-thirds of a hair.
14. The forehead, nose and chin areas, which tend to be oilier than the cheeks.
15. A hair weave is usually a hairpiece with layered gaps made into it.
16. Having no pigment. Possible causes: Genetic. Vitamin B deficiency. Drugs for treatment of arthritis. Other health factors.

A. WEAVE
B. EMULSIFIER
C. SOAP
D. MICRO DIFFUSE
E. DIATHERMY
F. ALOPECIA ADNATA
G. OUTER ROOT SHEATH
H. BODY
I. DRUG TREATMENT
J. CETYL ALCOHOL
K. WHITE HAIR
L. ELECTROLYSIS
M. BULGE
N. FUSION
O. T ZONE
P. HYDROGEN PEROXIDE

4. Find the hidden words. The words have been placed horizontally, vertically, or diagonally. When you locate a word, draw an ellipse around it.

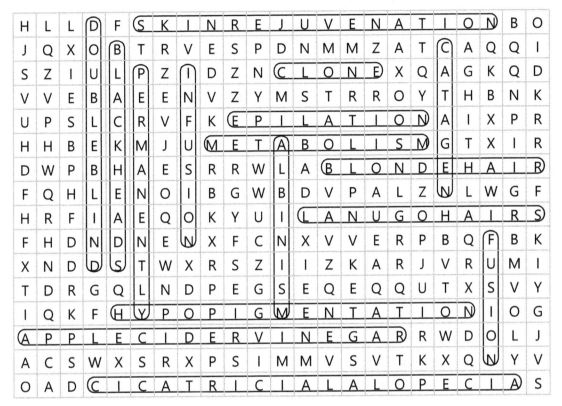

1. A clinical testing method in which neither patient nor doctor know what medication or procedure is being used.
2. The removal of hair below the skin's surface.
3. The process of attaching small pieces of human hair with a special adhesive and a thermal gun.
4. A group of genetically identical cells or organisms derived from a single common cell.
5. Are usually shed during the 7th month of fetal life following primary folliculo-genesis.
6. Tea made by steeping an herb's leaves or flowers in hot water.
7. A recessive hereditary trait which presents as white hair due to defective melanin production thought to be caused by a mutation within genes.
8. Combating the signs of ageing using the latest innovative, non-invasive treatments that give you visibly younger, healthy, radiant skin.
9. Is not as visible, but it's also harder to treat. Lasers have limited effects on it because of its lack of pigment, and it is difficult to see against the skin.
10. This is baldness due to scarring. The follicles are absent in scar tissue.
11. A natural solvent in oils and creams. It acidifies products.
12. Caused by an absence of melanocytes, whitening of the skin. Vitiligo is a common medical complaint.
13. Completely changing the natural color of the hair.
14. The body transformation of food into energy.
15. This is the end of the active growth period, and is marked by changes occurring in the follicle.
16. A type of clogged pore in the skin with a visible black plug.

A. ALBINISM
B. CATAGEN
C. FUSION
D. BLONDE HAIR
E. INFUSION
F. CICATRICIAL ALOPECIA
G. BLACKHEADS
H. DOUBLE BLIND
I. SKIN REJUVENATION
J. HYPOPIGMENTATION
K. EPILATION
L. APPLE CIDER VINEGAR
M. PERMANENTLY
N. CLONE
O. METABOLISM
P. LANUGO HAIRS

5. Find the hidden words. The words have been placed horizontally, vertically, or diagonally. When you locate a word, draw an ellipse around it.

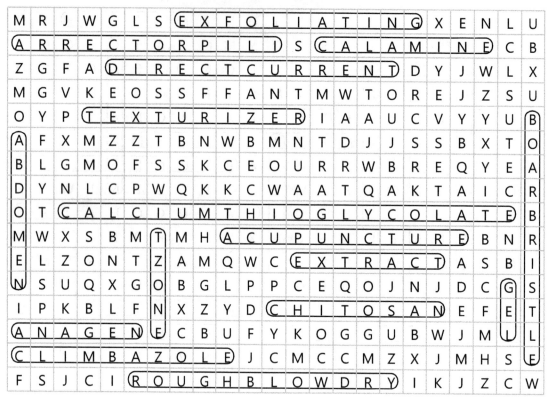

1. The active dissolving ingredient in many cream depilatories
2. A natural polymer obtained from sea crustaceans protects the hair.
3. A method of relieving pain by inserting needles into the skin.
4. a mild relaxing treatment. Instead of causing the hair to be 'bone straight,' this chemical treatment is left on for a shorter period of time.
5. A bristle commonly used in natural bristle brushes.
6. This is the growing phase of the hair cycle which lasts about seven years in a healthy person. The active stage in a hair growth cycle.
7. Highly effective active anti-dandruff ingredient. Combats bacteria on the scalp.
8. A pink ointment sometimes used to treat skin irritation
9. The forehead, nose and chin areas, which tend to be oilier than the cheeks.
10. Used to remove the moisture from wet hair.
11. a type of electrical energy that travels in one direction.
12. A process of removing the top dead skin layers to reveal healthier, newer skin underneath.
13. Creates "Goose Bumps" when stimulated.
14. The soft area between the rib cage and the pubic area. A common area for excess hair, often in a line from the belly button to the pubic hair.
15. An herbal concentrate produced by separating the essential or active part of an herb into a solvent material.
16. Jelly like material formed by the coagulation of a liquid. Semi-solid emulsion that liquefies when applied to the skin.

A. CALCIUM THIOGLYCOLATE
B. ABDOMEN
C. GEL
D. DIRECT CURRENT
E. T ZONE
F. CLIMBAZOLE
G. BOAR BRISTLE
H. ROUGH BLOW DRY
I. TEXTURIZER
J. ARRECTOR PILI
K. CHITOSAN
L. EXTRACT
M. CALAMINE
N. ANAGEN
O. ACUPUNCTURE
P. EXFOLIATING

6. Find the hidden words. The words have been placed horizontally, vertically, or diagonally. When you locate a word, draw an ellipse around it.

I	L	C	U	W	W	N	N	O	R	Y	V	U	M	C	V	A	R	G	F	P	R	I
X	F	F	W	X	D	M	T	L	P	Z	N	H	G	R	D	R	A	S	C	A	B	W
Y	T	B	G	W	O	Q	M	I	R	T	D	U	S	O	L	N	L	F	W	N	X	Z
S	B	U	D	R	L	O	O	I	O	E	Z	Z	C	W	E	E	V	K	E	T	E	C
Z	A	I	N	A	L	S	W	S	P	V	S	S	R	N	L	D	M	U	C	H	I	O
E	X	T	E	N	S	I	O	N	E	V	D	P	U	J	U	H	I	A	A	E	H	N
I	I	T	F	Y	Q	Q	D	H	C	B	X	X	N	R	F	B	C	J	C	N	L	D
V	T	S	O	W	P	S	W	E	I	B	V	A	C	G	O	U	R	F	C	O	S	I
I	F	R	L	C	Y	X	B	F	A	O	L	J	H	G	X	L	O	C	E	U	U	T
U	E	U	L	O	A	P	D	R	P	M	O	W	D	U	Q	X	D	S	N	P	H	I
S	E	L	I	J	Z	J	G	N	X	R	N	H	R	E	J	P	I	H	T	A	Q	O
S	F	C	C	H	I	R	S	U	T	I	S	M	Y	L	K	F	F	E	C	B	D	N
E	N	E	L	C	B	L	E	M	I	S	H	Q	J	A	G	P	F	Q	O	W	T	E
B	O	R	E	S	C	A	T	A	P	H	O	R	E	S	I	S	U	C	L	D	K	R
N	Q	D	I	S	C	O	M	F	O	R	T	R	J	B	W	N	S	G	O	W	H	G
B	C	E	T	Y	L	A	L	C	O	H	O	L	K	L	H	C	E	N	R	B	E	M

1. Esters found in sunscreen and cosmetic products that can make skin sensitive.
2. The brand name for finestaride. The only drug approved by the FDA to treat hair loss.
3. Usually a sharp, intense color used as a contrast or pickup for color scheme. It is used to add excitement to an overall effect
4. Blood or pigment based visible mark.
5. The hair follicle houses the root of the hair. A pore in the skin from which a hair grows.
6. Hair extensions are pieces of real or synthetic weaved close to the scalp in order to achieve greater length or fullness.
7. A gentle humectant, lather booster, and emulsifier. In hair products, it is used to smooth and soften the hair cuticle.
8. Area at the top of the head.
9. A technique for drying your hair which creates a style at the same time.
10. Optimum hold without overload.
11. An area of tissue erosion. They are always depressed and are due to irritation. They may become infected and inflamed as they grow.
12. Creamy hair product meant to be used after shampoo. Moisturizes and detangles hair.
13. Excessive hair growth, accompanied by enlarged hair follicles and increased pigmentation.
14. The forcing of substances into the skin from a positive to a negative pole. It is sometimes used after electrolysis to firm skin and reduce redness.
15. Varies greatly by individual and body area. Electrolysis is generally considered most painful, followed by laser, plucking, waxing and finally pulse light sources.
16. Aids detangling. Provides volume, control and shine.

A. PABA
E. FOLLICLE
I. ACCENT COLOR
M. BLEMISH
B. CROWN
F. EXTENSION
J. HIRSUTISM
N. ULCER
C. CETYL ALCOHOL
G. MICRO DIFFUSE
K. PANTHENOL
O. CATAPHORESIS
D. CONDITIONER
H. DISCOMFORT
L. PROPECIA
P. SCRUNCH DRY

7. Find the hidden words. The words have been placed horizontally, vertically, or diagonally. When you locate a word, draw an ellipse around it.

H	Q	D	W	K	X	R	L	H	B	P	O	P	V	Y	H	T	O	V	B	I	A	W
U	B	U	E	S	F	F	L	Z	A	A	E	Q	X	Q	U	P	D	X	N	U	Y	E
E	C	Y	U	I	S	S	M	P	L	N	S	N	O	S	M	A	Z	W	L	L	W	C
C	C	O	L	L	A	G	E	N	K	F	T	S	M	Z	I	L	I	B	Y	Q	Y	W
R	C	A	T	I	O	N	I	C	A	A	R	G	T	X	D	M	I	O	N	I	C	E
X	D	X	X	C	Z	J	C	S	L	Q	O	R	Y	L	I	R	H	B	R	B	F	F
S	B	K	S	O	S	L	S	C	I	Q	G	T	U	B	T	O	N	L	X	N	G	T
U	V	C	T	N	O	N	W	S	N	Z	E	N	C	U	Y	L	A	A	W	U	G	S
P	T	Z	Y	E	V	A	E	L	E	K	N	V	H	G	P	L	B	N	F	S	E	R
Q	L	A	L	P	H	A	H	Y	D	R	O	X	Y	A	C	I	D	C	O	I	R	E
F	S	S	F	J	Y	B	T	Y	N	L	T	Y	O	K	U	N	Q	H	Q	I	S	G
E	N	E	R	G	Y	D	E	N	S	I	T	Y	Q	D	Y	G	H	I	J	P	J	F
I	S	H	C	U	T	D	B	A	S	I	C	S	H	A	D	E	H	N	Z	C	M	T
N	H	B	P	L	M	I	C	R	O	D	I	F	F	U	S	E	U	G	P	H	W	U
Y	Z	Y	Y	O	O	U	X	Z	I	S	N	Q	V	D	Q	E	V	H	M	R	N	W
Z	S	I	B	I	W	D	E	P	I	L	A	T	I	O	N	E	S	C	H	A	R	P

1. Optimum hold without overload.
2. A substance with a pH greater than 7; non acidic.
3. A technique used to smooth out the shaft of a lock by rolling it, with or without product, between the palms of the hands.
4. The temporary removal of hair.
5. Possessing a positive electrical charge. Cationic detergents are often used in shampoos because they reduce static electricity and leave the hair manageable.
6. The amount of moisture available in the air.
7. Term used to measure the output energy for Lasers and Pulsed Light Sources.
8. Process where water molecules are broken down by ions into smaller droplets. This then allows the hair to absorb the moisture more easily.
9. A whitening of the skin sometimes caused by some types of hair removal.
10. A small temporary scab that occurs sometimes after electrolysis, especially after overtreatment.
11. These solutions are used as exfoliants. They can help reduce ingrown hairs and improve the look of skin.
12. Increases wet and dry combability.
13. Wefts are temporary hair extensions which are glued into your hair.
14. A female hormone sometimes linked to increased hair growth.
15. A natural or neutral color.
16. A protein that holds all connective tissue together under the skin.

A. WEFTS
D. ENERGY DENSITY
G. SILICONE
J. BASIC SHADE
M. ALPHA HYDROXY ACID
P. ESTROGEN

B. PALM ROLLING
E. COLLAGEN
H. BLANCHING
K. MICRO DIFFUSE
N. IONIC

C. DEPILATION
F. HUMIDITY
I. CATIONIC
L. ALKALINE
O. ESCHAR

8. Find the hidden words. The words have been placed horizontally, vertically, or diagonally. When you locate a word, draw an ellipse around it.

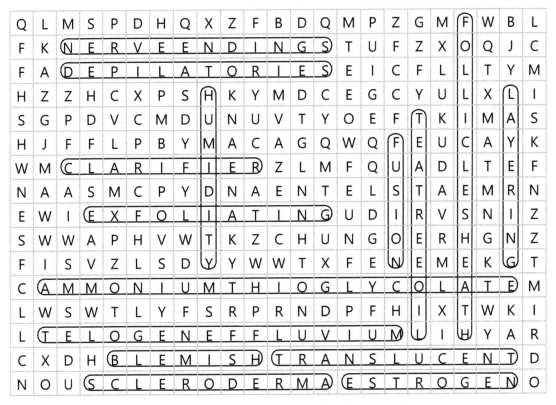

1. Blood or pigment based visible mark.
2. Protects the hair during its growth stage.
3. an extraction from the Melaleuca tree.
4. A female hormone sometimes linked to increased hair growth.
5. Hair shafts are produced by follicles within the skin in all but few locations
6. A process of removing the top dead skin layers to reveal healthier, newer skin underneath.
7. Substances used to dissolve hair above the skin's surface.
8. The amount of moisture available in the air.
9. A common ingredient in chemical depilatories.
10. The process of attaching small pieces of human hair with a special adhesive and a thermal gun.
11. A clarifying shampoo is slightly stronger than everyday shampoos and is designed to remove products, hard water or chlorine residue that have built-up over time.
12. Receptors which respond to touch, pain, pressure, heat and cold.
13. A disease of the skin and connective tissue that can cause hair loss over the affected areas.
14. A technique used by hairdressers to change the thickness of the hair, creating either a thinning or thicker appearance.
15. Allows some light to pass through.

A. BLEMISH
D. AMMONIUM THIOGLYCOLATE
G. EXFOLIATING
J. HUMIDITY
M. DEPILATORIES
B. TRANSLUCENT
E. TELOGEN EFFLUVIUM
H. TEA TREE OIL
K. FOLLICLE SHEATH
N. NERVE ENDINGS
C. ESTROGEN
F. SCLERODERMA
I. CLARIFIER
L. FUSION
O. LAYERING

9. Find the hidden words. The words have been placed horizontally, vertically, or diagonally. When you locate a word, draw an ellipse around it.

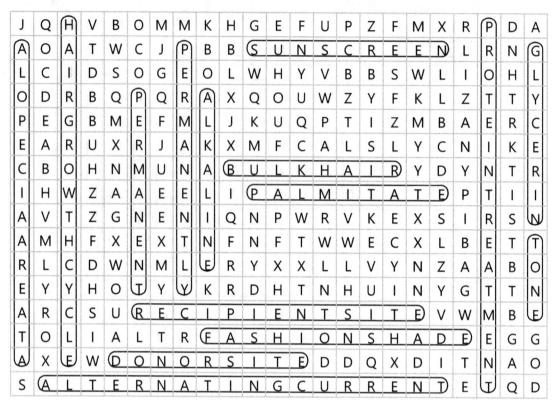

1. Hair loss which occurs in patches on the scalp.
2. Completely changing the natural color of the hair.
3. Products with ingredients that absorb UVA and UVB rays.
4. Distribution of ashen and warm pigments, visual effect of gold or ash in the hair.
5. A substance with a pH greater than 7; non acidic.
6. A humectant which absorbs moisture from the air to keep hair moist.
7. Site where hair roots are taken from during transplant surgery.
8. A definition set by the American FDA that most laser and intense light source manufacturers claim to meet for hair removal.
9. Hair passes through a series of cycles known as Anagen (growing phase), Catagen (resting phase) and Telogen (dormant phase).
10. Term for loose commercial hair. This hair is used for creating wefts or for services like fusion.
11. A treatment used on the hair. Designed to add strength and elasticity to the hair by adding protein to the cortex.
12. The type of electricity that comes from a wall outlet (AC), as opposed to direct current (DC).
13. Synthetic moisturizer.
14. A basic color with added tone.
15. The bald or thinning area where hair grafts or plugs a transplanted.

A. PERMANENTLY
B. PALMITATE
C. SUNSCREEN
D. PROTEIN TREATMENT
E. ALOPECIA AREATA
F. ALKALINE
G. BULK HAIR
H. FASHION SHADE
I. GLYCERIN
J. RECIPIENT SITE
K. PERMANENT
L. HAIR GROWTH CYCLE
M. DONOR SITE
N. TONE
O. ALTERNATING CURRENT

10. Find the hidden words. The words have been placed horizontally, vertically, or diagonally. When you locate a word, draw an ellipse around it.

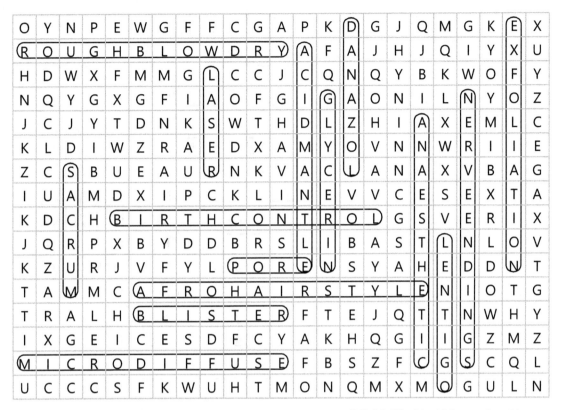

1. An acronym for Light Amplification by the Stimulated Emission of Radiation. A commonly used tool for cosmetic and surgical procedures.
2. The removal of dead skin cells to reveal softer skin underneath.
3. Optimum hold without overload.
4. Drugs that sometimes cause increased hair growth.
5. A flat, discolored area of skin similar to a freckle.
6. A substance used to relieve all feeling.
7. A drug sometimes linked to excess hair growth.
8. Bone in the lower back
9. A small fluid-filled bubble on the skin caused by heat from over treatment with certain types of hair removal.
10. A small opening of the sweat glands of the skin.
11. Receptors which respond to touch, pain, pressure, heat and cold.
12. Used to remove the moisture from wet hair.
13. A humectant which absorbs moisture from the air to keep hair moist.
14. The combination of sweat and sebum that provides the skin's protective coating.
15. A rounded, thick, tightly curled hair style.

A. ANAESTHETIC
B. LENTIGO
C. ACID MANTLE
D. SACRUM
E. BIRTH CONTROL
F. MICRO DIFFUSE
G. NERVE ENDINGS
H. EXFOLIATION
I. GLYCERIN
J. DANAZOL
K. ROUGH BLOW DRY
L. AFRO HAIRSTYLE
M. PORE
N. BLISTER
O. LASER

11. Find the hidden words. The words have been placed horizontally, vertically, or diagonally. When you locate a word, draw an ellipse around it.

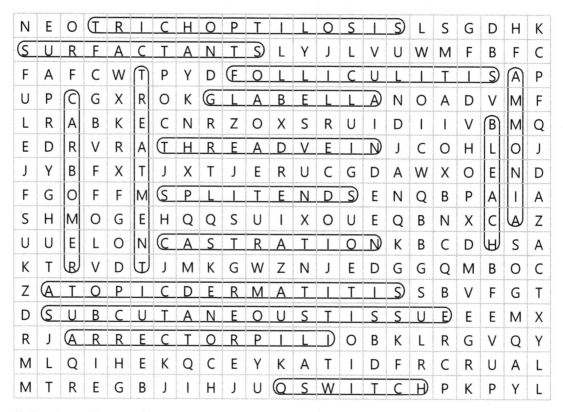

1. An alkaline ingredient used in some permanent hair color. An ingredient that results in a chemical action that decolorizes the hair.
2. used in between Shampoo and Conditioner to put protein back into the hair.
3. broken capillaries.
4. A polymer on the basis of acrylic acid. Provides a thickening, gelling action and consistency regulator for cosmetic products.
5. A device that produces short intense bursts of energy from a laser.
6. Split ends.
7. The space between the eyebrows.
8. Trichoptilosis
9. Creates "Goose Bumps" when stimulated.
10. Active agent that allows oil to mix with water. Used in skincare products like cleansers, wetting agents, emulsifiers, solubizers, conditioning agents and foam stabilizers.
11. The surgical removal of one or both testicles or ovaries.
12. A common disorder characterized by inflammation of the hair follicle.
13. Also known as eczema.
14. A method used to disguise (not remove) hair by lightening its color.
15. The body's shock absorber.

A. GLABELLA
B. ARRECTOR PILI
C. THREAD VEIN
D. BLEACH
E. Q SWITCH
F. SPLIT ENDS
G. TREATMENT
H. TRICHOPTILOSIS
I. CASTRATION
J. FOLLICULITIS
K. AMMONIA
L. ATOPIC DERMATITIS
M. SUBCUTANEOUS TISSUE
N. CARBOMER
O. SURFACTANTS

12. Find the hidden words. The words have been placed horizontally, vertically, or diagonally. When you locate a word, draw an ellipse around it.

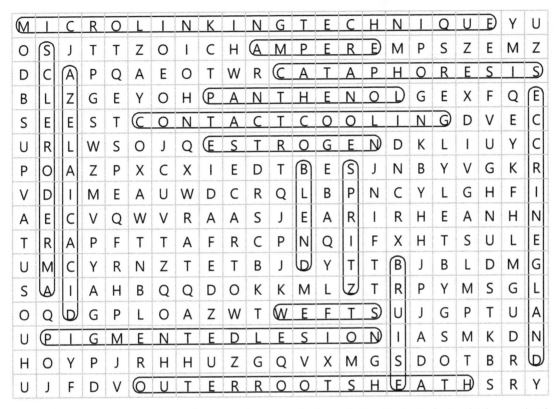

1. Commonly used in the treatment of acne and other skin conditions.
2. The forcing of substances into the skin from a positive to a negative pole. It is sometimes used after electrolysis to firm skin and reduce redness.
3. a light mist or spray, which when used as verb means to lightly spray your hair.
4. A method of cooling the epidermis immediately prior to laser irradiation in hopes of reducing or eliminating damage to the skin's surface.
5. A soft thin layer surrounding the lower two-thirds of a hair.
6. A medical term for sweat gland. These tiny pores do not contain hair follicles.
7. A female hormone sometimes linked to increased hair growth.
8. Aids detangling. Provides volume, control and shine.
9. A modality of electrolysis which uses both thermolysis and galvanic methods.
10. A discoloration of skin from blood, sometimes caused by electrolysis, plucking, or waxing. Also known as Purpura.
11. Variety of skin conditions mainly the result of excess melanin. Commonly known as Café au Lait stains, birthmarks, age spots and freckles.
12. A measurement of electrical current.
13. The process of attaching hair wefts without braids. The links are sewn on to the wefted hair. The user's natural hair is pulled through and locked secure.
14. Wefts are temporary hair extensions which are glued into your hair.
15. A disease of the skin and connective tissue that can cause hair loss over the affected areas.

A. PANTHENOL
D. SCLERODERMA
G. SPRITZ
J. CATAPHORESIS
M. AZELAIC ACID

B. BLEND
E. BRUISE
H. CONTACT COOLING
K. MICRO LINKING TECHNIQUE
N. PIGMENTED LESION

C. OUTER ROOT SHEATH
F. WEFTS
I. ESTROGEN
L. ECCRINE GLAND
O. AMPERE

13. Find the hidden words. The words have been placed horizontally, vertically, or diagonally. When you locate a word, draw an ellipse around it.

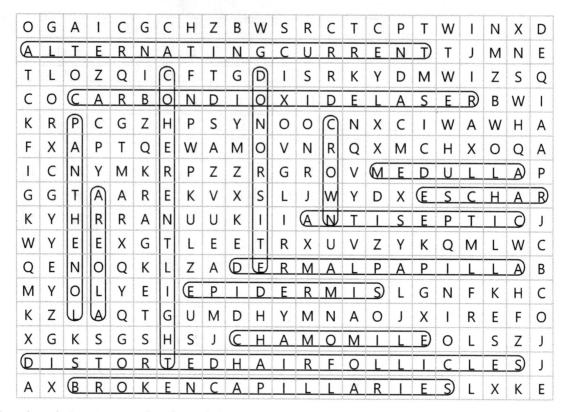

1. Site where hair roots are taken from during transplant surgery.
2. Light that stays focused, a property of lasers.
3. The type of electricity that comes from a wall outlet (AC), as opposed to direct current (DC).
4. Area at the top of the head.
5. These tiny blood vessels at the surface of the skin appear as streaks or blotches.
6. The thin outer layer of skin, on top of the thicker and deeper dermis.
7. A relatively rare condition in which the follicle is not straight.
8. The pigmented area surrounding the nipple. A very common area for hair growth.
9. Aids detangling. Provides volume, control and shine.
10. A small temporary scab that occurs sometimes after electrolysis, especially after overtreatment.
11. Used in many products for blonde hair to enhance color.
12. Situated at the base of the hair follicle. Contains nerves and blood vessels which supply glucose for energy and amino acids to make keratin.
13. Also known as a CO2 laser, these are commonly used to perform skin resurfacing.
14. A chemical agent that prevent the growth of bacteria.
15. The medulla is a central zone of cells usually only present in large thick hairs.

A. CARBON DIOXIDE LASER
B. ALTERNATING CURRENT
C. CROWN
D. DISTORTED HAIR FOLLICLES
E. PANTHENOL
F. BROKEN CAPILLARIES
G. ANTISEPTIC
H. CHAMOMILE
I. ESCHAR
J. AREOLA
K. MEDULLA
L. DERMAL PAPILLA
M. DONOR SITE
N. COHERENT LIGHT
O. EPIDERMIS

14. Find the hidden words. The words have been placed horizontally, vertically, or diagonally. When you locate a word, draw an ellipse around it.

G	S	C	P	Y	Y	K	V	O	Y	W	B	E	T	E	O	V	A	R	I	E	S	E
P	X	N	B	D	E	V	E	L	O	P	E	R	T	U	T	M	T	O	Q	S	E	I
Z	W	C	O	M	E	D	O	N	E	S	U	U	B	H	F	D	U	U	H	U	H	X
U	P	C	O	A	R	S	E	P	R	V	Q	F	W	I	N	K	I	K	M	N	Z	P
V	K	H	G	M	H	O	B	B	G	D	L	Y	A	U	D	F	U	W	Z	S	D	X
C	T	A	Y	M	A	R	J	K	L	R	V	G	O	Y	K	A	B	K	G	C	O	N
K	R	E	G	V	I	N	K	E	O	O	M	V	S	T	R	G	H	A	W	R	S	H
C	I	C	A	T	R	I	C	I	A	L	A	L	O	P	E	C	I	A	R	E	V	I
L	Q	S	B	M	C	W	S	A	C	U	P	U	N	C	T	U	R	E	E	E	T	R
L	T	O	R	J	L	S	B	W	S	Q	D	Y	F	X	C	J	K	V	F	N	T	S
T	T	K	A	J	O	R	O	U	G	H	B	L	O	W	D	R	Y	B	O	D	Y	U
V	V	O	S	F	N	O	N	I	R	R	A	V	D	T	H	I	A	P	K	P	J	T
S	T	M	I	Y	I	J	G	H	Q	R	Z	K	Z	A	J	S	N	E	V	H	E	I
H	M	H	O	F	N	B	Z	Q	D	M	E	D	J	A	L	O	P	E	C	I	A	S
E	B	Q	N	C	G	J	Q	W	C	H	I	G	N	O	N	H	G	S	Z	S	P	N
V	C	J	O	V	W	S	U	N	B	L	O	C	K	U	C	K	B	G	M	H	W	J

1. Loss of hair, especially from the head, which either happens naturally or is caused by disease
2. Products that reflect all the sun's rays, such as zinc oxide and titanium dioxide. They permit minimal tanning, and are a good choice for those who are sensitive to chemicals.
3. A method of relieving pain by inserting needles into the skin.
4. A technique under development which could make an unlimited crop of donor hair available for transplanting.
5. In women, a major source of female hormones. Certain conditions involving the ovaries can lead to excess hair growth, especially polycystic ovary syndrome (PCOS).
6. A product which oxidizes artificial color pigment.
7. A sophisticated, elegant up style, where long hair is twisted (either in a roll or knot) and pinned from the nape of neck.
8. The volume or springiness of hair.
9. A medical term for blackheads.
10. Excessive hair growth, accompanied by enlarged hair follicles and increased pigmentation.
11. Products with ingredients that absorb UVA and UVB rays.
12. A classification for stronger, thicker types of hair.
13. This is baldness due to scarring. The follicles are absent in scar tissue.
14. Used to remove the moisture from wet hair.
15. The process of scraping or wearing hair away. Causing partial or complete absence of hair from areas.

A. HAIR CLONING
B. HIRSUTISM
C. SUNSCREEN
D. DEVELOPER
E. ALOPECIA
F. COARSE
G. CHIGNON
H. COMEDONES
I. OVARIES
J. ROUGH BLOW DRY
K. CICATRICIAL ALOPECIA
L. BODY
M. ACUPUNCTURE
N. SUNBLOCK
O. ABRASION

15. Find the hidden words. The words have been placed horizontally, vertically, or diagonally. When you locate a word, draw an ellipse around it.

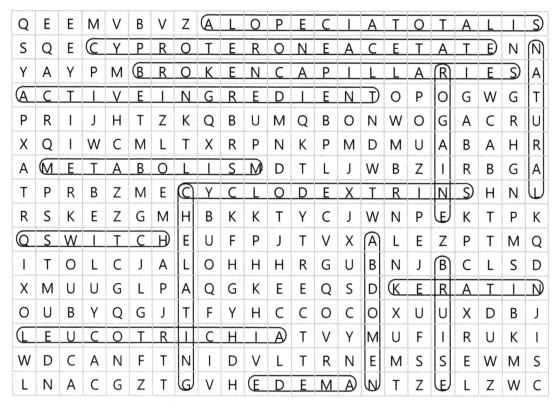

1. Produced from starch by means of enzymatic conversion and are used in a wide range of applications in food, pharmaceutical and chemical industries.
2. The body transformation of food into energy.
3. A deep cleansing process which strips the hair lightly before a chemical service. Also known as clarifying.
4. This drug is normally used to reduce sex drive in men who have an excessive sex drive. It is also prescribed to treat hirsutism and androgenic alopecia in women.
5. The soft area between the rib cage and the pubic area. A common area for excess hair, often in a line from the belly button to the pubic hair.
6. Refers to a congenital absence of pigment in a lock of hairs which will show as grey or white.
7. Ingredients extracted directly from plants, earth minerals, or animal products as opposed to being produced synthetically.
8. A fibrous protein found in hair, nails, and skin.
9. These tiny blood vessels at the surface of the skin appear as streaks or blotches.
10. The substance which, contained in a product, actually does the main part of the work that the product is used for.
11. A device that produces short intense bursts of energy from a laser.
12. A discoloration of skin from blood, sometimes caused by electrolysis, plucking, or waxing. Also known as Purpura.
13. The brand name for Minoxidil. A topical hair growth solution for hair loss.
14. This is the complete loss of scalp hair often combined with the loss of eyebrows and eyelashes.
15. A medical term for swelling.

A. BRUISE
B. EDEMA
C. Q SWITCH
D. METABOLISM
E. BROKEN CAPILLARIES
F. ROGAINE
G. ACTIVE INGREDIENT
H. NATURAL
I. CHELATING
J. CYPROTERONE ACETATE
K. KERATIN
L. ALOPECIA TOTALIS
M. CYCLODEXTRINS
N. ABDOMEN
O. LEUCOTRICHIA

16. Find the hidden words. The words have been placed horizontally, vertically, or diagonally. When you locate a word, draw an ellipse around it.

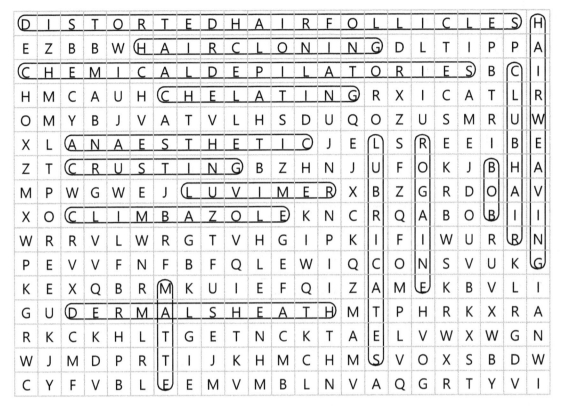

1. Powder or cream preparations that dissolve hair above the surface of the skin. Some find these products very irritating to the skin.
2. Highly effective active anti-dandruff ingredient. Combats bacteria on the scalp.
3. Makes smooth or slippery by using oil to overcome friction.
4. A technique under development which could make an unlimited crop of donor hair available for transplanting.
5. A process by which a hair piece is attached to existing hair on the head through braiding or a weaving process.
6. The brand name for Minoxidil. A topical hair growth solution for hair loss.
7. Dried fluid that seeps from skin in some clients following hair removal such as laser, electrolysis, and depilatories.
8. A substance used to relieve all feeling.
9. A non-shiny surface that absorbs light; a dead or dull finish.
10. A non-living hair in the last stages of the hair growth cycle, it is detached from the follicle but has not yet shed.
11. The classic look of the 50s and 60s; the style was short and straight but blow-dried and curled under.
12. A relatively rare condition in which the follicle is not straight.
13. Flexible resin.
14. A deep cleansing process which strips the hair lightly before a chemical service. Also known as clarifying.
15. A lining around a hair.

A. CHEMICAL DEPILATORIES
B. ROGAINE
C. LUVIMER
D. HAIR CLONING
E. BOB
F. CLIMBAZOLE
G. HAIR WEAVING
H. DISTORTED HAIR FOLLICLES
I. CLUB HAIR
J. MATTE
K. CHELATING
L. CRUSTING
M. LUBRICATES
N. DERMAL SHEATH
O. ANAESTHETIC

17. Find the hidden words. The words have been placed horizontally, vertically, or diagonally. When you locate a word, draw an ellipse around it.

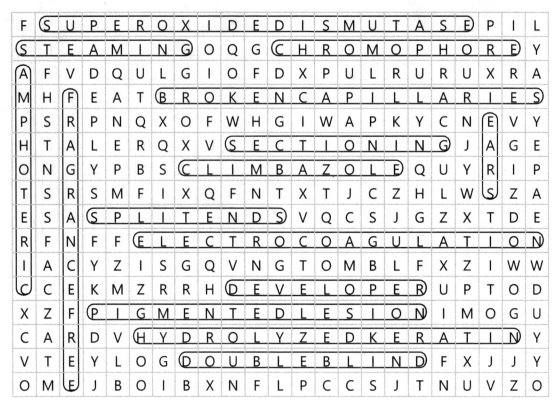

1. Highly effective active anti-dandruff ingredient. Combats bacteria on the scalp.
2. Variety of skin conditions mainly the result of excess melanin. Commonly known as Café au Lait stains, birthmarks, age spots and freckles.
3. A clinical testing method in which neither patient nor doctor know what medication or procedure is being used.
4. The enzyme superoxide, catalyzes the dismutation of superoxide into oxygen and hydrogen peroxide.
5. Trichoptilosis
6. A common place for hair removal in older males.
7. The process by which most synthetic fiber is curled at the factory.
8. Products so labeled may still contain small amounts of fragrances to mask the fatty odor of soap or other unpleasant odors.
9. These tiny blood vessels at the surface of the skin appear as streaks or blotches.
10. allows you to only pay attention to a particular area or panel of hair.
11. A product which oxidizes artificial color pigment.
12. The use of heat generated by electricity to change tissue from a fluid to a semi-solid, similar to cooking an egg.
13. A mild nonirritating surfactant often used in shampoos; leaves hair manageable and is gentle enough for chemically treated hair.
14. The substructure that is responsible for the spectral selective absorption of electromagnetic radiation.
15. The structural protein of hair.

A. SUPEROXIDE DISMUTASE
B. BROKEN CAPILLARIES
C. HYDROLYZED KERATIN
D. CHROMOPHORE
E. EARS
F. FRAGRANCE FREE
G. DOUBLE BLIND
H. SECTIONING
I. PIGMENTED LESION
J. STEAMING
K. ELECTROCOAGULATION
L. AMPHOTERIC
M. SPLIT ENDS
N. CLIMBAZOLE
O. DEVELOPER

18. Find the hidden words. The words have been placed horizontally, vertically, or diagonally. When you locate a word, draw an ellipse around it.

O	E	X	T	W	F	M	J	O	R	U	N	A	U	Z	F	E	F	T	Z	F	I	T
J	D	V	J	V	W	I	M	J	D	E	R	M	A	B	R	A	S	I	O	N	P	N
Y	A	Y	F	E	A	C	V	M	B	E	T	A	I	N	E	V	N	Z	N	Q	C	B
I	T	D	O	I	N	R	A	M	O	R	T	I	Z	A	T	I	O	N	A	W	T	F
U	U	T	X	M	T	O	K	M	B	H	F	Z	C	C	T	B	A	A	K	H	E	R
I	F	T	B	U	I	D	A	C	S	X	B	O	R	N	E	U	E	E	L	K	X	Z
L	A	X	F	L	A	I	P	I	G	M	E	N	T	E	C	Y	O	X	S	D	O	Y
S	R	C	W	O	N	F	A	R	C	T	R	A	C	K	M	H	U	T	E	G	Q	I
X	Z	X	P	P	D	F	M	H	T	Q	L	A	I	Z	V	L	J	R	P	J	C	V
Z	C	Y	P	K	R	U	A	L	O	P	E	C	I	A	T	O	T	A	L	I	S	S
V	N	D	G	T	O	S	Y	U	T	B	P	V	O	Y	L	L	Y	C	L	L	O	S
R	H	T	A	R	G	E	T	E	D	F	A	T	R	E	D	U	C	T	I	O	N	A
X	E	U	E	U	E	A	L	O	P	E	C	I	A	N	E	U	R	O	T	I	C	A
I	V	B	H	E	N	X	R	U	P	K	R	B	N	G	U	V	O	B	K	R	K	A
R	M	B	R	A	N	N	F	C	Y	U	B	A	R	B	A	Z	K	G	O	N	J	B
E	L	E	C	T	R	O	D	E	R	O	S	A	C	E	A	U	Q	I	B	T	M	F

1. Parting or a cornrow that establishes the placement pattern of wefts or strand additions.
2. Baldness following a nervous disorder or injury to the nervous system.
3. This is the complete loss of scalp hair often combined with the loss of eyebrows and eyelashes.
4. The process of converting one enzyme to another.
5. An inflammation of the skin, a result of over production of oil and bacteria.
6. A disorder involving chronic inflammation of the cheeks, nose, chin, forehead or eyelids. It may cause redness, vascularity, swelling or hyperplasia.
7. A natural conditioning substance for example: from molasses or sugar beet.
8. Optimum hold without overload.
9. An herbal concentrate produced by separating the essential or active part of an herb into a solvent material.
10. A cosmetic procedure used to smooth skin and reduce scars.
11. Color.
12. Medical term for beard.
13. In hair removal, a conductor through which electricity enters or leaves the body. An electrolysis needle is an electrode.
14. Metabolising stubborn fat deposits, typically in the lower body, using methods such as Eporex mesotherapy.
15. A drug or product that limited the effects of androgens (male hormones).

A. ELECTRODE
D. MICRO DIFFUSE
G. ACNE
J. BETAINE
M. BARBA

B. TARGETED FAT REDUCTION
E. ANTI ANDROGEN
H. ALOPECIA NEUROTICA
K. DERMABRASION
N. ROSACEA

C. PIGMENT
F. TRACK
I. EXTRACT
L. AMORTIZATION
O. ALOPECIA TOTALIS

225

19. Find the hidden words. The words have been placed horizontally, vertically, or diagonally. When you locate a word, draw an ellipse around it.

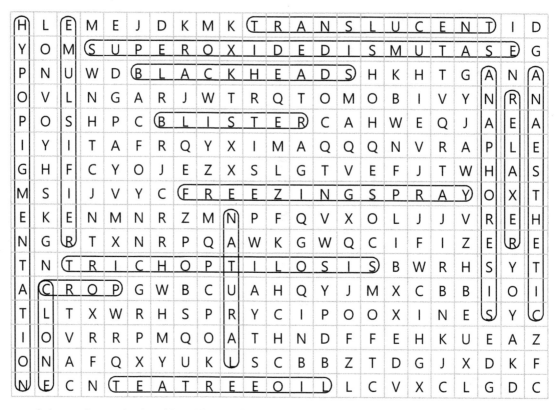

1. A type of clogged pore in the skin with a visible black plug.
2. The forcing of liquids into skin from the negative to the positive pole.
3. Caused by an absence of melanocytes, whitening of the skin. Vitiligo is a common medical complaint.
4. A small fluid-filled bubble on the skin caused by heat from over treatment with certain types of hair removal.
5. A substance used to relieve all feeling.
6. A group of genetically identical cells or organisms derived from a single common cell.
7. Split ends.
8. Ingredients extracted directly from plants, earth minerals, or animal products as opposed to being produced synthetically.
9. A hairspray with the firmest hold used to maintain style of hard to hold hair.
10. A thickening agent or binding agent added to products to change their physical composition (joins two or more ingredients together).
11. Allows some light to pass through.
12. An alternative to haircut, without any specific meaning to the style of the cut.
13. an extraction from the Melaleuca tree.
14. The enzyme superoxide, catalyzes the dis-mutation of superoxide into oxygen and hydrogen peroxide.
15. A chemical process by which the hair is permanently straightened. New-growth areas have to be maintained via 'touch-ups' to continue the straightened pattern.

A. TRANSLUCENT
B. RELAXER
C. FREEZING SPRAY
D. SUPEROXIDE DISMUTASE
E. HYPOPIGMENTATION
F. BLISTER
G. ANAESTHETIC
H. CROP
I. EMULSIFIER
J. TEA TREE OIL
K. BLACKHEADS
L. NATURAL
M. CLONE
N. TRICHOPTILOSIS
O. ANAPHORESIS

20. Find the hidden words. The words have been placed horizontally, vertically, or diagonally. When you locate a word, draw an ellipse around it.

F	D	M	T	Z	O	N	E	Y	P	A	U	R	S	P	R	I	T	Z	S	G	V
I	R	F	L	D	L	B	Y	Y	N	Q	T	V	W	M	T	O	C	A	R	Y	M	Y
N	Z	X	N	O	F	M	B	O	N	D	I	N	G	Q	J	D	M	S	Z	H	W	G
A	Q	R	P	H	L	I	B	N	I	Q	L	K	F	U	S	I	O	N	Q	I	M	V
S	S	M	R	C	I	C	A	T	R	I	C	I	A	L	A	L	O	P	E	C	I	A
T	E	Q	A	H	J	R	T	G	N	P	C	E	T	Y	L	A	L	C	O	H	O	L
E	C	X	W	I	P	O	K	E	B	V	F	O	L	L	I	C	U	L	I	T	I	S
R	T	P	P	D	N	G	X	K	P	Q	L	E	H	N	N	W	F	S	U	W	L	V
I	I	S	R	E	X	R	D	Z	C	B	O	F	F	T	G	H	I	U	S	W	I	O
D	O	H	B	P	J	A	P	R	O	T	E	I	N	T	R	E	A	T	M	E	N	T
E	N	W	F	T	L	F	S	A	S	R	D	N	S	Z	J	J	E	R	M	N	V	I
A	I	L	F	H	K	T	B	G	F	C	N	V	M	I	D	T	I	U	S	S	H	C
J	N	W	C	R	A	C	A	N	I	T	I	E	S	G	X	Z	Q	B	K	U	T	Y
A	G	Y	Q	U	J	M	V	Q	E	H	B	J	V	P	B	J	Z	U	G	S	Z	E
I	O	J	U	I	F	L	L	L	S	P	F	T	J	E	X	I	U	G	S	R	U	Q
R	L	I	Y	G	T	H	E	R	M	A	L	P	R	O	C	E	S	S	B	Q	N	A

1. a light mist or spray, which when used as verb means to lightly spray your hair.
2. The generic name of the brand name drug Proscar that is FDA approved for the treatment of benign prostate enlargement.
3. The forehead, nose and chin areas, which tend to be oilier than the cheeks.
4. A very small hair graft usually consisting of one or two hairs.
5. The greying of hair. A pigment deficiency frequently seen in middle-aged people of either sex.
6. To attach wefted hair to the natural hair with a latex or surgical type adhesive.
7. A common disorder characterized by inflammation of the hair follicle.
8. The process of attaching small pieces of human hair with a special adhesive and a thermal gun.
9. Used to measure acidity in cosmetic preparations.
10. allows you to only pay attention to a particular area or panel of hair.
11. A treatment used on the hair. Designed to add strength and elasticity to the hair by adding protein to the cortex.
12. This is baldness due to scarring. The follicles are absent in scar tissue.
13. A gentle humectant, lather booster, and emulsifier. In hair products, it is used to smooth and soften the hair cuticle.
14. The darkness or lightness of a color.
15. Temporarily straightening the hair with a heated iron.

A. FOLLICULITIS
B. FINASTERIDE
C. MICRO GRAFT
D. SECTIONING
E. CICATRICIAL ALOPECIA
F. PROTEIN TREATMENT
G. CETYL ALCOHOL
H. CANITIES
I. SPRITZ
J. THERMAL PROCESS
K. T ZONE
L. BONDING
M. FUSION
N. DEPTH
O. PH

Printed in the USA
CPSIA information can be obtained
at www.ICGtesting.com
LVHW082051200923
758757LV00053B/809